Eating the
Big Fish

Adweek Books is designed to present interesting, insightful books for the general business reader and for professionals in the worlds of media, marketing, and advertising.

These are innovative, creative books that address the challenges and opportunities of these industries, written by leaders in the business. Some of our writers head their own companies, others have worked their way up to the top of their field in large multinationals. But they share a knowledge of their craft and a desire to enlighten others.

We hope readers will find these books as helpful and inspiring as *Adweek, Brandweek,* and *Mediaweek* magazines.

Published

Disruption: Overturning Conventions and Shaking up the Market-place, Jean-Marie Dru

Eating the Big Fish: How Challenger Brands Can Compete against Brand Leaders, Adam Morgan

Hey, Whipple, Squeeze This: A Guide to Creating Great Ads, Luke Sullivan

Truth, Lies, and Advertising: The Art of Account Planning, Jon Steel

Under the Radar: Talking to Today's Cynical Consumer, Jonathan Bond & Richard Kirshenbaum

Forthcoming

Warp-Speed Branding: The Impact of Technology on Marketing, Agnieszka Winkler.

Eating the Big Fish

How Challenger Brands
Can Compete against
Brand Leaders

Adam Morgan

John Wiley & Sons, Inc.

New York • Chichester • Weinheim • Brisbane • Singapore • Toronto

Designations used by companies to distinguish their products are often claimed as trade-marks. In all instances where John Wiley & Sons, Inc., is aware of a claim, the product names appear in intial capital or ALL CAPITAL LETTERS. Readers, however, should contact the appropriate companies for more complete information regarding trademarks and registration.

This book is printed on acid-free paper. ∞

Published by John Wiley & Sons, Inc.

Published simultaneously in Canada.

This publication is designed to provide accurate and authoritative information in regard to the subject matter covered. It is sold with the understanding that the publisher is not engaged in rendering professional services. If professional advice or other expert assis-tance is required, the services of a competent professional person should be sought.

Library of Congress Cataloging-in-Publication Data:
Morgan, Adam.
    Eating the big fish : how challenger brands can compete against brand leaders / Adam Morgan.
      p. cm.
    includes index.
    ISBN 0-471-24209-8 (cloth : alk. paper)
    1. Product management.   2. Brand name products—Management.
3. New Products.   I. Title.
HF5415.15.M67   1998
658.8′27—dc21   98-28267

Printed in the United States of America.

10 9 8

For Ruth

When you're only No.2, you try harder. Or else.

Avis can't afford to relax.

Little fish have to keep moving all of the time. The big ones never stop picking on them.

Avis knows all about the problems of little fish.

We're only No.2 in rent a cars. We'd be swallowed up if we didn't try harder.

There's no rest for us.

We're always emptying ashtrays. Making sure gas tanks are full before we rent our cars. Seeing that the batteries are full of life. Checking our windshield wipers.

And the cars we rent out can't be anything less than lively new super-torque Fords.

And since we're not the big fish, you won't feel like a sardine when you come to our counter.

We're not jammed with customers.

© 1964 AVIS, INC.

Preface

They existed before Avis, of course: the second-rank brands, cruising the category reef in the shadow of the Big Fish. It was just that, before Avis, they always seemed just that—second rank. The brands we emulated, the brands we learned from, the brands we all wanted to be, underneath, were the brand leaders. "You know the new VP in marketing? I hear he comes from *Clorox*."

And then a car-rental company threw down a gauntlet to the brand leader in its category, and our view of what it meant to be number two changed. The strategy was smart, the image suddenly more desirable than even that of the brand leader: perhaps we were witnessing the birth of Number Two as Marketing Icon. Perhaps now we would start to see the marketing landscape change. Almost immediately, we enshrined the Avis story in legend: how the staff wore the badges of the slogan to enlist them in the cause, how the company used the little details to support a much higher emotional claim, how they weren't really number two at all, and that was the real brilliance of their strategy.

But Avis proved a false dawn. As second-rank brands went, there was some sterling support work in the years that followed from Pepsi—and that was it. Volkswagen was, well, the Beetle; and as much as everyone admired what it had done, it was hard to convince any marketeer that what they really wanted to be was another Beetle.

So the brand models remained the Brand Leaders. We read about Coca-Cola and Kellogg's, and all the other brands that had led their category since records began, and marveled. And if we wanted a number-two strategy, we had a choice of Avis or Pepsi: we could try harder, or go younger. But frankly, after a while that became a pretty thin diet for those of us working on second-rank brands. There were no real vitamins left in there, once everyone had taken a turn at chewing it over a few times. We had to go back to just trying to differentiate again.

And then, one afternoon in 1984, Apple bushwhacked IBM in the Redskins–Raiders Superbowl, and the Challenger brand was born again. People didn't remember the product details in the 20-page print insert that Apple ran the week following the game; all they remembered was a single 60-second commercial, and a girl with a hammer, and a declaration of intent that sent shock waves through the computer industry and imprinted Apple and Steve Jobs firmly on American popular culture. Hey, did you see that Apple ad? Apparently they only ran it *once*.

The little guy was back. Avis lived again.

The years that followed, the years of the bull market, were the years of the new entrepreneurs. Money men and women, yes, but also businessmen and women. Huizenga, Diller, Roddick, Branson, Murdoch. And with them came, it seemed, an explosion of new businesses and brands, challenging the hegemony of the old order. IBM didn't fall, but it wobbled, and suddenly it seemed as though anything was possible; the big brands seemed not omnipotent, but suddenly monolithic, immobile, old-fashioned, slow to react. The time of the new launch, let alone the number two, had come. The new marketing icons were not brands that had been market leaders since 1925; they were brands that had only been born two, three, five years ago and were turning the rules of their category upside down. Some stayed, some died, but the shape of the marketing landscape was changed forever.

Which leads me back to why I started writing this book.

For some reason, I have never seemed to work on brand leaders. I have worked on coffee shops and airlines, family cars and condoms, colorants and video games, but I have never seemed to find myself on the side of the big guy, the one with the muscles, sprawling confidently astride the category. Instead, I have always found myself in the opposite corner, picking up my gumshield on behalf of the number two or three—outspent, outpunched, and out to make a fight of it.

It was fairly obvious to me even as a novice in this situation that the model of the brand leader was not one it was wise to follow. Not simply was success impossible for a number two by following their strategy, but we couldn't even succeed by imitating their kind of relationships with the consumer. While "trust" and "reassurance" and "simplification of choice" might be of value to an established player with perfect distribution, they certainly weren't going to be enough to create preference for us. It would take a different kind of relationship to persuade our consumer to walk past the long, convenient rows of red cans and bend down to pick out the little blue one at the end.

But what were the alternatives? I feared for my sanity if I ever heard again the desperate injunction, "Let's all try to think outside the box"; surely the way to overcome the strategic difficulties we faced lay in something more structured than two hours of wild brainstorming. Equally worrying was the simplistic reduction of our approach to one-dimensional talk about "differentiation." Surely there was more than this to be learned from those who had passed this way before? Surely the iconic second-rank brands had done more to earn their success than simply try to be "different," important though that undoubtedly was?

Trying to find existing models to draw from didn't help. I could find lots of books about brand leaders, and brand leadership, that drew conclusions and compared one with another. But nobody seemed to have done the same with second-rank brands. There were books about individual companies and their founders, but no one seemed to have tried to trace what, if anything, the successful ones had in common. And this was curious, well, because surely there were so many more of us than them, the brand leaders. Because surely if one really thought about it, *we* were the rule and *they* were the exception: there is by definition only one brand leader in each category.

So I went looking for successful second-rank brands. They obviously must exist as potential models—some had become as iconic in their own way, after all, as brand leaders—but they just hadn't been grouped together as like things before; although as marketeers we had segmented and labeled consumers by every kind of attitude and behavior, we had remained curiously general in the way we thought about brands.

And this interested me: if I could find enough of these successful second-rank brands, what would they have in common? Could I glean from them seven or eight shared characteristics that, taken together, might in turn give me some guidelines as to how I should approach marketing my own brands and businesses? The beginnings of a more structured process?

The more I searched, the more the answer seemed to lie in what a colleague of mine gave the name of "Challenger brands": second-rank brands that had demonstrated growth in the face of a powerful and established brand leader. This book will look at some forty of these "Challenger brands" and the eight common marketing strands that the majority of them seem to share. In the opening chapters, I talk a little more about the situation facing second-rank brands and why it is that they need to think so differently about themselves. The bulk of the book is then given over to an analysis of these strands, which I have called "The Eight Credos of Challenger Brands."

The Eight Credos of Challenger Brands are:

1. Break with Your Immediate Past.
2. Build a Lighthouse Identity.
3. Assume Thought Leadership of the Category.
4. Create Symbols of Reevaluation.
5. Sacrifice.
6. Overcommit.
7. Use Advertising and Publicity as a High-Leverage Asset.
8. Become Ideas-Centered, Rather Than Consumer-Centered.

Although each Credo is important in itself, we will see that it is the relationship between all of them that makes the difference between a successful Challenger and a Paper Tiger. In particular, we will see that although most marketing books assume the central issue for brand success is marketing strategy, the eight credos suggest that successful challenger marketing is in fact made up of three critical areas: Attitude, Strategy, and Behavior. Having discussed each Credo in turn, therefore, we will look at the development of a Challenger process that encompasses these three areas. To this end, the penultimate chapter will offer a proposed outline for a two-day Off-Site Program that will attempt to kick start the Challenger process for a core group within a marketing or management team. Finally, I will close with some thoughts on the dynamics and spirit of the Challenger organization.

I made two key decisions early on. The first was to abandon any pretence of a statistically robust sample or scientific analysis: The sample is relatively small. I am unapologetic about this—I am not aiming at science or (god forbid) a formula. What I am hoping for us to derive instead is a sense of direction, a magnetic compass; and the sample, I hope, is large enough and colorful enough to offer that.

The second decision was to resist the urge to find entirely new case histories all the way through: Although I debated whether to include such relatively well-trodden ground as Saturn and the Body Shop, it seemed perverse to leave them out altogether. The value in their stories from our point of view will not lie, after all, in considering them in isolation, but in taking all of them together; what Saturn has in common with Absolut, New Labour with Wonderbra, even Gandhi, perhaps, with the Spice Girls.

For those impatient to start reading the Eight Credos, they begin in Part II, but I would encourage the reader to try the pages that intervene. Although I am aware that it is only the author of a business book who ever reads more than 20 pages of it, the purist in me would still contend that the most common cause of marketing error is a failure not to come up with the right solution, but the prior failure to correctly identify the problem—and in the first section of the book, I will begin by painting a more detailed picture of the specific business hurdles facing second-rank brands. And, more importantly, Challengers seem to succeed not just through original marketing thinking and strategy, but by carrying through that strategy into Challenger marketing behavior. And the attitude, the driving sense both of opportunity and need that Challengers establish for themselves right at the outset of their enterprise, is what drives that completion. It is to creating that attitude that Part I of the book devotes itself.

Contents

how could we apply them to our own situation to generate a source of personal business advantage?

This section identifies and discusses the eight common marketing strands these brands have shared and devotes eight chapters to discussing each in turn.

and role in the consumer's life. This chapter discusses some of the most strik-
ing of these symbols, what specifically it was about them that achieved the
results they did, and what divided them from being just another "publicity
stunt."

8 The Fifth Credo: Sacrifice   124

Challengers have less resource in almost every aspect of the business and
marketing mix than the Big Fish —what they choose not to do, to sacrifice,
is therefore as important to their success as what they choose to do. The na-
ture of this sacrifice and some of its key dimensions are the focus of this
chapter.

9 The Sixth Credo: Overcommit   138

The converse of sacrifice is overcommitment: the idea that, following the
process of sacrifice, if the marketeer or businessman has chosen to drive suc-
cess through one or two key activities then these must be successful—and to
achieve that success the marketeer must not commit but overcommit. This
chapter looks at examples of overcommitment, and how we can reframe our
own thinking and approach to key activities to ensure their success.

10 The Seventh Credo: Use Advertising
and Publicity as a High-Leverage Asset   155

For a Challenger, who is outgunned and outresourced in almost every other
area by the Market Leader, advertising and the intelligent pursuit of publici-
ty remain two of the very few remaining sources of competitive advantage
open—but only if they are systematically embraced as such within the com-
pany. In this chapter, what it means to treat advertising and publicity as high
leverage assets in this way is discussed, as well as the changes in the com-
munications development process that are required.

11 The Eighth Credo (Part 1): Become
Idea-Centered, Not Consumer-Centered   174

Success is a very dangerous thing—it causes brands and people to stop be-
having in the way that made them initially successful. The Eighth Credo,
then, encompasses how a Challenger maintains its momentum once it has
become successful, and in particular the moving of the organization from
being consumer-dependent to focusing on the generation and implementa-
tion of ideas—ideas that constantly refresh and renew the relationship with
the consumer.

16 Apple, Risk, and the Circle of Rope 261

The book concludes by discussing the more intangible characteristics of Challengers—luck, emotion, and the preparedness to embrace risk. After discussing the implications for leadership of a Challenger culture and team, it looks at the need for every serious Challenger to watch and analyze regularly the most vigorously fertile Challenger soil in the world—the West Coast of the United States.

PART I

The Size and Nature of the Big Fish

1

More Blood from a Smaller Stone

"Commercial incongruity is rife. Sainsbury's is a bank, Boots is a sandwich bar, and god knows what those pop-record people Virgin aren't into. But can anyone beat this flyer that came through my letter box today: 'Thames Water customers can now get cheaper gas from London Electricity.' I feel faint."
Letter to The Independent *April 1998*

In 1996–1997 the international advertising agency TBWA commissioned a piece of research among their own customers—their existing and potential client base—to look at the principal marketing challenges they saw facing them over the next five years. The clients ranged from marketing directors to chief executive officers and were predominantly from the marketing companies behind well-known second- or third-rank brands in the United States and Europe.

There was much talk among the people we interviewed of stress and change, of the difficulty of being asked to achieve more with less. But in particular they spoke of their having to confront and overcome *entirely new kinds of marketing problems*—types of problems that simply had not existed 5 to 10 years earlier:

1. **Certain markets had moved for the first time beyond maturity to overcapacity.** Even though the category was growing, the number of products and brands continuing to be introduced each year in surplus to natural demand meant that each individual brand was having to increase

3

demand to maintain per-store sales. Quick Service Restaurants in the United States, for example, is increasing distribution beyond natural capacity at such a rate that each restaurant will naturally see an approximate 5% *decline* in year-on-year sales if consumer interest in the brand simply remains at the same level. Or look at the projected overcapacity looming over the automotive manufacturers: Unofficially, Ford estimates 70 million new cars are being produced a year worldwide, in a global market with a natural demand for only 50 million.

2. Overcapacity meant there was not enough food to go around. To make their numbers, the bigger fish started preying more aggressively on the smaller fish. They have already reduced costs, reduced head count, and pushed distribution just about as far as it can go. They have explored global resourcing, search and reapply, panregional marketing efficiencies—and discovered the limits in the level of returns they will yield: continuous reduction in operating expenses as a percentage of sales is impossible now unless their sales go up. And those sales have got to come from someone else: the shareholder has to eat.

So the brand leaders turn on the smaller fry. We see Gallo, for instance, in court charged with imitating a little too closely with their Turning Leaf brand the minor success enjoyed by a fringe player in a market that Gallo dominates. We see Coca-Cola, unable to dominate Pepsi in Venezuela the way it did in the rest of Latin America, simply buying Pepsi's Venezuelan bottler and putting the world's number two out of business in that country overnight. In the summer of the same year, 1996, that same brand leader, Coca-Cola, offered the franchisees of McDonald's restaurants four digit bonuses if they dropped Dr. Pepper in favor of selling solely Coca-Cola's own products. Merely buying back the franchisee loyalty cost Dr. Pepper's parent, Cadbury, $6 million. We see British Airways, still awaiting the outcome of their proposed alliance with American Airlines, announcing they were to set up a subsidiary division offering a no-frills service branded "Go," specifically to compete aggressively in the segment pioneered by such small-scale entrepreneurs like Ryanair and Air UK.

These are fairly full-frontal assaults on a second-rank brand. But as Sun Tsu observed, a frontal attack is rarely the most effective strategy. Ask the British Office of Fair Trading, who in May 1997 began to investigate Dixon's, the United Kingdom's largest electrical retailer, over claims that it had been using an "unfair and anti-competitive" strategy to pressure the developers of out-of-town centers into denying floor space to Dixon's newer and lesser competitors.[1] In the summer of the same year came Compaq's deposition to U.S. Attorney General Janet Reno about Microsoft.

3. **And as well as turning their attentions downward, the Big Fish turned them outward.** The clients we spoke to faced *entirely new kinds of competition*—the brand leader from another category attempting to enter as a second-rank contender from the flank. One footwear manufacturer in Europe pointed out that their five key competitors hadn't even existed 10 years ago. Baskin-Robbins spoke about the impact McDonald's selling frozen yogurt and desserts had had on the casual walk across the road for ice cream after a cheeseburger. The photographic industry talked of Hewlett-Packard and printers as the threat in the digital age. Gas retailers in the United Kingdom talked of the threat of grocery chains—and now the number-one and number-two gas retailers in the United Kingdom are in fact those same grocery chains—Tesco and Sainsbury.

4. **As the big players moved downward, the retailers moved upward.** Marketeers in the research felt the ambitions of the retailer in their market were impacting much more dramatically on their own marketing requirements. Gaining market share from branded rivals *was no longer enough*—the retailer they depended on required them to also grow the entire market if they wished to retain quality distribution. Private labels flourished in certain countries (from jeans to bleach to stereos); in some, retailers had become considerable players in categories like financial services.

Now when the effects of each of these business dynamics are discussed in the press, the analysis is usually in terms of its implications for the brand leader. *Forbes* will discuss the implications of Hewlett-Packard's entry into digital photography, for example, in terms of its likely impact on Kodak. The *San Francisco Chronicle* will note the success of JCPenney's own label Arizona Jean in terms of its effect on Levi's. But ask yourself this: if Hewlett-Packard will seriously impact Kodak, how much greater will be its effect on the number-two brand, Fuji? And when Kodak and Hewlett-Packard become one and two, where does that leave the threes and fours, like Konica or Agfa? Or if Levi's is suffering in JCPenney, what has the success of Arizona Jean done to the sales and margins in that store of Wrangler and Lee—assuming that there is now a reason to stock those second-rank brands at all? Brand leaders moving across categories, pushing outside their territory to boost flagging home volume, means that we as a second-rank brand may swiftly find ourselves with not one, but *three brand leaders in our category*. It may not matter that two of these are, technically, brand leaders from other categories; the point is that if there's only room for a handful of profitable brands, then the existing middle ground is an increasingly vulnerable place to be.

When you look at the collective implications of these four marketing problems taken together—and add the velocity at which the marketeers we spoke to felt they were occurring—the simple conclusion is surely this: in the future, the middle ground will be an increasingly dangerous place to live. To allow yourself to continue to be *just another* second-rank brand is, by default, to put yourself into the mouth of the Big Fish and wait for the jaws to close. Caught in the new food chain between the new hunger of the brand leader, the speculative sharks from other categories, and the crocodile smile on the face of our retailer, the only path to medium- and long-term health is *rapid growth*. We are not necessarily seeking to be number one; there is a perfectly healthy living to be made as number two or three in our market (or large market sector). But to be one of those brands, we have to put some air between ourselves and the competition. We cannot be just another middle-market player; we have to be a *strong* number two.

And we can't get there by behaving like a smaller version of the Big Fish.

The Big Fish is a Different Kind of Animal

It may be thought at this point that I'm going to talk about the advantages of critical mass—the advantages at consumer, company, and competitive levels the brand leader enjoys over every other player in the game due to their size advantage. Well, these are of course enviable advantages: Who would not want the distribution power of Anheuser-Busch over the trade, or the ubiquitous consumer visibility of Coca-Cola, or the Research and Development resource of Procter & Gamble?

But this is not my point. Nor is the preference the social acceptibility of the brand leader lends it for the uncertain consumer; nor indeed the formidable trust and reassurance it enjoys; nor yet the power of its monstrous marketing budget relative to ours. These are odds we know and understand. These all merely lead us to talk generally about "trying harder" and "differentiating in our advertising," and "focus." Everything we are already trying at the moment.

What I am going to talk about is how, even knowing all this, we are still underestimating the situation: *The true dynamic is actually worse than this*. For it is not just that brand leaders are bigger and enjoy proportionately greater benefits: the evidence we are going to consider suggests that the superiority of their advantage increases almost *exponentially* the larger they get.

The Law of Increasing Returns

The easiest way to illustrate this difference is to map out the brand-consumer relationship into three stages (albeit rather crude ones) and look at the relative performances of the brand leader at each stage relative to a second- or lower-ranked brand in the same category.

Stage One: Consumer Awareness

First, awareness. Who does our target think about first?

Top-of-mind awareness, sometimes called *salience*, is the proportion of consumers for whom a certain brand comes to mind *first* when they are thinking about your category. An acknowledged key driver of purchase in lower-interest or impulse markets, like burgers and snacks, top-of-mind awareness is also an underestimated factor in shopping higher-interest categories. General spontaneous awareness, on the other hand (the proportion of people who are aware of your brand at all without prompting), is obviously important at some level to a brand's success—people rarely

Figure 1.1 **Top-of-mind awareness versus total spontaneous awareness**

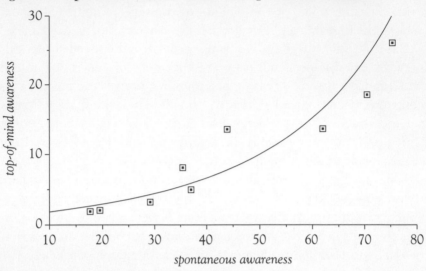

Source: U. van de Sandt/Ammirati Puris Lintas

buy an unfamiliar brand—but tends to reflect brand size and share of market: it often corresponds roughly to market share.

The assumption marketeers generally make is that the relationship between the two is a linear one—one's total spontaneous awareness and top-of-mind awareness will rise in roughly equal proportions. Figure 1.1, however, taken from work done into the relationship between the two among packaged goods brands in France by the advertising agency Lintas (now Ammirati Puris Lintas) in 1990,[2] shows otherwise.

What is striking here is that top-of-mind awareness increases quasi-exponentially in relation to total spontaneous awareness. That is to say, if I as brand leader am twice as big as the number two or three, and spontaneous awareness is linked to market dominance, my top-of-mind awareness is on average close to *four times* as great. And by the same token if I as brand leader starting from a higher base increase either of these, my return will be almost exponentially greater, gain for gain, than a Challenger making the same gains lower down the scale.

Not only, it seems, do brand leaders have more muscle and resource to start with, but it earns them almost twice as much top-of-mind awareness in return. Udo van de Sandt, the French Strategic Planner whose

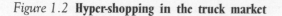

Figure 1.2 **Hyper-shopping in the truck market**

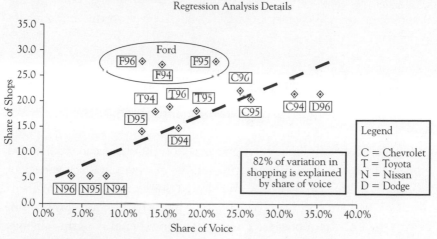

Source: C. Scott/Allison Fisher[3]

work this was, found the same relationship existed between "spontaneous brand awareness" and "usual/preferred brand." We may have to differentiate more sharply than we thought.

Stage Two: Shopping

What happens when the consumer leaves the house?

What happens is that this "Law of Increasing Returns" is translated directly into shopping behavior. Imagine our consumer is shopping for a truck, for instance. Well, from a marketing point of view, you would expect that the more you advertised your new truck, the more footfall in store you could generate compared to the competition. And this is true, up to a point. If one takes the the U.S. compact pickup market, for instance, and plots the relationship between advertising spend and shopping (Figure 1.2), there will be a close fit along a straight line for every brand—except the Ford Ranger. It alone does not obey the normal laws of proportionate returns.

Why? Because the Ranger is the compact pickup segment leader and as such enjoys a dramatically higher share of shopping even when supported by a comparatively low share of voice.

It looks as though, as an ambitious number two, we will need to be a greater source of differentiation not just into our image, but into the shopping process. We cannot compete effectively with the brand leader under the existing rules.

Stage Three: Purchase and Loyalty

So a picture is emerging. It translates even into purchase and loyalty, albeit in a less dramatic fashion.

"Double Jeopardy" is a brand phenomenon that has been studied and modeled by researchers in marketing for over 35 years across a variety of markets in cultures as diverse as the United States and Japan. It refers to the combined effects of two benefits that high-share brands profit from relative to low-share brands. The first of these benefits is the obvious one: high-share brands enjoy higher penetration (i.e., simply have more buyers) than low-share brands. The second, more interesting observation is that the buyers of high-share brands *buy them more often* than the buyers of low-share brands purchase those same low-share brands (see for example Figure 1.3).

Figure 1.3 **Annual penetrations and average purchase frequencies (Leading brands of U.S. instant coffee in their market-share order)**

Instant Coffee (USA, 1981)	Market Share	Penetration	Average Purchase* of Brand	of Any
Any Instant	100%	67%	—	7
Maxwell House	19	24	3.6	9
Sanka	15	21	3.3	9
Tasters Choice	14	22	2.8	9
High Point	13	22	2.6	9
Folgers	11	18	2.7	9
Nescafe	8	13	2.9	10
Brim	4	9	2.0	9
Maxim	3	6	2.6	11
All other brands	13	20	3.0	9
Average brand	11	17	2.8	9

*purchases per buyer of the brand

Source: MRCA/Professor A.S.C. Ehrenberg/R & DI[4]

The cumulative effect of these two factors taken together leads to relative scale of increase in the number of purchases tending toward the exponential effect observed in the work on salience shown in Figure 1.2. (Some researchers, indeed, have claimed to observe variances for very high-share brands greater even than this.)

The Consequence: Profitability

What, of course, all this leads up to is brand leaders making more damn money than we do. Figure 1.4 is taken from the PIMS database; it shows the return on investment for a brand leader (split into two different kinds—dominators and marginal leaders) compared to second- and third-ranked brands.

Look at service businesses, the fourth column in Figure 1.4: While a second-rank brand makes a fifth as much profit again as a third-rank brand, a brand leader that dominates the category makes *twice as much profit as either of them*. Or take durables: A second-rank brand makes twice as much as a number three, but a dominator almost doubles that again. I bring this up not just as a stockholder issue, but as a further compounding of the difference in resources between us. Those with an aversion to data tables may find the profitability of a market dominator illustrated a little more vividly by the remuneration of Roberto Goizueta, the late CEO of Coca-Cola, who became the first CEO to earn $1 billion in salary and bonuses alone. That has yet to happen at Pepsi or Dr. Pepper.

If profit allows a company to make choices, to invest resource in finding sources of future competitive advantage, then this disparity serves to

Figure 1.4 **Return on investment % (average over 4 years)**

Market Rank	United States	Europe	Industrial	Service	Durable	Non-Durables
Dominator	39	36	35	52	40	42
Marginal Leader	27	26	26	29	29	28
Rank-two	22	21	20	26	21	26
Rank-three	16	12	17	12	11	11
Follower	12	9	12	17	10	9

Source: PIMS Database of performance of 3,500 businesses, 1998.

widen the discrepancy between the chips the brand leader has at their disposal and the pile we have to play with. And as we have seen, each of their chips seems to win them twice as much as ours.

Which is one of the reasons why so many Brand leaders in FMCG markets, for instance, are exactly the same brands that were market leaders 60 years ago.

So what?

The point of all this is not to suggest that it is hard for a second-rank brand to catch the number one; as we will come to see, that is rarely their objective anyway. Nor is the point that at a crude level we as second-rank brands are outgunned more comprehensively than we thought (though we are).

What the Law of Increasing Returns means is that we have to swim considerably harder than the brand leader *just to remain in the same place*. Up to now this has largely translated itself into conversations about relevance and focus: decisions about communication strategy and customer targeting.

But what if staying where we are in the future will not be enough? What if profitable survival in our category requires the achievement of rapid growth, in a probably static market, in the face of three new kinds of competition? Knowing that to follow the model of the brand leader is to help them increase their market advantage?

It would mean that we would need to abandon conservatism and incrementalism and start thinking like a Challenger just to survive healthily. It would mean we would have to behave and think about the way we marketed ourselves in a completely different kind of way. Find a different way of thinking about our goals and strategic objectives. Require, in fact, a different kind of decision-making process altogether.

A Bear Stearns analyst was quoted approvingly recently in *Financial World* for commenting, "There is a certain trust associated with the McDonald's brand name." "Of course," continued the magazine, "[the analyst] has paid McDonald's the ultimate compliment a service brand could hope to receive."[5]

A service brand? Any service brand? A brand leader, maybe, but certainly not a number two or three looking for growth. The currencies of reassurance, simplification, and trust, though they may well have been adequate until relatively recently for brands like AT&T and IBM, are woefully inadequate as the basis for the kind of relationship we are going to need with our consumer. Facing the Law of Increasing Returns, number-two brands are going to need to deal in altogether more potent currencies: those of curiosity, desire, and reevaluation. To succeed, they are going to have to create an emotional identification, a strength of belief in the brand, a sense that we are one to watch or explore—*active* expressions of choice and loyalty that will make someone walk by the big, convenient facings of the brand leader and lean down to pick out the little blue can at the side. As a second-rank brand, we don't just want to create desire, we want to create *intensity* of desire. Harley-Davidson's legendarily loyal customers, for instance, are not putting their trust in the brand's motorcycle engineering—they can buy a higher-performance bike at a highly competitive price—nor are they people who appear to be desperately in need of reassurance or simplification. They buy one because they want to feel Bad. And no other bike in the world lets you feel Bad like a Harley.

And what this demands is a different kind of marketing altogether, a different approach. We will come to see that it will demand a change, in fact, not just in strategy but in the attitude that precedes that strategy and the behavior that follows. Fundamental to each decision taken and each way of thinking will be the concept of Mechanical Advantage— the physical principle describing a machine that manages to create greater output from the same or lesser input. Getting more results, in short, from less resource. Not only is this going to be the framework for our entire way of thinking, but it is also going to be the brief for the way we rethink the internal working structure, processes, and behavior of the company and people behind the brand.

And at the heart of Mechanical Advantage in marketing—its currency, in fact—are ideas.

2

The Consumer Isn't

"The past is another country; they do things differently there."
L. P. Hartley

If Consumerism was a brand, we would say that the person on the street has developed significantly different usage, attitudes, and behavior toward that brand over the last three decades—and yet the vocabulary we still use to talk about it remains essentially unchanged. The old underlying structures and concepts that we still refer to implicitly every time we use words like *consumer* and *audience* and *category* are thus now left fundamentally flawed. These were concepts, after all, coined at the beginning of the packaged goods mass market, when families watched television together and being a consumer meant something because—certainly in the United States—consumerism was embraced by the general public as a healthy sign of being part of, or aspiring to, the middle class. But although our vocabulary fails to acknowledge it, the world is very different today. Consider what has happened to just those three basic concepts—audience, consumer, and category—over the last 30 years.

The Audience Isn't

Much has been written about consumer's sense of stress today, to the point of it becoming a cliché. But the fact that it has become a cliché should not blind us to the fact that it is profoundly true and is having a considerable effect on the way that consumers interact with marketing activities, communications, and ideas. One of the most important shifts that has resulted from our point of view is the relationship that people are looking from in the media they use.[1]

In a 1991 poll, 94% of all American adults stated that a primary use of their free time was to recuperate from work. If true, this is one of the most important pieces of marketing data to have emerged in recent years, and it describes a profound shift in the way consumers use one of the principal marketing tools as our disposal, namely, the television. It implies that there has been a profound shift in our society, from a work/leisure society (i.e., one that self-consciously divides itself between two basic types of activity, work or leisure) to one that divides its time between three: a work/recuperation/leisure society.

Why is this important to us? Because recuperation is a very different thing from leisure. You use recuperation time in a different way, look for different kinds of experiences. Figure 2.1 shows how television has subsumed all other activities as recuperative activity over recent years.

Note how significantly the gap has widened. Now, one might argue that in a stressed world, television has subsumed all other activities precisely because it is *not* an activity—it is passive, a "vegging out." But it is more than this—if we think of it as active recuperation. Of those who saw recuperation as a primary function of their leisure time, 75% did not

Figure 2.1 **What activities are the one that you usually enjoy or look forward to during a day?**

	1988	1996
Watching Television	61	62
Checking the Mail	59	53
Going to Sleep	52	43
Taking a Shower/Bath	50	41
Getting in the House	46	40
Making Love	*	39

* Not asked

Source: Roper 1997

even classify watching television as leisure. For them, I suggest, it has gone further than that. It has become necessary therapy.

Look at yourself. Exhaustion is, in every sense, a great leveler. At a very profound level the consumer is yourself on a Thursday night after a tough four days. What kind of advertising do you want to watch? The answer, of course, is none at all. At nine o'clock on a Thursday night, all you want to do is escape a little. Relax. Eat peanuts and scratch your stomach.

It is not simply a question of boredom thresholds or tolerance levels decreasing—even in serious relationships (with a local divorce rate running at 68%, one county in the American Midwest is considering *compulsory prenuptial counseling* before granting a marriage licence). It is a question of the pace at which we live profoundly impacting quite basic levels of human need. We live in a world in which 10 years ago the average American said they have six close friends; today they say they only have four. We live in a world in which companies are monitoring the amount of bathroom tissue that is used to demonstrate that people go to the bathroom less often when they are working more intensely. So if man, a social animal with physical needs, is cutting down on both those basic requirements in order to get through the day, what slack are they going to cut *us?* In this context, when their prime evening motivation is recuperation and escape, advertisers have moved beyond being clutter. They are no longer in the communication business, they are in a new kind of business altogether: The Nuisance Business.

Which means that the audience is not an audience. To call them an audience presupposes they are listening. In fact, we, the brand, are merely one of the three or four acts that are on stage simultaneously, each vying for the attention of the potential audience. Children, conversation with one's partner, food, magazines—video research of the consumer "watching" television shows that they are anything but a captive audience, even when the programming is on. One study suggested that 23% of U.S. golf programming *plays to an empty room.* And their attention to advertising is getting even more selective (see Figure 2.2).

And this in turn, of course, is because they pay even less attention to the advertising than they do to some of the programming (see Figure 2.3).

Audience, then, although it is a word that is used almost interchangeably to refer to our target, is fundamentally flawed. Our target is

Figure 2.2 **Adult evening viewers able to name a brand or product advertised in show just seen: no prompt**

Date	Can't name any product/brand seen (%)	Name brand/product in show seen (%)	Name brand/product in other show (%)
1965	60	34	6
1974	72	24	4
1981	80	13	7
1986	80	12	8
1990	84	8	8

Source: Newspaper Advertising Bureau.[2]

not an audience, for that would presuppose they were watching or listening. While it may have more usefully described our target at the beginning of the intersection of mass marketing and television (and even this is arguable), it certainly does not do so now. The audience isn't.

And neither, in fact, in any very useful sense, are they a consumer.

Figure 2.3 **Viewer's response to commercial break**

Stimulated channel change	19%
Muted commercial	14%
Ignored commercial	6%
Alternating attention	53%
Attended to commercial	7%

Source: American Academy of Advertising

The Consumer Isn't

Implicit in the idea of a *consumer* is someone who is engaged in an activity—namely consuming. Basking in this, as marketeers we eagerly add rational information for them to absorb and inform themselves with our packaging, brochures, in-store material, and direct mail. Don't put it in the body copy, we say, confidently—we'll get our consumers to pick it up in the nutritional information.

In fact, consumption of anything other than the product itself is passive at best, and with very rare exceptions, it is centered around the actual moment of purchase or use—people don't have the energy or in-clination to be continuously engaged with regard to a product. They are simply using your product and getting on with their lives. In most cases, the smaller the interaction—the less they have to react—the better. There is evidence to suggest that people want less nutritional claims, less choice, less information to have to deal with in the things they buy every day.

Jack in the Box, a fast-food chain operating primarily on the West Coast of the United States, put into focus group research a new range of in-store material talking about product improvements. In the groups, people responded well to the tent cards and posters—they were seen as informative and attention-worthy. Jack in the Box then mocked up one of their restaurants with the new material—which screamed out (to their eyes and ears) the benefits of key new menu improvements—and conducted the research again in the form of random exit interviews with regular consumers who had been into the restaurant to buy a meal for themselves. In this second piece of research, most of the consumers in-terviewed had no idea what we were talking about. What in-store posters? they asked. Tent cards? Were we sure? They had just come in for a burger and fries; they didn't know they were supposed to be reading the stuff on the walls as well.

Why the inconsistency? The first piece of research assumed the Jack in the Box eater was a consumer—and respondents played the game ac-cordingly in the focus groups. The second piece of research treated them like people who bought fast food at Jack in the Box—and the limitations of the concept of "consumer" started to become apparent.

Furthermore, the Jack in the Box story suggests that to say they are willing consumers of a product is *not to say they are necessarily open-minded consumers (or even consumers at all) of its marketing*. It is well known that the happy coexistence between marketeer and consumer of the 1970s and early 1980s has been strained by the cynicism toward in-stitutions of all types (from the government down)—to the point where they have become inoculated against many of the marketing claims in each category. It is not simply that people are marketing-aware in con-cept and vocabulary (the knowledgable 1990s consumer is the exact an-tithesis of Vance Packard's unprotected innocent), it is that as victims of hype and oversell by flagging players in maturing or overmature markets, they don't intend to trust anyone but themselves. One might forgive them for scoffing at advertising images of smiling flight attendants pouring drinks, when the evidence of experience has denied the gloss for so long; more startling is the disbelief when a genuinely superior product comes onto the market. When Sony PlayStation, for instance, tried to talk as a possible launch route about its genuine product advantages (360-degree movement, 3-D graphics, and higher resolution), the teenage target exposed to these concepts simply sneered—not because these were not things to be desired, but because Sega and Nintendo had tried to sell their ailing 16-bit technology on such claims and lied. Burnt once, twice, the target was not about to get fooled again.

So how much of your marketing does your consumer *really* want to consume? I suggest to you that your consumer isn't consuming in any really useful sense. I suggest that the golden age of marketing is over. The consumer, in fact, isn't.

And neither, perhaps, is your category.

The Category Isn't

To begin with, we are all much too close to our own categories: Consumers simply don't see them in the clearly defined way that we see them. If one lays out 16 products in front of focus group respondents and asks them to sort the products by which criteria they—the product users—regard as being the same and others as being different, one frequently finds that what we would regard as the "category" groupings are the least interesting, least useful (and often emerge surprisingly late) in the different ways the products can be sorted. Where we as marketeers see each product category as being substantially different from another, the target very often doesn't. They are making comparisons of relative use and value across categories that transcend the crude ways we ourselves divide them. A woman asked in group to sort out female toiletries divided them into two piles: one she called "Pretties," and one she characterized as "Things you throw in the basket with the frozen chicken."[3] Quite apart from being a more accurate portrayal of her relationship with, for instance, underarm deodorants than our own physical description of what the category offers, this is also a far more revealing and useful way of thinking about the problems and opportunities for your brand. Instead of considering minor pack changes for relative standout compared to the competition, for instance, our time might be better spent considering how we would turn something that was just for "throwing in the basket with the frozen chicken" into a "pretty."

In any case, the most powerful brands have an emotional role that transcends their historical category usage (if Wonderbra's real benefit is self-confidence, does its category remain underwear?). We are limiting the potential of our own brand by thinking purely in terms of our own category.

Furthermore, what boundaries they do draw are not always the ones we ourselves live by; they are in fact being encouraged by product development within even apparently complementary categories to break down the walls even further. Technology is an obvious example—if one offers the consumer a machine that is simultaneously a phone, answering machine, fax, and copier, what category are we in? And this blurring is not limited in any way to technology. Historically, for instance, you would have said that the hotel business and the luggage business were complementary—greater use of one encouraged greater need of the other. But 1996 saw the beginning of them as competitors for the first time: As Samsonite reinvigorated its product range for the travel-jaded road warrior, making it lighter, faster, more convenient to carry and stow, the Four Seasons Hotel in Chicago introduced a "No Luggage Service," where, far from needing to minimize your luggage, you can in principle travel with *absolutely no luggage at all*—you can have the clothes you walk in wearing cleaned, while you put on one of a range of men's or women's apparel that the hotel lends out. The Four Seasons had realized, it seems, that the question one typically asks of consumers in luggage focus groups—"What kind of bags do you really want?"—is in a very real sense starting too far downstream: people these days simply don't want to have to deal with the hassle of carrying bags *at all*.

Besides, in certain key respects, consumers don't *want* to see categories as being entirely different; in many ways they want their service aspects, for instance, to have more in common. Twenty or so years ago, every service category had developed its own rules of engagement with its consumer—car dealers treated you one way, fast food treated you in its own fashion, airlines were airlines, and so on. And the consumer, in turn, generally accepted this. But today, consumers have become aware of what is possible—and indeed what they should be expecting for their money—in *any* category. Educated by quality of service or experience in one business, they transfer those expectations to every category in which there is a service transaction. A respondent at a recent focus group on airlines put the case with some verve:

> You know, I have a dry cleaner at the end of my street. It's just a little Italian guy doing his own thing, no big company or anything. I took him a work blouse on Monday, and I needed it in a hurry. "No problem," he says. So on the way home I picked it up in the evening and it turns out it's missing a button and he's replaced it with another just the same, without even making a big deal about it. Doesn't charge me anything extra; like it's all just part of the service.
>
> Well, then on Wednesday I get on the flight to New York, and I ask for an extra packet of peanuts because I haven't eaten any lunch, and the flight attendant tells me I can't have any more because she only has one bag of nuts per passenger to give out. And that doesn't hold up for me. When I look at how much more money I give the airline each year than my dry cleaner, and how many more people they have working for them, and the infrastructure and everything, I just don't understand how they can hold their heads up and say stuff like that.

Ask them in focus groups in Des Moines what the blueprint for a new telecommunication company would be like, and they answer the name of a car company: Saturn. In the 1990s, quality of experience and the expectations that engenders travel beyond the category they were first experienced in.

Our category, in summary, isn't.

In conclusion, then, the language that we use everyday in our jobs is a legacy from a past that is no longer relevant, leaving that same vocabulary and the concepts it represents fundamentally flawed premises for the new world marketeers say they are beginning to find themselves in. Implicit in those concepts are numerous assumptions that may have been correct when the language was first coined but are dangerously misleading now. Now, I am *not* going to attempt in the rest of this book to pursue this caution into the invention of a replacement vocabulary—it would make for tiresome reading, besides distracting us from the principal thrust of the book, which is the study of Challenger brands. For the moment, it will serve to remain keenly aware of those implicit pitfalls and think of the old marketing language we still use as like a rotten wooden floor—it will take our weight as long as we realize we have to walk gingerly and understand the nature of the drop beneath.

Which brings us back to the imperative of Mechanical Advantage and the importance of ideas.

Communication Doesn't

The shift in the way we need to think about the category, the audience, and the consumer suggests that we should not be thinking of our marketing goal as communication. The sum of all this is that communication doesn't, or rather, that communication doesn't *necessarily*. Communications suggest active listening, but our target doesn't want to be communicated to, isn't waiting for a further message. Put bluntly, therefore, anyone who talks about "communications" or "integrated communications" is again using a flawed concept in the current business environment. The only business to be in is the *ideas* business (integrated or otherwise); for implicit in the ideas business is not simply the idea of communication, but also that of *engagement*—seizing the audience's imagination.

The combination of category blurring and the consumer's changed relationship with television has significant implications for advertising: In a very real sense, our competition in this new world, particularly this new world of recuperation is now *all* advertising, not just our principal competitor's share of voice. If total ad spending in the United States was $162 billion in 1995, and we are a brand that spends $20 million on advertising a year, our real share of voice is 0.012%. If we are in the laundry detergent business, our competition is not the other appalling commercials our competitors deploy for laundry detergents, but the other commercials our target are engaged by, and respond to, across *every* category: pizza, batteries, cola, beer. A competitive advertising review must be all the competitive advertising the target sees: our action standards measured in terms of which of those—*whether within or outside what we call "our category"*—the consumer finds relevant and appealing.

Which is why, as a Challenger, we need ideas. Implicit in the concept of ideas, quite apart from the content, is that they are engaging, provocative, and self-propagating. The unexpected pairing that an idea consists of seizes or engages the attention and imagination of the target, rather than assuming that ears are already waiting to hear; it provokes a response, rather than allowing the listener's indifference to be maintained; and it is self-propagating in that, once seeded, it does not allow constant external feeding to flourish.

This concept of ideas will run throughout the book. Indeed, most of the Eight Credos have at their heart the development and implementation of ideas.

3

What Is a Challenger Brand?

Not least among the difficulties in abandoning—as we are attempting to—the natural reactions we fall back on in times of marketing adversity is the daunting prospect of facing a journey we have not made before, and a journey that seems almost by definition to be one for which there is no map or precedent. It takes more time, energy, and effort to create something new than it does something old, and these are the three commodities of which we feel most deprived. We need new brand models to guide us, to give us an overall sense of direction—an intuitive marketing compass we can fall back on in the fog of war. We look enviously at the precedents of the legal world; would that we had new precedents of our own to help short-cut decision making.

Well, we do. They're just not the precedents we used to use—the brand leaders. Instead, we have to look to another kind of model—from a type of brand that is far more relevant to us. The criteria for a brand we (as, at best, a number two in a category) should be looking to emulate are three:

1. They should be *at best* a second-rank brand themselves.
2. They should have demonstrated a period of sustained and dramatic growth.
3. They should be from a category other than our own.

These kinds of second-rank brands we shall call Challenger brands.

Who Is a Challenger Brand?

The expression *Challenger brand* may be thought to simply evoke a number-two or number-three brand who is up against a much bigger and more muscular brand leader—the *Establishment brand*. Images of David against Goliath come to mind: attitude and a single shot against confidence and power. And isn't the Challenger naturally the number two to the Establishment brand, rather than any rank lower? Can one really challenge from the position of fourth, fifth, or sixth?

One might have agreed with this up until the 1960s. But when Avis, which explicitly introduced the whole concept of the number-two brand to modern consumer and marketeer alike, launched the celebrated "we're number two, so we try harder" positioning, the brand wasn't quite in the close second place its advertising suggested; it was certainly in the following pack, but at some distance from Hertz. The brilliance of the strategy was that its *claimed* position took it out ahead of the chasing pack, apparently snapping at the heels of the gigantic Hertz. One would get the impression from the advertising, in fact, that they were the only two players of any significance in the market at all. More recently, Richard Branson's Virgin Atlantic has played the same game with British Airways in its home market. Although British Airways has far more serious potential rivals, even in its home market, in the major U.S. and European competitors, Virgin has created the impression for the domestic consumer that there are only two choices on the routes they fly: themselves and British Airways.

The classification of brands we will examine throughout the rest of the book are consequently deliberately broad, both in the ranking of the Challenger within its market (if it has one—Starbucks, for example, effectively created an entirely new market) and indeed in the definition they embrace of what is and is not a brand. The reader immediately comfortable with Las Vegas, the Spice Girls, and the British Labour Party alongside Absolut and Wonderbra as brands, and Cirque du Soleil and Starbucks alongside Lexus as Challengers can move directly to the First Credo and Chapter 4. For those who prefer a greater preliminary clarity, the rest of this chapter will offer some definitions: first, what I mean by a "brand," and second, who is and isn't a Challenger brand.

The Expanding Universe of Brands

"The X-Files has been a very carefully managed brand."
Pat Wyatt, President of the Fox Licensing Division[1]

The Marketing universe is exploding. What was once perceived to be the province of packaged goods and retailers is now systematically embraced by institutions and products as diverse as theme parks, cities, charities, gaming software, volunteer organizations, films, programs, sports, artists, and public figures. Even within the rather simplistic idea of packaged goods as things that are found on supermarket shelves, one would now be forced to include U2 and Madonna as brands. When a new release from U2 went straight to the top of the singles chart, it was not simply because of quality of the melody or the lyrics—the product quality—it was because the brand that was packaging this product had a residual equity in the minds of consumers considerably hotter than the young unknowns loitering hopefully at number 29. For his part, Michael Jordan says that Nike has turned him into a dream—and what are brands if not dreams in one way or another? How far, then, is he from fitting David Ogilvy's definition of a brand as being "the consumer's idea of a product"? And if the presence of a cologne bearing his name is not enough to convince us of Jordan's stature as a Living Brand, what do we make of Martha Stewart?

Marketing has even overtaken historically creatively driven categories as diverse as fashion—the fashion editor of the *New York Times* was quoted recently in connection with the resurrection of Gucci as saying: "The fashion industry *is all about* marketing now"—and programming (as the remark at the head of this section from the head of Fox's licensing division testifies). If, as we will go on to see, we can learn more from looking at other categories that we can from studying our own, this is an invigorating time to be a part of marketing and brands: For as the universe of brands expands, so does the universe of marketed categories—and this in turn means there is a greater fund of fresh thinking we can learn from.

Embracing the riches of this expanding galaxy, I am going to define a brand as an entity that satisfies all of the following four conditions:

1.   Something that has a buyer and a seller—the Spice Girls, but not the Queen. (Buying and selling in this sense doesn't have to be a *financial* transaction to be of value to both sides. Political parties and the Boy Scouts both have sellers and buyers who derive value from a transaction between them.)

2.   Something that has a differentiating name, symbol, or trademark—Tide, but not sugar or bleach—but also something that is seen as being differentiated from other like products around it *for reasons other than* its name or trademark—the Los Angeles Police Department, but not the Fourteenth Infantry Division.

3.   Something that has positive and or negative opinions about it in consumers minds for reasons other than its literal product characteristics—Cirque du Soleil, but not Concrete.

4.   Something that is created, rather than naturally occurring—*The X-Files* and Las Vegas, but not Adam Morgan or the Blue Grass of Kentucky. (People, in fact, are difficult in this regard. Ronald Reagan and Margaret Thatcher, if not created, were styled and boosted by spin doctors. Andy Warhol re-created and marketed himself with much of the panache of a brand entrepreneur. Steven Spielberg appears an executive producer credit on a film in a way that one would normally think of a brand as adding value.)

There are two temptations the above list has tried to avoid. The first is to define a brand as "anything that is marketed." I have resisted this because the only person who can define whether something is a brand is the *buyer*, not the seller. Wishing something is a brand, and even spending money behind marketing it, does not make it one. Most U.S. telecommunication companies and cellular providers, for instance, would regard themselves as brands, yet they are little more than recognized names or commodities with trademarks. The lack of real competition masks the consequences of the consumer's inability to distinguish any real difference between them, or indeed, in the case of cellular providers, to be aware of the role of the brand in their lives at all. I suggest if we are unhappy with the concept of "consumer" and feel it has fundamentally changed from when the word first became marketing currency, then this definition of a brand is something we should reject as inadequate, too. For if a brand by its very nature only exists in the consumer's

Figure 3.1 **Types of marketed concepts (examples)**

Traditional Brands	New Generation of Brands	Marketed Entities	Trademarked Commodities
Kellogg's Corn Flakes	Las Vegas	Ronald Reagan?	Most Utilities
Heinz Ketchup	Cirque du Soleil	Michael Jordan?	Many cellular
	British Labour Party		providers
	The Spice Girls		

mind (a can of Coke on a desert island is just an aluminum can full of sugared water), then when the consumer begins to retreat from the marketing relationship, a brand must start to demand more of itself, just to stay in the same place. Existence and intent are not enough. In order to pass muster as a brand at all, it has to have made someone have a positive or negative opinion about it.

The second temptation I have tried to avoid is far more seductive: it is the definition of a brand as "something the consumer wants to buy," as opposed to the product of a company or organization. The reason for rejecting this is far simpler: some brands have largely negative equity. British Telecom, some of the major utilities, Skoda, the Los Angeles Police Department all have struggled with largely unfavorable consumer opinions—and it is that they have this negative equity, rather than that someone wants to buy them, that makes them brands as well. Indifference is the characteristic of the commodity, not rejection.

Four types of marketed concepts are illustrated in Figure 3.1. For the purposes of this book, our marketing universe includes the two types of brands in the two columns on the left, but not the two on the right.

The Three Criteria for a Challenger Brand

There are three criteria for a Challenger brand—a state of market, a state of mind, and a rate of success:

1. State of Market. Challengers are by definition not the number-one brands; nor are they niche.

2. State of Mind. This is what really characterizes all these players—being number 2 (or number 6, or 18) is simply an accident of birth. Challenger brands have a mind-set that encompasses two key differentiators:
- Ambitions that exceed their conventional marketing resources, and,
- A preparedness to accept the marketing implications of the gap between their ambition and their marketing resource.*

The latter is an important distinction—ambition in a marketing plan is not enough; being smaller and hopeful, without a preparedness to behave *in whatever way is necessary* to fulfill that ambition will lead to nothing but being small and disappointed. And note that in talking about a "Challenger mind-set" we are not necessarily talking about aggression. Taking a historical perspective, both the Sex Pistols and Gandhi were Challengers, but only one of them was aggressive; a determination to change the status quo doesn't necessarily require a full frontal attitude.

3. Rate of Success. The final criterion for a Challenger has to be—for our purposes—success. There is no point in imitating an aggressive brand that has failed—this is not challenge, merely arrogance or misguided ambition. We shall require of all our brands that they have enjoyed significant and sustained growth through their marketing actions. This is not to say that they are *still* always growing at the same rate (Oakley, for example), but that there is a period of their life we can learn from, a period in which they enjoyed *rapid* growth. This is what Challengers can offer us over the brand leaders—an illustration of how to do it *quickly*.

The antithesis of the Challenger brand is the Establishment brand. The most dominant example of this is the brand leader, but other brands—even long-standing number-two brands—can fall into this category if they lack either the ambition or the acceptance of the marketing implications.

---

* I make the distinction between 'resources' and 'marketing resources' because of Saturn. Saturn's marketing resources are in proportion to their size. But their birth and many of the physical characteristics of their distribution base, for instance, were the gift of an enormous investment by a gigantic parent company.

The Principal Challenger Brands Considered Here

I have chosen brands that I have been able to get good primary or secondary data on, or have worked on myself. Although, therefore, not a scientific study in the sense that the brands can be said to be a representative sample of all brands, I have attempted to include a broad mix of the following:

- Launches (Lexus, Absolut, Goldfish) versus relaunches (Wonderbra, Tango, Harley-Davidson, Jack in the Box).
- U.S. brands versus international brands.
- Challengers that continue to enjoy strong growth (PlayStation) versus Challengers that have displayed strong growth in the past, even if recent performance has plateaued (The Body Shop).
- Categories as diverse as, for instance, packaged goods, credit cards, fast food, automotive, and entertainment.

I have included some brands the reader may not be familiar with, either as being regional brands within the United States (Jack in the Box), or as brands from countries and markets with which the reader understandably may be unfamiliar (South Africa, for instance). These are included not simply to leaven their more familiar costars, but because each has an enviable growth rate that has strikingly outperformed the category—and the brand leader—they compete against. Jack in the Box, for instance, was one of only two U.S. fast-food brands to increase per-store sales in 1996; it has increased sixfold its parent company's stock price in three years. Equally, Goldfish is a U.K. credit card, which in its first year has come to count for more than 20% of all new credit cards issued. These are brands I have felt it is worth trading a small amount of explanation for in order to reap the rewards of their experience.

Category aside, these fall into four kinds of groups, shown in Figure 3.2. Each of the four sections of the grid represents a different kind of Challenger. Most of the discussion in the book will center on Group A, who are launches or relaunches that have challenged the Brand Leader in the category. Group B are brands that have either

Figure 3.2 **Challenger Brands Table**

A. Challenger Brands	B. "Challenger" Brands
Launches or relaunches into a category with an existing brand leader (e.g., Tango, PlayStation)	Challengers that have succeeded through creating their own category (e.g. Starbucks)

C. Challenger "Brands"	D. Historical Challengers
New brands that have become brand leaders (e.g., British Labour Party, the Spice Girls)	Historical Challengers (e.g., Gandhi, Alexander the Great, America 1776–1941, Andy Warhol)

created their own category or succeeded by moving outside what had been thought of as their "natural" category altogether. They accomplished growth in slightly different ways from Group A—if growth is caused either by increasing their market share or increasing their market, then brands in the top right of the grid increased their market: Cirque du Soleil, for instance, redefined its competition from other circuses to be "every other show in town" and aimed to attract the occasional show goer by being one of the two things they went to see that year. Brands in the Group A (e.g., PlayStation), on the other hand, were as likely to take share from the brand leader as they were to grow the market.

What's a Coffee Shop Going to Tell Me about Selling Sheet Metal?

The problem with marketing case histories such as the list of Challengers we have just mentioned is this: If they are in our category, we already know all about them, and they have long since lost the ability to stimulate or inspire (far fewer offer an opportunity to derive competitive advantage). If, conversely, they are outside our category, we don't know what to do with them. Take the most discussed launch (or, technically, relaunch and expansion) of the last 10 years: Starbucks. Much featured, much feted, but what do we make of it if we don't sell beverages? Or

Absolut: The vodka market is fascinating, but it's an image market, and I'm competing on service. Oh, and don't talk to me about Wonderbra— my distribution system is nothing like lingerie. Like looking through a piece of textured glass, one thinks one grasps the application of the point the author is trying to make, but it doesn't really seem to match the lines and structures we actually live with every day. And so we put this other marketing world down and forget about it, the bridge unfinished between them and us.

Yet a key thrust of this entire book, and the strategic process we are going on to create, is that there is at least as great an advantage to be gained from watching the players in *other* categories as in analyzing the players in one's own. In order to flourish under the dynamics of the new, more voracious marketing food chain, the new brand models we should be watching and learning from are not the other brands in our own category, and certainly not brand leaders, in our category or anyone else's. They are instead:

- Second-rank brands.
- Outside our category.
- Who have demonstrated rapid growth.

If this is to work, we have to find a way of constructing a bridge from an apparently unrelated marketing category to our own in a way that is genuinely useful. So let us try to construct a bridge between two such businesses, and in doing so derive the first of a series of exercises that will form the building blocks of the Challenger strategic process later in the book.

Starbucks is an interesting case for a number of reasons. One is that if you had researched it, you would never have come up with the concept as something of mass appeal—it would have done well among a few high-end gourmands, but the general population would not have been able to respond to the concept (expressed verbally, for the sake of argument, on a board in focus groups). Why? Because of course they are not selling a cup of coffee, they are selling a coffee experience. And, put simply, it is impossible for you or me to evaluate our reaction to that experience without actually experiencing it. So our starting point for learning from Starbucks might be this: Whatever lesson or product idea I draw from Starbucks for my business, I'm not going to be able to research; I'm just going to have to do it somewhere and see what people make of it. Then I'll decide if I do it everywhere. Because it's a lesson about selling an experience for two dollars, not a product.

Fine, you say to me. But I'm trying to sell more cars. What do I actually do with this? Well, let's start somewhere else. Imagine it is eight years ago. You have been recruited to a focus group somewhere in Los Angeles to talk about coffee; I, by a curious coincidence, am the focus-group moderator.

We begin. I tell you that there is a coffee company that is about to open in Los Angeles called Starbucks, and that they will be selling coffee at $2.50 a cup, and that they would like your business, preferably everyday. You look at me, incredulously, and ask me what on earth would justify spending two bucks everyday on a cup of coffee.

What do you think? I say. You consider this. It must be home delivery, you say, something like that. They come to you, straight to your door.

No, I say. Actually you have to go to them. And to start with, this is going to mean a bit of a detour on your way to work—you may even have to double park—but it's a detour you'll be happy to make.

You consider this again. Well, maybe it is about instant service when you get there, you say: as soon as you arrive, you get a great cup of coffee exactly the way you want it. No, I'd say to you, I'm afraid you're going to have to wait in line, sometimes for seven, eight minutes at a time. You look a little puzzled. But here's the thing, I continue—actually, that waiting in line is in many ways the best bit. In many ways that's what they're actually selling. Because (stepping back to what we in fact, eight years on, now know the Starbucks' experience to be) it is: the anticipation of the choice, the smell of the coffee, the world of beans and the names of exotic blends that surround us as we step outside our pedestrian world for a moment, the exotic language the baristas speak that we now understand, the strains of jazz that make us feel sophisticated without being threatened, the lore of the bean that we savor and learn as we wait our turn—hey, I don't even drink coffee and I'd pay two dollars just to go and wait in line for 10 minutes. That, it seems to me, is the real brilliance of what Howard Schultz did with Starbucks: He took the part of the process a time-starved consumer should in principle hate most—

waiting in line—and he made it one of the most rewarding parts of the experience.

To cars, then. The least favorite part in buying a car for many consumers is the long four hours sitting on a plastic chair waiting for their credit to clear. One of the questions the Starbucks story would put on the table for us, then, is this: How does one make that moment, the part of the process they currently most hate, not simply less painful, but the piece of the process they actually enjoyed most (apart, of course, from physically driving the car off the lot)? A part of the process that got them talking to their friends around the water cooler the next day about it? About, even, how they wished they could do it all over again?

What would it take? More than a couple of dog-eared copies of *Readers Digest*. You would need to learn a little more about what gives your type of consumer pleasure. For some it might be play—perhaps in an out-of-town dealership having a go-kart track out back. For some it might be learning—perhaps a computer with a simulated advanced driving course, or free lessons in off-road techniques for truck purchasers. If all you have is a video, a film on how police drivers are taught to handle high-speed chases. Something that gave each person a better feeling about the interaction and a reason to talk about it to their friends, from making the down time valuable rather than simply no longer irritating.

In other words, the relevance of the Starbucks case to us has nothing to do with coffee. If we match what Howard Schultz created against consumer expectations from that kind of category—and then translate the points at which he gained advantage into the parallel points in one's own category—the relevance is not hard to find. In fact, we will go further. We will create the first of a series of exercises that turn a key point of relevance from the brand outside our category into an exercise we can apply to any category, regardless of the superficial differences and anomalies.

These exercises take the form of intransitive verbs. The first such verb is this:

Schultz *vb:* To take the least-favorite part of consumer's interaction with our brand and turn it into the part they most enjoy.

If we can translate each key case history discussed within each of the Eight Credos in this way, we will begin to develop a group of exercises that allow us to apply profitably the breakthroughs in thinking from other categories to our own and thus replicate their challenge and growth.

And as second-rank brands, of course, we need rapid growth, whether we want to challenge or survive. The middle ground is going to be an increasingly dangerous place to live.

The Eight Credos

We shall start with a series of observations about what these brands all seem to be doing and then construct a new kind of strategic process and series of exercises we can apply our own brands.

It will be, of course, an enormous postrationalization. None of the people behind the brands we are discussing consciously sat down and said, okay, team, I think I've worked out the eight credos we have to follow. They did it instinctively, often because they had to, rather than of their own volition. But that doesn't matter for our purposes; we are learning from their experience curve. And in some cases, like Timberland, they will be challengers whose mistakes are as valuable as their successes.

Finally, at the heart of being a Challenger is precisely the fact that marketing is not a science but informed judgment—there is opportunity in there being no marketing absolutes anymore. A friend went so far as to suggest that the cover of the book should offer a photograph of Herb Kelleher, dressed as his occasional business alter ego, Elvis Presley, with the title "Does This Man Look Like a Scientist?" In the spirit of that informed judgment, then, while I have substantiated the core hypothesis as rigorously as possible throughout, at certain points I will leave the tarmacked road and offer a point of view about the future of marketing and the consumer; I will telegraph these more subjective observations as clearly as possible as they occur.

PART II

The Eight Credos
of Successful
Challenger Brands

4

The First Credo: Break with Your Immediate Past

"The problem is never how to get new, innovative thoughts into your mind, but how to get the old ones out. Every mind is a room packed with archaic furniture. You must get rid of the old furniture of what you know, think, and believe before anything new can get in."

Dee Hock[1]

The Vitality of Inexperience

Looking at the list of the great Challengers that have really impacted their individual markets, the first thing that strikes one is how many of them are launches: that is to say, how many of them (and more specifically, the people behind them) lack any previous experience in their chosen category at all. Richard Branson, for instance, used the money he made from selling rock albums to start an airline business: Virgin Atlantic. Michael Dell was a college student in Austin, Texas, when he realized he could beat both IBM and Compaq by focusing on the delivery system rather than the product; by 1997 Dell Computers was worth $12 billion. Jim Jannard of Oakley was making motorcycle handgrips when, while watching post-race interviews with Nascar drivers, he noticed that the camera close-ups cut out all the sponsors on the cars and clothes to focus on the face; the next week he started work on branded eyewear.

Ian Schrager's only previous experience was in nightclubs, yet he created the three hottest hotels in New York (the Paramount, Royalton, and Morgan). Wayne Huizenga made his first million in waste disposal, yet he transformed the video market's every structure before selling Blockbuster to Viacom; with the proceeds, he set up in an altogether different category again—automotive retailing. Howard Schultz was selling Swedish kitchen equipment before he acquired a little Seattle coffee shop called Starbucks and changed the way Americans thought about coffee. Circuit City thought the car business should be no different from retailing hi-fi and set up CarMax. Anita Roddick has in fact gone a stage further: In developing the Body Shop, she claims *always to try to do exactly the opposite* of what the industry experts do.

We are taught that category experience is valuable, perhaps essential. There is a natural tendency in a company to think of its sphere of business or category as being special, with its own rules, intrinsically different from everyone elses. And whenever one changes jobs, or moves within the same job onto another category of business, there is always that grimly predictable moment when the old hand leans across the table and explains over the course of an hour or two (rather patronizingly, in my experience) why this business is like no other business you have ever worked on. Our enthusiasm and fresh thinking is understandable, it seems, but misplaced—and when we know the business a little better, we'll understand why.

In some rather limited respects, of course, they are sometimes right. There are often lead-time differences, or distribution structures, or union agreements, or even (very occasionally) consumer purchase cycles that shade things a little differently here or there—if one knows a great deal about the subject and thinks about it from the manufacturer's point of view.

But the consumer hasn't had the benefit of working on the business for a number of years, either. They don't think that what they experience in one market has to be necessarily any different from what they like in another. Indeed, in many ways they'd *like* the experience they get in some categories to be more like those they get in another. As we saw earlier, if they could find an airline that treated them like their local restaurant, they'd fly it every time; if you ask a focus group in Peoria what they'd like a new telecommunications company to be like, they'll give you the name of a car company from Spring Hill, Tennessee.

Which is exactly why people have responded so strongly to many of the challengers on our list. Far from category inexperience being a drawback, it has proved to have a vitality that has allowed the new players to envision fresh possibilities in the category, possibilities that those who have worked for years in the category have grown too close to be able to see.

And the same is true, I would suggest, of you and me. After all, do we not really feel underneath that we understand the possibilities of a market better in the first month we work on it than we do three years in? In those first few weeks, we are absorbed in and focused on the questions and opportunities, uncalcified by the category shibboleths and uncluttered by the petty details and manufacturing perspective that obscures our judgment later on. It all seems so wonderfully simple and clear; we open up the market instead of closing it down. We ask "Why not?" and not simply "Why?" We see no real reason why the questions our five-year-old daughter would ask of the category are any less valid than those we pay our research department to ask: Why are watches such boring colors? Why do they all look more or less the same? Why do people only wear one at a time? And this beginning is the time, if at all, when we tend to change things. Look at Branson, Schrager, Dell: Innocence, intelligently applied innocence, has changed the face of business more profoundly than all the MBA expertise in the world.

This goes beyond marketing. My English literature teacher used to claim that the finest writers in the English language in the last 200 years were Conrad and Nabokov—neither of whom had English as their first language. It was indeed, he contended, the very fact that both of them started from another culture, another tongue, that the possibilities of the English language opened themselves up to them in such a striking and unusual way. So also the creative breakthroughs of the 1960s, the golden age of U.S. advertising, were credited by some New Yorkers at the time in strong part to an influx of minorities with strong cultures of their own into a profession historically dominated by the WASP. Creative thinkers from strong Italian and Jewish cultures, the theory went, were able to bring fresh insight to familiar categories that those already within more mainstream U.S. culture were too close to see.

Which is why the preparation, the mental preparation of Breaking with Your Immediate Past, is the First Credo for Challenger brands. Even for those of us still in the market.

This is ridiculously easy for someone new, of course; there is no furniture to get rid of in the first place. But how do you make yourself inexperienced in your own category? And how do you create that climate in others?

Andrew Grove fired himself. In 1985, when, far from being a brand leader or even a challenger, it looked as though Intel, then a player principally in the memory-chip business, was unable to match the Japanese price/value offer and remain in profit, Grove reached a personal crisis. To demonstrate emotionally to himself the need to wipe the slate genuinely clean, he began again by inviting his chairman to walk out of the Intel building with him as if they had both been fired; they would reenter the building not as Andrew Grove and Gordon Moore, but *as the newly recruited replacements for themselves*.

Sitting down afresh in the boardroom they had just mentally vacated, they looked with new eyes at the business they had been managing for the last few years and identified immediately the key issue the company faced: namely, that it was in the wrong business. It had to get out of memory and put the entire emphasis of the company behind what had up to now been a secondary priority, namely microprocessors. In one dramatic moment Grove created the ability to see through innocent eyes the solution to a problem they had both been wrestling with for months.

At this point, then, we shall invent the second of our new set of intransitive verbs. These, you will remember, are intended to collectively define the sequence of actions that will take place in the two-day off-site at the end of this book, actions that will be involved in turning us into a Challenger.

The new verb, then, is this:

Grove *vb*: To fire oneself, reenter the building as one's hard nosed successor, and identify the core issue facing the company.

In other words, identify the Big Fish. We have talked about it up to now as of it were another major competitor, but in fact it may not be quite as simple as this. It may be that the threat or success of this major competitor is a *symptom* of the problem, rather than the problem in itself.

We then have to instill this sense of innocent vitality not simply in the individual but in the whole team around us, or at least enough of them to drive the difference through the thinking of the company. The way to foster that culture in those around you, as we shall see, is to ask of them different kinds of questions, questions at a higher level. Swim upstream.

Swimming Upstream

In October 1997 Richard Branson announced the launch of Virgin One, Virgin's bank. Over the previous few years Virgin had already introduced to the U.K. market a number of relatively small-scale financial products—a Tracker fund, a Personal Equity Plan, a pension—with some success and established not simply a visible presence but an image of being no nonsense and straight talking, as against the paternalistic image of the established U.K. banks. Now Branson proposed to take on the Big Institutions more directly. His ambition for the new bank, he announced in his press conference, was simple: "We want to change the way the nation feels about money."

This is a striking remark, as much for what Branson didn't say as what he did say. He didn't say, for instance, that he wanted to "change the way the consumer thinks about long-term high-yield deposit accounts" or "the way this or that demographic use automatic teller machines." He made no mention of the need for financial advice, or opportunities in cashier services, or the hidden virtues of the equity market. Instead, Branson proposed to base his new brand on his desire to change the way "the *nation* feels about *money*"; he set as his starting point for the new enterprise not the satisfaction of unmet savings needs or checking requirements but *the changing of an emotional relationship with the whole category*. He swam upstream.

It is hard to imagine an Establishment brand such as Wells Fargo, or Bank of America, or Barclays asking themselves such a question or setting themselves such an ambition as a central objective. They have become too close to their own business to become wave makers; we all get trapped in midstream thinking the more we work on a piece of business, particularly if that business becomes quietly successful. But asking the question, setting the goal at Branson's higher level changes one's entire approach to the task ahead. Let's consider if we were set the task by Branson, for instance, to change the way people felt about money. How would we go about it?

Well, we would certainly have to think about a different kind of exploratory research; much more open-ended than we are used to. We couldn't do a Usage and Attitude study, for instance, because such a structured piece of quantitative research presupposes that we know what the questions are—and therefore implicitly that we think we know in all probability what the answers are. We would have to get people into a room and just ask them about what's on their minds, and see how soon they mention money. Instead of a three-page discussion guide, we would want to sit back and just listen for a few hours, letting them set the agenda—what they like and don't like about money, what'd they'd change, what relationship one kind of monetary decision has to do with another. We'd listen for the vocabulary they use, the analogies they bring out, the emotions they reveal. Even getting them into a room with a viewing facility would probably change things too much—money is a difficult subject to be honest about. You'd want to go to their houses, live with them for a bit. See how they used money, ask them as they spent and saved and planned how they were feeling. Catch them when they were up and when they were down. And so on.

When Tom Ford was handed, with the Creative Directorship of Gucci, the difficult task of restoring Gucci's credibility after the cliché it had almost become in the 1980s (the sprawling cliché, in fact—at one point it had stamped its name on 14,000 different items), his first show was clearly pivotal. Although haute couture accounts for less than 10% of Gucci's sales, it defines the fashionability of the rest of the brand— and the world's media were waiting to judge the fashionability of Gucci from Ford's first outing.

Fashion works in trends. Almost as a collective, the fashion world tends to create one predominant climate or another, and at the beginning of the 1990s the climate was asexual clothes and political correctness: clothing styles were getting almost cerebral. Ford felt dissatisfied with this; instead, he swam upstream. He asked himself the deceptively obvious question—"Why do people wear good clothes?"—and kept coming back with answers that had nothing to do with the fashion climate of the time. Good clothes were, surely, all about attracting people. It wasn't complicated; they wore them to feel sexy. Ford felt this was an opportunity for Gucci, so instead of loose-cut greens and beiges, he produced a look instead that was very aggressive, sleek, sexy, and glamorous. Tough chic. It was an instant hit with both critics and the public.

Sometimes, of course, the consumer is as close as the brand is to the preconceptions about the category. They cannot tell you what they want because the category has effectively defined it for them. Before the Swiss watch manufacturers faced extinction from the new Japanese pretenders, for instance, their approach to watches and watchmaking had defined watch culture around the world for centuries: Time was to be respected, so watches were to be respected. Watches were durable, heavy, expensive, carefully crafted, and worn singly as a high-status item. Cheap watches were for children, who did not understand the importance of Time.

To Eat their Big Fish with Swatch, Nicholas Hayek and the Swiss broke with almost every aspect of the legacy of Swiss watchmaking that had been so carefully nurtured and reinforced over the years. They began to make cheap, almost disposable watches, instead of high-value items; they made them of bright rather than subdued colors; they molded them of plastic rather than carving them from metal; they gave them a spirit of fun rather than a sense of formality; and they encouraged multiplicity—even to the point of wearing two at the same time. They launched new collections twice a year, in line with the fashion seasons. The consequence? Swatch became not just an icon of popular culture, but one of the great business success stories of the last 30 years.

The breakthrough came from the question they asked right at the beginning: "What business are we in?" Hayek's answer to that question was not "Timekeeping," or even "Status," but "Fashion." Once one asks a different level of question and answers that question in a fundamentally different way, everything else flows. In this case the question was more important than the consumer because the consumer could not necessarily see the category any more clearly than the Swiss watch industry. It took an outsider to ask the question that made the difference.

It was being *forced to reenter* the market that made the Swiss countenance this higher level of question. Hayek commented later in an interview on the reaction to his proposed new watch: "If ASUAG or SSIH had been making one franc of profit, they would have thrown me out the window. [They would have said,] "You're crazy, what do you know about watches anyway?"[2] But the situation they faced forced them into challenge.

Asking this kind of question, then—swimming upstream as a mental preparation for challenging the category and the brand leader—allows you to see what business you are really in, or *could* really be in. I remarked earlier in this chapter that Challengers brought no experience to their category. In fact, this is not true—they frequently brought experience of *another* category to their category, and sometimes this gave them a new angle into the category they entered. One of the reasons that the Royalton and Paramount hotels have become the success they are is Ian Schrager's belief that hotel lobbies are the nightclubs of the 1990s; this is not a random thought—he had founded and managed New York's Studio 54. Again, the consumer would never have made this observation to him; it was applying the possibilities of one category to another that created the thought. (In the same way Jerry Springer's surge in talk-show ratings past Oprah Winfrey has come because he doesn't see his product as a talk show—he sees it as "more of a circus."[3] Like Schrager, this is born from Springer's previous category experience; he used to be in politics.)

An opportunity to invent another of our intransitive verbs: Schrager.

Schrager *vb*: To ask of your category how someone from another, essentially "different," category would approach its marketing *if they attempted to transfer their perceptions of that category onto your own.*

This exercise can work at one of two levels. The first is the general, category level. Take pasta sauce as an example: How would Bill Gates sell it? Suppose he were put in charge of the number-two brand. What would he do? How would he make it the overwhelming consumer standard, applying his learning curve from the software market? Or what if someone came over from Lexus? They attempted to redefine the consumer's notion of luxury by setting new performance standards: How would they do that with pasta? What might be the equivalent of "champagne glasses on the hood" in the pasta market? What is the red sauce equivalent of that heavy thud of the closing door that tells us we are surrounded by a substantially-built piece of automobile? Come to think of it, why is it that a new luxury car flatters all five senses, but a jar of pasta only three? How would you be able to hear the quality of a pasta sauce?

In many ways this is of course something we do instinctively when starting a new job—describing it in terms of the old brands and the old segmentations from the category we have just left. But doing this continually through the lens of one other category is dangerous; the value comes not just from thinking about our category from the perspective of software, or just thinking from the perspective of luxury cars, but from the point of view of a diverse range of other categories in sequence. What about the lens of the Body Shop and "well-being products"? What of Absolut and white spirits? What of Cirque du Soleil: How would you make pasta as fun and unpredictable as a contemporary circus?

The second level of the exercise pushes this idea a stage further. Schrager applied the concept, strictly speaking, not to hotels but to a part of the hotel or hotel experience—the lobby. You might want instead to break your brand down to five key component parts, applying the exercise to each of the parts individually.

There are two values to "Schrager." One is that it may lead to seeing one's brand or category in a different way, particularly if one asks the consumer the same kinds of questions. There is a story that General Motors, dismayed by the financial impact of the Japanese on their historical user base, were doing work some time ago on GM cars and the competition in a focus group. The moderator asked consumers what a car would be like if made by Sony; finding the response enthusiastic, the moderator asked them to choose between a car made by Sony and a car made by General Motors. What seems a no brainer to you and me was a shock to General Motors—the consumer apparently chose the technological sexiness of Sony over the mechanical experience of a U.S. automotive manufacturer. From this shock the need for some kind of response was realized, and what became the Saturn project began.

The second value to the exercise is that the very act of asking questions of the category prompts one to move higher, even if those questions are wrong. Tom Ford of Gucci talks of how he likes to walk the streets and look at people whose clothes combinations he *doesn't* think work—the people whose clothes sense really makes him wince. He then sits in his office and tries to work out why; he finds this as valuable an exercise as starting from what he knows to be aesthetically in tune.

Besides asking different kinds of questions, then, we should be looking for the answers in different sorts of places. The chances are that the company's traditional wisdom has been calcifying because it has been asking exactly the same questions in substantially the same ways for years.

This doesn't have to be complicated. cKone was an attempt by Calvin Klein to challenge the hegemony of the big perfume manufacturers by producing an androgynous perfume aimed at a slightly younger, 18- to 25-year-old age market. One of the key problems facing the marketing team was the elusive, impulsive nature of their audience: How could they get the product in front of them fast enough to give the launch critical mass? Instead of conducting quantified research into the behavior of the target market, the marketing director of Calvin Klein simply called in all the junior brand team members to the Calvin Klein boardroom and asked them what they had in their pockets, wallets, and purses. Surprised, the team emptied everything out on the table. Among the combs, dollars, and lipstick were concert tickets, compact disc receipts, clothing ads, haircare products. The marketing director pointed: That, she said, will be our distribution base. If the company couldn't rely on their target to take a detour to come and find them, they'd have to put the product in the paths they were already taking. The next week the sales team rang Tower Records.

Putting Everything In Play

So Challengers see and realize places to stand in the market that other brands have not seen or realized before. *Seeing* them depends on making oneself innocent again. *Realizing* them depends on divesting oneself of all the baggage a brand acquires over the years in terms of all those individual marketing elements that *do not in themselves make a difference*, but are thought to be important collectively in differentiating the brand from the competition and maintaining consistency with the past. So even for existing brands, Challenging is about beginning again.

Beginning again when you already have a brand that is substantial and not yet in critical decline is a hard thing to contemplate. Much of what has been written about Brand Management concentrates on consistency over time—recognizing your current equities and maintaining them through your marketing activities. And indeed our natural human reaction is to protect what we have once we think it has achieved a certain basic value; studies have shown that as human beings we are not so much risk-averse as loss-averse—the more you already have, the more your inclination is *not* to gamble it. Which is why, of course, the risk-taking entrepreneurs tend to be the people who start with nothing.

But if we want to Eat the Big Fish, protecting what we already have for its own sake seems out-of-date thinking in a Challenger mind-set. Challenger brands seem to deliberately break with their own immediate past (if they have one)—they intentionally reinvent key aspects of themselves in order to force rapid reappraisal from the consumer. To do so they become first prepared to break with every equity, every preconception about the market, and every current marketing strategy for every current marketing tool, and then they need to sacrifice minor equities to create major differences.

Again, this seems counterintuitive; we are taught to protect and nurture marketing and advertising equities. But ask yourself this: if any of them were all that valuable in the first place, why aren't we in a better position now? As we go through the process of reexamination, what is important in our past will rise to the top again; but we won't see it if we're swimming surrounded by the flotsam and jetsam of the immediate past. The question for us about such equities is not "Are they valuable?" but "Are they valuable *enough*?" Are they valuable enough for the change in growth rate we now need to achieve?

When in 1992 Nissan relaunched their midprice sedan, they had the courage to abandon the old name, the Stanza, and start again. The Stanza had significant historical equity—but not enough to realize Nissan's volume ambitions for the new car. As we saw earlier, the gap between ambition and resource is sometimes the Challenger's best friend: Confronted by the daunting existing equity enjoyed by the Honda Accord and Toyota Camry, Nissan eventually walked away from the Stanza's entire past and started again. The renamed and repositioned car, the Altima, went on to become the best-selling new nameplate that year.

Politics is a particularly pure test for Challenger marketing, since by and large there are only two players in the running: the Brand leader and the Challenger. Leading up to the last election, and faced with 16 years in unsuccessful opposition to the Conservatives, the British Labour Party took a more radical route to power than they had ever attempted before. They broke dramatically with many of the fundamental structures and philosophies of their own past—solidarity with the trade unions, a respect for the hard left (the break with Militant Tendency), key policies like Unilateral Nuclear Disarmament, and High Income Tax—in order to reinvent themselves and claim victory for the first time in 16 years. (One of the interesting aspects of this election was the noted prominence of Peter Mandelson, essentially Tony Blair's Marketing Director, within the Labour Party. Marketing has gone on in politics for many years, but it has rarely been so open or so dramatically successful.)

The video-game category, conversely, is an example of the *failure* of brands and companies to reinvent themselves fast enough because they clung to their past: Atari failed to understand the importance of the icon (Nintendo's Mario); Nintendo failed to understand the new importance of being cool as playground currency (Sega's 1992 advertising); Sega failed to understand the importance of abandoning 16-bit technology and focusing on the next, 32-bit generation when the launch of Sony's PlayStation raised the category experience gold standard to a whole new level.

The important equities have a habit of reemerging in the process of reexamination. Swatch kept "swiss" as a part of its DNA because it gave the watch technological impeccability; the sober connotations of the word also served as a delicious foil to the flagrant neon plastics of the watch design. Harley-Davidson went back to its core values; Nissan, in looking at everything again, identified the spirit of "Mr. K" (the founder of Nissan in the United States, Mr. Katayama) and the latter days of Datsun as being the spiritual heritage of the U.S. brand. Breaking with the immediate past is not the same as mindlessly throwing everything away. It is simply a way of freeing yourself to focus on the questions and possibilities that will make the difference between being a Challenger and being an Establishment brand.

So, if current marketing equities are in fact still significant, they will float to the surface again as one reenters the upstream/downstream questioning and listening. But they may be masking something more important that you already have in your past. And the effort and resource consumed in retaining it may dilute the force of the new direction one is about to assume.

Naive Listening

Asking innocently is one thing. Listening well to the answers is quite another. We have become so "sophisticated" in our marketing and research that we filter and interpret too much; sometimes the most important attitudes to the category are ignored simply because they come out of the consumer's mouth first. "They always say that," we murmur to each other, chewing dismissively on another M&M. "Let's send a note in and get the moderator to dig a bit *deeper*." Educated one and all to become good Freudians, where what really matters is underneath, we lose sight of what is right in front of our noses. Before one is five minutes into a focus group on frozen-ready meals, for instance, the group will volunteer and concur with the feeling that such meals are "too small." In automotive groups the first consumer remark in discussing car advertising is either that it is all rather oppressively the same, or, if one finds oneself in New York, that it all sucks.

Yet our reaction in the back room in these situations is to ignore such remarks—because we feel we have heard them before and that they are therefore somehow not a deep enough insight. In fact, they may well be the most important things that are said all night: the frozen meals remark means, for instance, that as far as the consumer is concerned, these brands are not in fact offering *proper meals at all*, which has profound implications for how one markets oneself in the (wrongly titled, it seems) Ready Meals category—and the consequent opportunities for a Challenger. If we want to challenge, then we have to learn to lose some of this so-called sophistication, to listen more naively.[4]

Giants and Children

The famous giant killers of folklore tend to be children. Whether their names are David or Jack, it does not occur to them that a small round stone cannot successfully take on an eight-foot spear. (If you are going up against an eight-foot spear, the one weapon it is foolish to choose is a four-foot spear; if you can't match the length, you need something different.)

The first foundation of challenge, then, is not experience, but innocence. The ability to step back upstream and question all the old assumptions afresh. Challenge them, in fact, and see which can really withstand the inquisition.

Then, if one views strategic thinking in terms of upstream (questions about the fundamentals of the category) and downstream (refinements of product of service offering), most Challengers have to deliberately attempt to compete either *significantly upstream* or *significantly downstream* of the Establishment brand. The brand leader, having established the codes and conventions of the category, does not revisit or attempt to change them in terms of upstream thinking; equally, they are too large and cumbersome to arrive at or implement innovative downstream thinking with any speed. Once one has made oneself innocent, perhaps the first decision to take about eating the Big Fish is whether the real opportunity to attack them lies upstream or downstream: do we overturn the category basics (as Swatch) or develop the product to a point they have yet to reach (Virgin Atlantic's in-flight entertainment at launch)?

Breaking with the immediate past has four purposes in this regard:

1. To establish afresh what the core issue facing the brand or the company (The Big Fish) really is; taking a step back and more accurately defining the problem.
2. To help define, therefore, what business we should really be in.
3. To free ourselves up to see all the possibilities of the category.
4. To allow us to see clearly both opportunity and threats, and to create the momentum to push Challenger strategy into Challenger behavior.

It is thus both a valuable mental exercise in itself and critical to making a Challenger a brand of action, rather than just a company of talk.

Finally, some companies, believing that fresh insight is one of the last unfair competitive advantages a brand can possess, have gone so far as to institute new kinds of team relationships within their culture, specifically geared to harness the benefits of innocence to the strengths of indepth knowledge, and to keep this process perpetually occurring. One of the leading multicultural advertising agencies in the United States, for instance, attaches two people to each project—one "on culture" (that is, belonging to the culture the marketing activity will take place among) and one "off culture" (belonging to a culture other than that of the target audience).[5] It is from the combination of the deep understanding and the fresh perspective that the new opportunities and ideas come.

5

The Second Credo: Build a Lighthouse Identity

"The primary role of advertising is to say who you are."
Don Hudler, *vice president of marketing, Saturn*

The second characteristic of Challenger brands is that they do not attempt to navigate by the consumer. Instead, they invite the consumer to navigate by them.

There is a certain school of advertising one might call "That's why" advertising. You can spot an example by the presence of those two little words in the middle. Such a television commercial might, for instance, go something like this:

"At Champion Healthfoods, we know how upsetting finding cat fleas in your bed can be."

(We look up from our newspaper to witness a scene of a man and woman sobbing hysterically over their pajamas. Small black objects gleefully leap about on their bed. The harrowing voice-over continues:)

"*That's why* we've introduced new Champion Kittymunch with ZX4. It's packed with the rabbit liver that kitty loves *and* contains a secret ingredient that eradicates fleas."

(We return to the husband, who in desperation has gone to the all-night grocery store, still in his pajamas. We see a look of hope and wonder on his face as he discovers Kittymunch. We cut to cat eating same. We brace ourselves for an invigorating endline; it does not let us down.)

"New Champion Kittymunch: Liver 'n' Let Die."

(We finish. The couple is smiling, the packshot is generous, and the cat is asleep. Perfection.)

"That's why" advertising navigates by reference to the consumer. It holds up a mirror to their lives—or what the advertiser supposes are their lives—and gives them a reason to believe the product we are selling contains something that will make their day better in some regard. It is very tempting advertising to pursue for both agency and client, because it is so hard to fault if examined logically. Together we have identified a real problem—people get upset when they find cat fleas in their bed; we have shown the consumer that we understand how they feel about that problem (we've shown them sobbing, for goodness sake—they can see that we are almost living this thing with them); and we've given them a practical solution—they can give little Milo the rabbit liver he loves so much, and it also contains a mildly toxic ingredient that eradicates cat fleas.

And yet the Challengers we are looking at tend not to do any of this. They don't do "That's why" problem-solution advertising; in fact, in many cases they don't really talk about the consumer at all. Instead, they talk about themselves; they invite the consumer to navigate by them. They behave as what we shall call Lighthouse brands, with a Lighthouse Identity.[1]

First, let us look at the idea of lighthouses, and why they might be important. Then we shall take the four key dimensions to being a Lighthouse brand—Identity, Emotion, Intensity, and Salience—and discuss the importance of each of these in turn. Finally, we shall discuss the roots of being a Lighthouse brand—namely, overperformance and self-belief.

Navigation, Not Communication

It's not that the world is more complex these days. It's that it's falling apart. It is hard to overdramatize the recent steady collapse in people's

Figure 5.1 **Top six U.S. prime-time television shows, 1960 versus 1995**

1960–1961	1995–1996
1. *Gunsmoke*	1. *ER*
2. *Wagon Train*	2. *Seinfeld*
3. *Have Gun, Will Travel*	3. *Friends*
4. *Andy Griffith Show*	4. *Caroline in the City*
5. *Real McCoys*	5. *NFL Monday Night Football*
6. *Rawhide*	6. *Single Guy*

Source: TV Dimensions[2]

frameworks for living—the breakdown of families, the disappearance of job security, the disgrace of respected public figures and institutions, the financial embarassment of former business icons, the enduring shock at the suddenness and effect of Black Friday, the displacement of basic social needs such as friends and family life by pressures of work, the personal sense of being nearly overwhelmed by the legion of pressures we cope with every day—be one a soccer mom, merchant banker, or magistrate. This sense of collapse is fanned every night by the most consistently skeptical and graphic media commentary the Western world has yet known. As a single striking instance of the part the media plays, consider the results of a survey taken at the end of the Gulf War, which attempted to identify the most vilified figure on U.S. national radio over the previous year: the president of Iraq, Saddam Hussein, who had shot, bombed, and threatened with chemical warfare the sons and daughters of the United States and Israel, only managed to come in second; the president of the United States came in a handsome first. (This is not a moral judgment on the media, incidently: A glance at their company reports would suggest that at some level they understand their audience very well.)

The fact that we are so close to this structural collapse ourselves sometimes makes us snowblind to its effect. But consider some of the symptoms. Look, for example to the comparison of top prime-time television shows in Figure 5.1.

The first column, 1960–1961, is essentially one of Western grit and heroism, how America was made. The second column, with the exception of *ER* and *NFL Monday Night Football*, contains comedies about losers, how people like us hilariously fail at the hurdles of everyday life. And of course, neither of these columns covers the glorious paranoia of *The X-Files,* the all-encompassing cynicism of *The Simpsons,* or the colorful couch commentary of *Beavis and Butthead,* the three most influential programs on youth culture to come out of the United States in the last 20 years.

This is not a lament for the passing of civilized society; it is an observation with practical consequences for us. People today lack certain core frameworks that have helped structure previous generations' lives, and it shows.

In human societies goods have always been a form of communication—to the outside world and to oneself. Now I would go a stage further; I would suggest that brands have become a form not simply of communication but of *navigation.* Although it is too glib to say that brands and products are what increasingly provide meaning in uncertain times, it does mean that the brands that flourish today are those that have a very clear sense of *who they are*—that is to say, not simply a distinctive identity but a strong and self-referential identity; they stand out from the competition by their intensity and their confidence in themselves. If we were to pursue the image of the consumer adrift on uncertain waters, then we might say that the brands that flourish in this uncertain environment are those that have what we call a Lighthouse Identity.

The reader might challenge me at this point. They might object to the navigation metaphor on the grounds that since there are categories that palpably retain low consumer interest, a navigation model makes no real sense. For high-status or value items such as cars or sneakers, perhaps it might work, but floor cleaners? Fast food? Batteries? The reader might throw the T-shirt test at me: If a consumer is prepared to wear a brand logo on a T-shirt, then it is a brand the consumer is proud to be associated with; if not, however, then the whole theory of brands as lighthouses must be questioned.

In answer, I would simply point to two forms of social currency enjoyed by low-interest brands, which pass the T-shirt test in their own way. Jack in the Box is a fast-food brand: Fast food is not a high-status category for its younger heavy user—you eat it, and get on with your life. Fire and forget; end of story. Yet Jack, the clown in a three-piece suit, whom we will see in Chapter 7 apparently blowing up his own boardroom and taking control of the Jack in the Box fast food chain again, has become an icon in his own way. Three months after introducing the new brand identity, the company produced an antenna ball in the shape of Jack's head, which could be mounted on the tip of a car antenna, sold at Jack in the Box outlets for a price of 99¢. In the first year more than a million people in southern California and Texas chose to pay 99¢ for the pleasure of driving around with a small clown's head permanently attached to the end of their car aerial, from Ford Ranger to Nissan Z; the number is now up past 1.5 million.

The Energizer Bunny, equally, has become a part of the popular culture. Referenced in films, television programs, and political cartoons, he has come to own the category generic of "long lasting" for the company. In the film *Die Hard 3*, for instance, Bruce Willis dryly rebuts the villain's exasperation at our hero's inability to lay down and die by comparing himself to the Energizer Bunny, who just keeps going and going. This, like all the other media references the Bunny collects, is not a result of paid-for placement. Nor is it because batteries are a high-interest category, or because the writer or viewer are themselves avid battery purchasers. It is because, in its own way, Energizer—like Jack in the Box— is a Lighthouse brand, to the point where what it stands for has become a social currency that the user is happy to be a part of.

Do these two brands have profound meaning in shaping their consumers lives? No. Do these brands represent a new structure for people to hang their lives around? No, again. But have they become commonly understood reference points by having a clearly forged and insistently communicated identity? Absolutely. And does the consumer ascribe a social value to being a part of that brand and that meaning—even though they come from low-interest categories? Undoubtedly—their success in fact suggests that there are no such things as low-interest categories; there are only low-interest brands.

That consumers find the self-confidence of such brands appealing should be no surprise. In life, people are drawn to strength and to people of character who are true to themselves. In marketing life, in using goods as communication or even navigation, people are drawn to strong brands. As number one, this strength can come from the familiarity and ubiquity of a brand leader; if you are a second-rank brand, it comes from an intense projection of who you are.

Jack as Icon

The Defining Characteristics of Lighthouse Brands

Identity, intensity, self-confidence—we should start getting a little more specific about the principal characteristics of Challenger brands with a Lighthouse Identity. There are four:

1. Self-Referential Identity: The predominant purpose of Challenger brand's every marketing action is to tell us where *they* stand. They don't attempt to tell us something about ourselves—and they certainly don't attempt to navigate themselves with reference to *us*. (This is important: The Consumer Isn't.)

2. Emotion: They aim to create an emotionally rather than rationally-based relationship with consumers. Challengers do not tend to succeed through the satisfaction of rational needs; instead, through a Lighthouse Identity, they invite a realignment of emotions.

3. Intensity: They offer intense projections of who they are in everything they do. Weak preference will not cut it for a late entrant: Challengers need to be vivid.

4. Salience: They are highly intrusive; one cannot avoid noticing their activity even if not actively looking in their direction—that is, shopping their category. (Important: The Audience Isn't.)

In the remainder of this chapter, we will discuss each of these in turn, along with where the roots of identity may lie and indeed, how one arrives at a strong identity in the first place.

Self-Referential Identity

Challengers do not seem to plot their path by the rest of the world; they are confident enough to invite the world to navigate by them. Saturn's vice president of marketing has been the most public about this in his definition of the role for advertising, and indeed, such was the company's belief in the importance of identity that they spent months straightforwardly laying it out before the public in advertising before the product was even available. (One should bear in mind that the previous history of the U.S. car business in prelaunch advertising has lain in showing us undiscernible shapes below dustsheets and an enigmatic voice-over.)

They have a very clear sense, first and foremost, of who they are, not as a sense of their own external image, but as a sense of their own internal identity. This is often because they have a founder at the center, many of whose personal beliefs they reflect and amplify. Richard Branson is offering his own personal culture within Virgin: the smiling revolutionary, the entrepreneur in a fluffy jumper, the debunker of the establishment. Anita Roddick's personal beliefs and ideals are famously enshrined within the Body Shop.

Everything else in the company flows from this—behavior, image, communication, culture. But the other Challenger brands we are considering with a less obvious (or nonexistent) founder—Absolut, for example, or Wonderbra, Lexus (at launch, certainly), Gateway 2000, Fox, Diesel, Swatch, Orange, Oakley, and Goldfish—are all other brands that in their own way evince an enormous self-confidence, a sense of who they are, without any permission from or reference to the world around them. Whether they express themselves most effectively through design (Swatch, Oakley) or communication, their reference point is themselves—no comparative or "That's why" advertising here. The delineation between themselves and those around them is bold and clear: the differences in identity that mark out these challengers are not the subtle differences that emerge from weeks of discussion within the marketing/agency team over nuances of this or that word used to describe the brand's personality. They are differences that are immediately observable; they are highly defined, in or out of their category context: an orange fish in a sea of faceless financial services (Goldfish), a jeans company with its own philosophy of living (Diesel), a mass-market television network with a fondness for adult cartoons (Fox), a telecommunications company without a "com" or "tel" anywhere in its genetic makeup, but named instead after a color (Orange).

Indeed, some brands I researched have achieved such a highly defined state of identity that they are *unable to describe themselves with reference to anything other than themselves*. So, Las Vegas has been through a number of positioning statements for itself and the public, from "The American Way to Play" and "No One Does It Better" to "The Entertainment

Capital of America." But now they have arrived at such an extraordinary uniqueness of product, brand identity, and attitude that they simply claim "Las Vegas Is Las Vegas." So also Taco Bell protects itself internally from moving into product areas that would stray into the province of its burger and chicken competitors by defining itself to everyone working in the company as "Fast food in a world all its own." Lighthouse Identities are their own countries, with their own languages—make mine a grande half decaf double tall skim almond mocha. Did I say decaf? My language slipped for a moment there. I meant, of course, unleaded.

Look, by contrast, at a second-rank brand that has failed to establish its own identity, either to itself or its consumer, and the effect it has had on their success. Reebok is a second-rank brand that has continually failed to define who it really believes itself to be, and thus it poses a weak challenge to Nike's dominance of the footwear market. Instead of accepting that Nike has appropriated the high ground of athletic performance (and has more claim to it anyway, given the origins of the Nike brand in college sports versus Reebok's origins in the aerobics fashion) and uncovering another, genuinely differentiating place for itself to live, Reebok has spent the last few years as a weak Nike wannabe. It is a brand that lacks an identity, lacks self-belief in who it is or can be, and it shows. Born from a group of traders, it has no true north; consequently, it has failed to make any ground on the leader. Nike, sprung from the loins of an athlete, has an identity and a direction that feels confident and real.

To say that Challengers develop or build a Lighthouse Identity is not to say it was in place right from conception (or reconception). While some challengers like Virgin Atlantic and Absolut come out of their corners with the identity more or less complete in their minds from the first bell, for others the emergence and exact nature of their identity hasn't always been evident straightaway, even to themselves. When Cirque du Soleil, for example, first left their Canadian base and crossed the border into an unambiguously English-speaking audience (the Niagara Falls area), they carefully changed their name back to something more conventional, translating it into "Circus of the Sun"; they were concerned that a U.S. audience might find French name too outré. The name change proved a disaster: the management was inundated throughout the season with requests for refunds from disappointed customers who had thought from the (translated) name they were paying to see a conventional circus, complete with lion tamers and elephants. Cirque du Soleil learned from this that part of their identity lay in playing up the differences with conventional circuses, rather than playing them down, both inside and outside the Big Top. Far from changing their name when they travel, they now dramatize the sense of difference between themselves and what the audience is used to seeing, to the point where every show is completely different in mood and style—not simply from any other circus the audience is familiar with, but even with the previous Cirque du Soleil show that played two years ago the last time they came to town.

Fox in the United States, which has a very clear brand image now (young, irreverent, iconoclastic), was at the beginning simply looking to find commercial acceptance as a fourth network. The initial belief at Fox among the small group under Barry Diller was that if they simply offered original, well-produced programming, that would be sufficient. Original though much of the early programming was, it was of mixed quality and character—from *The Reporters*, a low-rent news magazine, via *Beyond Tomorrow*, an Australian futuristic magazine show, to *America's Most Wanted* (which only made it onto the schedule because of a writer's strike), *21 Jump Street*, and *Married with Children*.

Then, over the course of the first couple of years, the ratings started to paint a picture of where the network's opportunity might lie. The Fox shows that mirrored traditional network material performed significantly below those that broke from the conventional path in some way—the mockery of *Married with Children*, most notably, or the young Johnny Depp in *21 Jump Street*. "For the first six months to a year, we tried to be like the other networks in programming," Garth Ancier, Fox's first programming director, said in an interview 10 years later. "Frankly, what we learned is that if you try to be like other networks, then there is no reason for viewers to try you."[3]

Learning they needed to be different was the first step. A more precise conception of who they really were was still to come. Initially, it seemed to the small group to lie in the series of comedy programs they were scheduling on Sunday nights in opposition to the "Disease of the Week" movies playing on every other channel. From this, the idea of Fox as the "comedy alternative" started to develop. Marketing it as such

Cirque de Soleil–Quidam North American Tour

Photo: Al Seib

Cirque de Soleil—Hoops/Cloud Swing

Costumes: Dominique Lemieux

brought another dimension to life: Looking at creative ideas for the press advertisements the agency presented to them, which included a picture of the recently disgraced Jim and Tammy Faye Bakker underneath the line "Now that they're gone, we're the funniest thing on television," there was an attitude in the advertising that struck a chord with those that worked at Fox. This was a place to stand they could be confident in.

They followed this with an adult cartoon—*The Simpsons*. Then came a sequence of landmark shows: *Beverly Hills 90210, Melrose Place, The X-Files, Party of Five,* each of which tackled material one simply wouldn't see on other channels. The network's identity rounded out a little further into something more than just comedy—distinctive, risky, sometimes risqué, edgy, rebellious, counterculture, antinetwork. The result is that what Brandon Tartikoff once dismissed as "the coat-hanger network" has become arguably the only real brand in television.

Now, such is strength of the brand's identity, consumers have expectations of what is and isn't a Fox show. Two shows launched in 1996, *Partners* and *Ned and Stacey,* were thought to be well-made, well-written, and well-acted shows, but ratings disappointed. It was said at the time that there was nothing wrong with the material in itself, that *Partners* would have been a success at NBC for instance, but that it failed to fit what had become a Lighthouse Identity for Fox.

The Fox story demonstrates that it isn't necessary for the identity to spring fully formed from the marketing team's temples at birth. But the drive for an identity as a foundation for all other activity does have to be a credo—something one believes in and actively moves toward. Although the identity wasn't clear for Fox at the outset, it is something they, unlike Reebok, have sought and moved toward—seeking differentiation from those around them. It has been well observed that once you have the identity established, every other aspect of the brand's communication and behavior should flow out if it. Image, for instance, is often discussed as something that can be invented or reinvented at will. In reality, consumers' noses have evolved: They can smell a fraud. An image rooted in identity is the difference between reality and marketing posture. This is not to say that the image cannot evolve or offer radically new ways of thinking about the brand, but that it has always to be rooted in the brand's identity, rather than be something created or marketed as a discrete entity in itself. Indeed, with Challengers, *everything* has to flow out of the identity: image, behavior, product innovation—and not least, the internal culture. And this is the reason founders can be so critical to a Challenger's success—not simply as icons or as focal points for publicity, but because they root the belief system, as well as providing a source for it and continual propagation of it.

The Consumer Inside

In looking at the underlying appeal of a lighthouse, we suggested that the primary value lay in the strength of appeal to one's end user; this is not, in fairness, the principal advantage challenger CEOs themselves would advance. One of the remarkable things about the so-called "consumer-centred" age of marketing is that neither successful brand leaders nor successful challengers in actual fact regard the end user as their primary target. The brand leader treats the end user as secondary because the shareholder is the priority; conversely, many Challenger CEOs regard the end user as secondary because the (stated) primary target is their own staff.

Herein lies for many of the brands we are discussing the most important value in identity of all: Challenger companies talk not of management or empowerment of staff but *inspiration* of staff. This is not youthful enthusiasm on the CEO's part; it is a question of necessity. Just as we observed earlier that the gap a Challenger faces between ambition and resource demands greater marketing creativity, so that gap demands within a Challenger organization's employees the urgent sense that this is more than just a job—they are about to turn the category, or indeed the world, on its head. Returning to Roddick's vision of Body Shop, her avowed desire is to create an electricity and passion (her words) that bond her staff to the company; she wants them to feel they are doing something important, and in doing so create a kind of motivation that she could never achieve if they were just selling shampoo and body lotion. To a brand leader her remarks might seem almost ingenuous, but one sees this sense of "importance" in Challenger companies early and everywhere—in Silicon Valley, for instance, Steve Jobs' unforgettable cri de coeur to John Sculley ("Do you want to sell sugared water for the rest of your life, or do you want to change the world?") has its children in the way Microsoft employees talk urgently about work projects as "jihads," holy wars against the infidel. While Brand leaders like to have a mission statement, Challengers have to live a mission.

Easy to say about computers? Look at how the fledgling Starbucks educated its people to feel about coffee: professional competence, a 24-hour training in correct temperatures, timings, and techniques for the perfect espresso, was not enough—the so-called baristas are required to extend their knowledge about the art of brewing coffee to their customer as well.

And in this respect a strong identity is a powerful recruitment tool and motivator for those already developing or promoting the brand. Despite the reality of Challengers often paying less, they need their people to deliver more, particularly if much of their competitive advantage, as we shall come to see, lies in the experience they deliver. Better people, motivated for the right reasons, more passionate about what they are doing, are more likely to create an intense relationship between customer and brand. Mechanical Advantage again.

This very clear sense of identity encompasses not simply who the brand is, but also what business it is really in. Wonderbra, though apparently lingerie, made itself a business and consumer icon by moving into the confidence business—or, more strongly put, the power business. An uplift bra whose virtues had remained effectively unsung for years, Wonderbra began its restaging to the consumer with a black and white photograph of a (then) unknown Czech model exuberantly displaying Wonderbra's product benefit, accompanied by the line "Say goodbye to your feet." The advertisement that really set the direction and identity of the brand, however, was the one that followed. In this, the model, still clad only in a Wonderbra and briefs, holds the viewer's eye with a coolly amused smile; beside her are the two words "Hello Boys." Not for the Wonderbra user, it seems, the traditional lingerie concerns about comfort or a quiet continental sensuality: This was for someone who wanted to enjoy not just a bigger bust but the power it gave you—the power to behave badly.

We noted earlier that Ian Schrager, the founder of the Paramount and Royalton Hotels in New York, regards hotel lobbies as the "nightclubs of the nineties." What most people see as transitional space, somewhere to have a drink before dinner or wait for a cab, Schrager's vision has turned into a destination, and thus a driver of competitive advantage. It shows. He employs different kinds of staff, different kinds of decorations, a different kind of lighting. Consequently, he succeeds in attracting a clientele who come just for the atmosphere. The lobbies— not the restaurant, service, or rooms—are the beating heart of those hotels. Certainly, the rooms are also cool—Philippe Starck is never dull—but it is the other people one sees nursing Absolut in the lobbies that convinces one of one's own good taste. (Mind you, Schrager is a man who has always taken cross-category thinking to a different level: He envisaged the door policy at Studio 54—the legendary New York club he cofounded in 1977—as like "tossing a salad," deliberately mixing the individual clientele admitted to create a whole that was more appealing than merely being the sum of its parts.)

Identity Drives the Organization

The combination of identity and business definition in turn drives every aspect of the organization, down to recruitment—for an organization cannot hinge entirely on the will or ethos of one person, even if, like Bill Gates, that individual can communicate his or her will to every employee in the world simultaneously and in what amounts to real time at the depression of an e-mail key. Challengers specifically look when recruiting to maintain the core characteristics the founders feel are essential. Oakley looks for people who have, besides technical competence at their job function, serious sporting interests outside work. That way insists its CEO Mike Parnell, in producing sports eyewear they feel like they'll be working on something that will actually impact on their own lives and loves. (It also, incidently, means they are young and extremely competitive—a distinction Parnell is careful to draw with rivals Ray Ban. "I'm sure they are nice guys at Ray Ban," Parnell will tell you with a wry smile, "but I don't want to go for a drink with them." This sense of competition is casually fostered within the culture by "fun" but aggressively contested daily competition: lunchtime cross-country mountain bike rides, games on a full-size indoor basketball court, staff ski weekends and so on.) For Oakley, the competitive identity of the desired employee reflects the competitive identity of the brand.

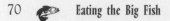

Lobby of Royalton & Paramount Hotel

© Todd Eberle

Emotion and Intensity

The purpose of a strong identity is to invite and create a more intense relationship between challenger and user, however the latter is defined. Brands and the value of branding are sometimes described as something along the lines of "facilitating and making more effective the customer's choice process,"[4] but as brands who are by and large entering or reentering a mature category, we are a long, long way from that. A Challenger brand does not break through in a mature category by being more convenient or trustworthy. It succeeds because it offers the consumer an emotional reward and/or relationship that the Establishment brand cannot match. While certain aspects of the product mix may satisfy certain rational needs, then, Challengers do not tend to succeed through the satisfaction of those rational needs (there are rarely many rational needs left in any given mature category anyway); instead, through a Lighthouse Identity they invite a realignment of the consumer's emotions.

The Challenger brand has to possess a stronger, emotionally based relationship with the consumer than the brand leader does—*for whatever reason*. As strong is not enough. Indeed, I suggest there is a graduating scale of positive affiliation with a brand that looks something like this (let us leave aside negative equity for the moment):

- **Indifference.** A decaying brand is treated with indifference. It becomes a commodity or dies.
- **Reassurance.** A well-established brand leader that has failed to renew itself offers reassurance. This is valuable for a while in new categories the consumer is afraid of, like technology or telecommunications, but it is inadequate in categories wherein a consumer is more confident, like gourmet food.
- **Weak preference** is vulnerable to competitive pricing or other aggressive retaliatory tactics. It may be sufficient in high-volume, low-interest categories like fast food but will probably be insufficient for a Challenger that needs to build momentum on change buying behavior in spite of distributional disadvantages.
- **Enthusiastic preference** should be the benchmark to which a Challenger aspires. In a very few categories this is what the brand leader already enjoys—Lexus, for example, in the import luxury market. Nike's stated aim was to create customers like fans: "Nobody roots for a product."
- **Identity** is where the preference is such for the user to identify themselves with what the brand offers. Harley-Davidson users offer an extreme example—to the point of actually having the brand name tattooed onto their skin—but Apple, for instance, has enjoyed the

same emotional identification. The apparently innocent statement "I'm a Mac User" masks a host of other related beliefs in the user's own creativity, perspective on the world, and originality of thought.

- **Enhanced self** is where the brand finds itself not simply so in tune with what the user wants to be or do that it builds identification, but where it actually confers something on the consumer they didn't realize they wanted but makes them feel, once they experience it, more than they were. Starbucks or Wonderbra offer this sense of enhanced self. The Starbucks user is not just buying coffee; he or she is buying a moment of sophistication, of being in the know, of feeling classy in a frazzled day. Wonderbra offers not just an apparently fuller figure but a sense of confidence and even power that the wearer does not normally enjoy.

We can see, then, that as far as a brand is concerned, in all practical respects the opposite of love is not hate; it's indifference. Indifference is certainly dangerous to a Challenger, but so is weak preference. Enthusiastic preference is *the least* a challenger should be aiming for.

In order to achieve this degree of preference, you have to have and project a very clear sense of who you are and what makes you different. Sympathy and solutions, characterized by "That's why" advertising, offer the consumer a mirror but not an identity. They may build short-term sales on problem-solving, but they will not create a strong enough affiliation to the brand to build medium-term momentum.

Nicholas Hayek of Swatch puts it eloquently: "Emotional products are about a message—a strong exciting, distinct, authentic message that tells people who you are and why you do what you do. There are many elements that make up the Swatch message. High quality. Low cost. Provocative. Joy of life. But the most important element of the Swatch message is the hardest for others to copy. Ultimately, we are not just offering watches. We are offering our own personal culture."[5]

Salience

The final characteristic of a Lighthouse is that it intrudes on one's consciousness: One notices it even if one is not actively looking for it. So, while you may not be a vodka drinker, you will be able to tell me what Absolut stands for. You may never use Strawberry Guava Body Lotion, but you could explain to a Latvian what Body Shop's values were. You may not switch over to *King of the Hill*, but you know what Fox is all about. You may not be the battery purchaser in your household, but you could write down three words that summarize the personality of Energizer.

This is partly to do with the identity itself, and partly with the way the Challenger expresses that identity through its marketing communications and behavior. The whole issue of salience and how Challenger brands achieve it are covered much more in Chapters 6, 7, and 10 later in the book; simply note at this point that its importance to a Challenger is rooted not in the motherhoods of good business practice but in two specific issues challenges observed in Chapter 2: The Category Isn't and The Consumer Isn't.

The Source of Identity

Seeing Nicholas Hayek talk of his own personal culture, it is apparent that an individual drives an identity and its cultural manifestations in a way an idea or a group cannot. In a founder-driven company such as Starbucks, for instance, the employee benefits package is born out of a deeply personal aspect of Howard Schultz's life. Talking of his father in an interview in 1995, he said, "He never made more than $20,000 a year. I watched my dad's self-esteem fracture and I watched his self-respect fracture. It had a lot to do with how he was treated in the workplace as a blue-collar worker."[6] Consequently, Schultz regards his staff as his most important audience, and the creation of Bean Stock, whereby each and every member of staff has equity in the company, springs from deeply felt personal ideals, not a management toolbox. While Schultz is at the helm, this is clearly not something that is going to change with each new personnel director.

But what do the rest of us do about this, attempting as we are to transform ourselves into Challengers? Not many of us have a "strong personal culture"—or at least one that is instantly apparent to the casual acquaintance. But an organization can have one, indeed *must* have one, and that, in turn, can create our own personal culture within the organization. What, then, is the source of a highly defined identity for an aspiring Challenger, if there is no founder or central visionary?

Identity doesn't hinge on having a real living founder—look at the identity-that-is-the-bottle in Absolut, or the myth of Harley-Davidson. Broadly speaking, if there is no founder within the organization, or strong CEO, there are four possible sources for a strong central identity to emerge from: the overlooked past, the relationship with hard-core users, the competition's weaknesses, and the advertising or marketing idea.

The Overlooked Past

Some have said that the role of brand planning on a mature brand is not to add value, but to *extract* value[7]—that is, to find and amplify a part of the brand's history and essence whose relevance and potential power has been lost sight of.

As an example, consider the story of The Cooperative Bank in the United Kingdom. A long-standing bank with a clientele historically more working class and less affluent than the U.K.'s Big Four, it needed to be able to regain share and build its customer base in Current Accounts and also play profitably in the expanding financial services arena; in particular, it wanted to be able to compete successfully in the credit card market. Two obvious problems faced it: first, the difficulty of launching yet another credit card so late in the market, and second that of credibility—what was a working class bank doing launching a credit card particularly, as was the case here, a gold card? Yet this remained a business imperative; the bank accordingly put the problem out to competitive pitch.

The agency that won the business (Partners BDDH) looked at the brand's past as a way to resolve the problem. It discovered that in the brand's past identity was a story considerably richer than the diluted concept of a "working man's bank" that consumers and indeed employees tended to think of it as. The Cooperative Society had begun in fact as a retailing arrangement between a group known as the "Rochdale Pioneers," who rejected the sharp and unethical business practices common in 1820s England: "short weighting," for example—where the customer was fooled into believing they had bought a greater weight of goods than they really had—or the contamination of basic foodstuffs such as flour with husks and other detritus in order to dishonestly increase the weight of the flour bag. In looking at the company's foundations, the agency realized that the heart of the identity of the bank lay not in alignment to a particular stratum of the population, but in being an ideals-centered institution taking a stand against unethical business practices. Looking therefore not at replicating the original identity, but *translating its meaning* to the present day, they asked themselves—were the bank to re-found itself today, what ethical position on business and prevalent current business practices might at the same time attract a market? From this grew the idea of an "ethical bank" that took a position on, for instance, animal testing. Research encouraged the belief that the ethical position was an attractive one, and the roots of the claim in their identity imbued it with a credibility none of the Big Four U.K. banks had, or could have. The results? The Cooperative Bank doubled its brand share over the period 1992–97 and transformed a £16 million loss into a £55 million profit over the same period. By 1997 they had become the largest issuer of gold Visa cards in Europe. And they had redefined the identity of the company to the internal as well as the external consumer.

Sometimes it takes a catalyst to see this. The company itself was too close to the everyday reality to see who it really was, and how that might be translated into the 1990s; it had become overgrown. Hence the agency and client team working on the gold card project did not so much add value as extract it. And because the identity was intrinsic and founded in a truth about the company, albeit one that had become overgrown, it was infinitely more powerful than anything they might have tried to bolt on.

The Relationship with Hard-Core Users

In many cases the brand has developed a very clear identity among a small group of hard-core users or early adopters: This identity has arisen almost despite active marketing, because these users have found or projected something onto the brand from the context in which they have come to know it.

Such was the case with the Australian lager Fosters, which in the early 1980s, prior to its national U.K. launch by Grand Metropolitan, was a niche brand enjoying cult status, particularly around London's Earl's Court—the home of the Australian backpack community. While other brewers before Grand Met had flirted with launching an Australian beer before, the imagery explored had typically been around the image of Bondi Beach, surfing, and sun. What the team found in launching Fosters was that the brand had become among its hard-core early adopters synonymous not with the bland clichés of the Australian lifestyle, but with the straightforward and dryly humorous attitude to life of the Australian beer drinker—drawn either from their own experiences of Australians or from an admiration of such Australian icons of counterculture such as Barry MacKenzie. From one of these two sources the users had developed a very clear sense of the brand's identity: down-to-earth, authentic, irreverent, a model of unpretension in swimming quietly against a tide of continental European lager beers. The launch advertising, in fact, created a spokesperson very close to the expatriate drinker that had so influenced the perspectives of U.K. early adopters, in the form of Paul Hogan.

The value of this relationship between diehard early adopters and the brand in defining its identity for a broader audience is not confined to launches, of course: For Harley-Davidson these hard-core users were the people who kept the identity alive, even when those at the company were trying to turn it into something else. And when the company was forced to become a challenger again, in the face of Japanese dominance in the category, these were the values they resuscitated, and this was the identity the company promoted.

The Competition's Weaknesses Define the Identity

Saturn is the counterpoint to the Motor City. It shapes the positives out of its oppositions to the defining characteristics of the competition:

Traditional U.S. Automotive Company	Saturn
City of Industry	Small-Town America
Hard Sell	Soft Sell
Law unto Itself (e.g., price negotiable)	Consumer category like any other (e.g., one price, no negotiation)
Selling Sheet Metal	Offering an Experience
Salespeople as Businesspeople	Salespeople as "Friends"
The One-Off Deal	The Relationship

And so on. The very clear identity in the consumer's mind of the rest of the category, allowed the brand to adopt an equally clear and compelling identity as the photographic negative. This approach is relatively easy in what I will come to talk about as "Diseased" categories (see Chapter 12), where the consumer is readily and articulately dissatisfied with key aspects of service or product in the category. But it is not confined to such categories: As we saw, the Body Shop also consciously defines itself by being the opposite of the mainstream cosmetics industry.

The Idea Defines the Identity

A fourth source of identity is to use a big enough advertising or marketing idea as a touchstone to shape the internal culture as well as the external perception. When Jack in the Box's relaunch advertising propelled Jack the founder-with-a-spherical-plastic-head into the public and the company's consciousness, his value to the company internally was more than just an entertaining spokesperson. He was an agent of change within the company. And, spherical head or not, the creative director behind Jack had imbued him with such a developed attitude toward what he would and wouldn't accept from the company he regarded as his, that the question "What would Jack do in this situation?" actually made sense. Made sense to the point, in fact, where proposals such as corner cutting on the quality of tomatoes in the Jumbo Jack, for instance (a relatively high and seasonally volatile part of the unit cost of a burger), were overturned in internal meetings on the basis that faced with this decision, Jack would insist on good-quality ingredients in his signature burger.

The Roots of Identity: Overperformance and Self-Belief

"Product Obsession is Primary."
Jim Jannard, Oakley

There are two necessary foundations to a Lighthouse Identity, other than a clear sense of who you are and what business you are in; they are product performance and self-belief. One fuels the other: If a clear identity gives differentiation externally, it also gives self-belief internally—as long as that identity is founded on concrete product performance. Knowing that one is different, better than the Establishment brand one is taking on in some key dimension affects not simply one's own performance and attitude but the relationship with one's customers.

Brand leaders operate a "just enough" strategy. Just enough mushrooms in the sauce, just enough thoughtfulness in the ergonomics of the bottle, just enough quality control in the product sourcing, just enough courtesy at the check-in desk—and only one packet of peanuts per passenger per flight. There is a story about Henry Ford that dramatizes the "just enough" philosophy nicely: Ford used to send his people out to scour the scrap heaps of America looking for old Ford engines. Dragging them back to Detroit, they would look for the parts that hadn't worn out and then downgrade the specifications to save money.[8]

While "just enough" is at some level simply good commercial sense for a brand leader, it creates an opportunity for the Challenger—to create product enthusiasm, not just product satisfaction. Robin Wight has observed that brands that enjoy an iconic status in consumers' minds are not so much engineered (in the broadest sense of the word) as overengineered: They offer not just product performance but product *over*-performance—that is, they honor the brand promise by offering the consumer in their product *dramatically* superior performance on some dimension chosen by the Challenger. Absurdly generous quantities of chocolate chunks amid the ice cream, a product that is sourced only from three islands in the Honduras, a free chauffeur-driven limousine to take you to the check-in desk in the first place. Wight believes such brands have their own design standard, one that is based not in research telling them the nature of their consumer's wants and needs, but their own, almost obsessive sense of how the product should perform, how it should be able to be experienced. A Land Rover, he will tell you, has a design standard that requires it to be able to drive 4,000 miles continually off-road without requiring anything further than more gasoline. It is actually hard to find 4,000 miles of off-road driving these days south of the Arctic circle, but that is the design standard of the people building Land Rovers. (And in some almost osmotic way, even if the Land Rover purchaser is never specifically told this, they understand the machine's extraordinary capabilities.)

Many of the Challengers we are discussing reflect Wight's concept of overperformance—indeed, they parade it. They are more deliberately extreme than the brand leader not simply in the emotion and intensity of the way they talk about themselves, but also in the product performance they offer. When driving a car, for instance, the occasions on which one needs to be able to balance three tiers of champagne glasses on one's hood as the engine approaches 6,000 rpm are relatively rare, but Lexus's launch advertising offered you the ability to do that. To the computer cautious businessperson in the 1980s, simply to have a drag-and-click function was a relief; to then be presented by Apple with a dustbin icon instead of a little drag-and-click box marked "delete" was translating their computer tasks into the language of their day-to-day household life. When requiring a little food comfort, Ben & Jerry's offered not quantities of chocolate chunks, but absurd quantities of chocolate chunks; they had their own ideas about what pleasure should mean in ice cream. In the travel business, Virgin Atlantic took entertainment to great lengths in economy—not just the choice they offered on the headset, but continual screening of classic BBC comedy on the screen in front (at a time when other airlines offered one film on an eight-hour flight), and as if that were not enough, live entertainment—jugglers on certain flights to New York and back. Perhaps even more interesting was Virgin's offering in their Business Class—Upper Deck. While most airlines tried to outdo each other on leg room, Virgin's Upper Class offered neck masseurs, chauffeur-driven limousines, a bar you could sit at in mid-air—they treated you like a real high flyer.

Lexus, Ben & Jerry's, Virgin's Upper Deck: Does overperformance mean premium? Not necessarily. Even Southwest Airlines, in its own way, overperforms—it overperforms on enthusiasm and friendliness. It may not be to everyone's taste, but it is very engaging to those who like it.

Fashion offers a multiplicity of further examples. Although fashion has historically been regarded as driven by aesthetics, many of the younger fashion brands have begun their lives with a credibility rooted in a better product idea. Mossimo began with a better idea for volleyball shorts—roomier in the seat and looser around the legs. Redsand started life in the shape of an optic yellow volleyball. Oakley started from a motorcycle grip that curved to fit the shape of a hand. Teva sandals were developed by river-rafting guides as water-friendly rafting shoes, to overcome the difficulty of negotiating white water in soggy tennis shoes. Dr. Marten's became chic partly through fashion and partly through their orthopedic soles; extreme product performance in the world of fashion is cool. (Indeed, Timberland went so far as to explicitly market themselves on this platform at one point—"More shoe than you'll ever need.") And, returning to one of the Lighthouse Identities we have already spent a little time on: Underpinning the dayglo plastic fashion statement of Swatch was a very high quality of engineering. All Swatches were water resistant and shock resistant; an $80 Swatch chronometer could perform at all the levels a $300 Tag chronometer could, but it cost $80. Oh, and it was also bright green, which jellyfish all over. One of the reasons it fought off the competition from the number of imitators (Lorus and Bonjour, for instance) who quickly flooded market was the degree of its technical excellence. It overperformed.

What is the value of overperformance to a Challenger? It is partly that it turns early adopters into justified apostles. But there is also something else. I will use the example of a brand we haven't discussed at all so far; a brand that occupies the unusual position of being both brand leader and challenger—Warburton's.

Warburton's is a family bakery in the northwest of England that began life when Ellen Warburton baked the first loaf for public sale in 1876. Still a family-run bakery, Warburton's has grown to become unsatisfied with remaining in its native Lancashire and has pushed into four new areas, the most recent in 1996. Warburton's is a premium loaf in price and quality; to make their bread the best in the business, they use better quality ingredients than any one else in the business, importing a specific variety of top-grade wheat directly from Canada that no other baker in the world has access to—not even Canadian bakers. The degree of commitment this represents is demonstrated not just by the price they are prepared to pay for the raw material—this variety of wheat is one of the most expensive in the world—or by the fact that they import every last grain when there is lesser wheat available on their own doorstep, but by the lengths that David Henderson, then Warburton's technical director, was prepared to go to in order to secure the deal. To create this opportunity, Henderson had to meet with and lobby each member of the Canadian Wheat Growers Association individually—and the Canadian Wheat Growers Association is *500 members strong*. (The strength of this commitment is highlighted by the fact that at the time when Henderson concluded the last interview, the chairman of the U.K. Brand leader had yet to even set foot in Canada.)

Now the benefit of this commitment to Warburton's is clearly a superior-quality product. And there is a consumer whose relationship with the brand Jonathan Warburton, the marketing and sales director, believes is profoundly affected by the knowledge of this commitment to quality. This consumer is not the general public, who buys and eats the bread; the exceptional quality of their ingredients is not something that the company ever communicates to their end customers, who believe good bread is to do with the skills of the baker, not the ingredients that make up the bread. There is a different consumer on whom Jonathan Warburton believes this commitment to ingredient quality has a profound effect—the internal consumer within the company.

Kevin Ainsley is the sales manager for one of Warburton's five operating regions. Ainsley knows that David Henderson has been to Canada and done something special for his company's bread that makes it better than anyone else's. He doesn't know *what*. He couldn't tell you the variety of wheat, or the effect on the loaf's rise or butterability. All he knows is that Henderson has gone to extraordinary lengths to make sure Warburton's bread is the best in the world. This knowledge allows him to operate differently from the way he would approach "selling in" for the competition. In negotiating and handling new accounts he has absolute self-belief, because he has absolute confidence in the product's success. If, once a new account is gained, the product mix doesn't work at first, he swiftly reconfigures it until it does. His self-belief is infectious. He knows he's better; he feels like a winner and is selling a winner even before he walks into the room. This is one of the reasons, perhaps, that in 1997 Warburton's became the biggest-selling bread brand in the United Kingdom, even though it is stocked in only half the country.

Overperformance, then, has many benefits for a Challenger. It is not simply an extreme point of difference that justifies the emotional position the Challenger adopts. It is not simply to create fanatics and apostles in the user base (and therefore mythology—see Chapter 10)—although all these are important. Its other value is to create supreme self-belief and conviction within the company, and this is something that can be detected by those outside the company.

Overperformance shows the company really cares about the product, which in turn means it is committed to delivering on the brand promise. And it gives the company the confidence to be a Lighthouse.

Implications for the Challenger Organization

In short, successful challengers do not seem—publicly, at least—to navigate with reference to the consumer; instead, the strong sense of their own identity that they actively and intensely communicate at every point of interaction with the brand invites the consumer to navigate with reference to them. Like a lighthouse, one notices them without looking for them.

If we begin to put the first two credos together to create the first steps of a Challenger process or strategic approach, we are faced immediately with an apparent contradiction: How are we to resolve the tension between the need for knowledge as to who you are as a brand and company (Building a Lighthouse Identity), and the need for an intelligent innocence as to the confines and opportunities of the category (Break with Your Immediate Past)? Both need to exist and be vital within the company in order for the Challenger to flourish—the latter so that we can see the opportunities for growth, and the former so that we can realize and own them—but how? Through process or personnel we will need to find ways of creating intelligent collisions between knowledge of the brand and inexperience of the category; Chapter 12 will look at how a Challenger company manages such apparent tensions in their systematic manufacture of dynamism and ideas.

6

The Third Credo: Assume Thought Leadership of the Category

We tend to talk about Brand Leadership as if it were only true of one brand in each category—the largest. In fact, there are two kinds of brand leader in each category. One is the Market Leader, the biggest player, the brand everyone lives with—and, chances are, the brand they probably grew up with.

But there is also another type of brand leader: the Thought Leader, the brand in the category that everyone talks about. While not the biggest, it is the brand that is getting the most attention. It's the one that is seen to be picking up momentum, entering the popular culture. At one distant point in its life, the existing market leader was this brand. But with very few exceptions, once the brand leader reaches the top, it stops making waves.

Most of the brands we are looking at effectively took the decision that if they weren't the first of these, they needed to be the other; if they couldn't be the Market Leader, they needed to be the one everyone talked about. The one that was seen to be dynamic.

They aim to achieve Thought Leadership not just through product innovation or advertising strategy, but through *behavior:* by surprising the consumer in selectively breaking not all, but one or two of the conventions of the category they were entering or reentering so late.[1]

Behavior That Breaks the Conventions of the Category

The first law of Marketing in the real world is this—everyone *talks* about being consumer focused, but no one really does it. Mission statements the world over talk about "Surprising and delighting consumers" with their customer service, yet the gap between what the consumer wants and what the consumer gets remains large in any category.

Instead, marketeers surround themselves with rules or conventions that govern the marketing of their product within the category: you have to show two women side by side in the kitchen if you have a detergent commercial, for instance, or some relationship with dentists if you are in toothpaste. If you are in financial services, you need a serious brand name; if in airlines, a livery that impresses. Consumers have, it seems, expectations one has to deliver on to play in the category: If one goes to a circus, for instance, they expect elephants, and someone who puts their head into a lion's mouth, and ladies on horseback, and men with big trousers and flappy shoes who run round and round and squirt water in each other's faces. If they are going to buy a luxury car, they expect a prestigious marque. And so on.

But the point about these conventions is that they often have little to do anymore with understanding what the consumer really wants, or rather *might want*: They have been invented by marketeers (and the market leader) for reasons now forgotten and so by default become the status quo. In turn, some secondary brands in each category have eked out a comfortable but unspectacular living by playing to the existing conventions established by the brand leader; and this repetition by the Establishment brands has in turn shaped consumers' expectations of how that particular product should be seen and how products of that sort are marketed. The research the established players commission from time to time often confirms the validity of these conventions because the questioner is too close to the category to ask the questions in a way that doesn't presuppose the same old answers, and the consumer has never really seen what else might be on offer.

But a Challenger enters (or reenters) a market almost by definition late. In entering late into a market, one has to differentiate oneself more strongly: One has to offer the consumer a powerful reason to choose you. An identity has to be justified.

Finding that strong reason is not easy: While there will be times a genuine product innovation (such as the Dyson Cyclone vacuum cleaner) precedes the creation of a brand, more often now the concept for the brand precedes the notion of the shape and nature of the product. If one looks at the telecommunications business, for instance, deregulation creates the opportunities for greater choice of brands, but in the main those brands have little idea in the early days of what their real product differences might be. This means that the marketeer cannot rely on being given something physical, patentable, or enduring that they can point to as their reason for being chosen—they will have to create it at the same time as they create (or re-create) their brand.

Category conventions offer a natural point of leverage to create this differentiation: The Challenger has to find a genuinely innovative insight into what the consumer really wants—and then play to that by taking one or two of those conventions and deliberately breaking them in the way it markets itself. This offers short-term leverage as the Challenger enters the market. It also offers drama, if that break is highlighted through publicity or advertising. (This is one of the core philosophies behind the martial art of Aikido—that one uses one's opponent's strength to own advantage.) The length of time the convention has stood and the degree to which the consumer assumes it is just the way the category operates adds to the drama of the convention being genuinely upset.

But it is important to stress that this kind of convention breaking is not just about making a splash to gain attention. While one is certainly looking to be noticed, the short-term aim is also to use the break to communicate with impact one's identity and positioning. And, longer term, the goal is to reframe the category territory, in particular the consumer's selection criteria, to territory the Challenger has defined themselves, and therefore to their own longer-term advantage. Changing the rules in their favor for ever.

There are three kinds of conventions that surround every category:

1. Conventions of Representation.
2. Conventions of Medium.
3. Conventions of Product Experience.

As we will see in the following examples, breaks in convention are rarely created through whim or even desire; more often they are forced on the challenger because of limitations in their own resources, typically those of advertising budget, distribution base, or just the time the trade will grant them to build up critical mass before making a decision about their future. Yet the forced change precipitates the very behavior that intrigues and seduces the consumer. As well as changing the rules for everyone else.

Conventions of Representation

Conventions of representation are those that surround how and where you portray yourself and your identity. These embrace advertising (yogurt advertising always has a close-up of a spoon going into a mouth), packaging (mineral water is always in clear bottles), logo, and name. (Advertising conventions are not discussed in this chapter; the reader interested in pursuing the breaking of advertising conventions will find the subject admirably and comprehensively discussed in another volume in this Adweek series by Jean-Marie Dru called *Disruption*.)

It is rare that we get the chance to choose our own names. When we do, at a launch, it proves a tortured luxury, and the inclination for the newcomer is, more often than not, to take one's cue from the others. When Fox launched as the fourth U.S. television network, for instance, the original plan was to call it FBC. It is not hard to see why—this was how channels branded themselves, it seemed. ABC, NBC, CBS: These had surely set the stage for any newer player to walk on if they desired consumer success.

Yet, before the three initials hardened and set in the fledgling company, Barry Diller and his core launch team reconsidered. Although the sense of brand personality and identity were only to be fully developed and articulated several years later, it became clear to the team even before the launch that they had to have something different about them. While not yet confident enough to take this differentiation into all their programming straightaway (the launch program was, after all, Joan Rivers), the decision to change the name from FBC to Fox heralded in an important sense the desire to be a brand, rather than just a network—and, longer term, a brand that changed the way television marketed itself.

Goldfish was another brand to launch late, into a market where the rules had apparently been defined by the existing players. When Gold-brand Developments, the parent company, first approached advertising agencies about the imminent launch of a new credit card in the United Kingdom, naming research had thrown up "Vantage" as the proposed name for the new card. The winning agency took the view that in the light of the extraordinary competition already fighting for share in a mature marketplace, real differentiation would be imperative, and the name would have to be considerably more radical if it was to invite consideration from a consumer already bombarded with more new financial brands than they understood or needed.

A name like Goldfish for a financial services product is a brave choice. People with years in the business would have told you that it was in fact a dangerous choice. Money is a serious business, they would say; if you can't have something with financial authority or weight, at least choose something neutral. What you certainly must avoid is the irreverent or apparently lightweight.

Yet, with 400 cards already on the market, and another 140 launching that year, breaking the convention proved the most sensible and low-risk decision to take: High differentiation was a business necessity. Goldfish has achieved success in a number of ways, but the first and most important was to call themselves something that was unconventional, yet that still communicated its purpose: a credit card that would be everyday, universal, and accessible, rather than elitist. With 600,000 users in the first year, 80% awareness, and a user base that uses it more often than any other card, it appears to be succeeding.

The Virgin name is now an accepted part of the landscape. It came into the airline business out of rock, but even in rock it is easy to underestimate now Branson's flair for publicity in calling it something like Virgin. He founded the original company at a time in Britain's life when only a few years previously someone (Branson himself, as it happens) had been taken to court by the government for using the supposedly indecent words "venereal disease" in a printed flyer for a woman's clinic he was promoting. If "venereal disease"—essentially a medical term—was thought to be something the Great British Public needed protection

Goldfish Card

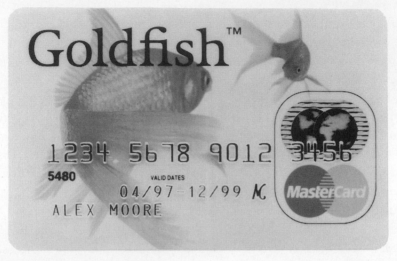

Supplied by Goldfish Credit Card.

from, to call oneself a name like "Virgin" was to walk a splendid line between shock and respectability. Even now, as we witness enormous and aggressive companies calling themselves invented nonsense (in the literal, rather than pejorative, sense of the word) like "Diageo" because they mean nothing in particular—whatever the naming company tells you—one cannot help feeling that the name of Branson's empire helps set the agenda for much of the identity and attitude that makes him successful more often than not.

For other Challengers, walking away from conventions of packaging has been a more defining part of the brand identity than the name. For a relaunch, where the name is often the only real point of continuity, the packaging is usually the first point of fresh departure. The U.K. soft drink Tango has become famous for its advertising, but the packaging is equally interesting: It is predominantly black. Black is a color long rejected for food; the reasons for this are variously given from its simply being funereal to the more elaborate explanation that we are wired as animals to look for food that is gold and red (the color of health and ripeness) and shun that which is black or purple (the predominant colors of rot and disease).

Tango Can

Supplied by Britvic Softdrinks Ltd.

Yet Tango chose to fly in the face of all this. A long-standing middle-order player in the U.K. soft-drinks market, they had tried advertising with attitude for a number of years and failed to make any impact on the bigger players. Developing new packaging and advertising simultaneously, they needed drama, and the use of the color black helped give it to them. First, it was a color that dramatically highlighted the fruit graphic in the center of the can representing the Tango taste "sensation." Second, it gave them dramatic standout on shelf—a block of black to fight

Coke and the wannabe colas' vast block of red (soft drinks suffer particularly from distribution dominance). Third, it was packaging that aroused a strong reaction—people actually argued about it in research groups. To some consumers it seemed simply wrong, and to others it was this very wrongness that made it intriguing, iconoclastic, attractive. But to flourish Tango needed to be a brand that elicited strong reactions, and Britvic (Tango's parent) chose to be noticed. The new launch, fuelled by the advertising, has doubled sales in six years.

In breaking with the conventions of packaging, the Body Shop went beyond graphics. The existing category players believed that since body products essentially represented a little female luxurious pampering during an otherwise unglamorous day, then the packaging should glorify and lend status to the product—in many ways, in fact, the packaging was what you were really paying for. Anita Roddick, however, bottled her liquids in cheap plastic bottles, with simple green labels stuck on the front. What she was aiming for was a different kind of emotional value—an internal one rather than an external one. Her bottles wore no makeup, as it were, because it took away from the real heart of the brand, which was a natural, spiritual well-being rather the superficialities of the big cosmetics houses. While there may have been all kinds of financial merits for a newly launched retail concern in low-cost packaging, the positioning advantages were at least as great: the focus/identity would have been far harder to dramatize for the consumer had Roddick played by the packaging rules and tried to communicate the difference purely through advertising—assuming, of course, that she believed in advertising in the first place. Making the bottle unimportant threw attention both on what is inside the bottle and what is outside the packaging; it forced the consumer to notice instead—and the company to develop instead—new criteria for choice: new emotions in the product (fruity descriptors that sounded like luxurious desserts, for example) and new emotions in the store around one (a philosophy of spirit and nature, communicated through posters and informational leaflets). The Body Shop offered not just differentiation, but a little journey of learning and experimentation; it achieved this partly by breaking the convention of packaging to force attention on the new grounds for choice. Now, no new body-product brand is complete without a leaflet setting out their philosophy about naturalness and the body.

The Body Shop Bergamot Body Wash

© The Body Shop International PLC

A recent Challenger in the mineral water category achieved tempo-rary momentum by breaking the conventions of packaging in an inverse way to the Body Shop. Mineral water is always in clear bottle, to wor-ship the purity of the fluid inside and propagate the illusion that it is more than just water. Since France had historically been the home of

The Body Shop Bergamot Lavender Oil

© The Body Shop International PLC

mineral water, Ty Nant (like Absolut in its own market) made no attempt to justify the provenance of its water. Instead, it produced a bottle where the water was invisible, because the glass itself was a deep cobalt blue. This aroused enormous curiosity, and a surprising relationship with the bottle started to form the basis for trial and experimentation with the new brand: The outside became more prized than the inside. Fashion shops as far from its native Wales as Los Angeles started using the cobalt blue empty bottles to adorn their windows. While Evian was busy developing plastic technology to facilitate their bottles' disposal, Ty Nant bottles were being kept as empties to decorate hairdressers' salons in Santa Monica. This in turn spread the desirability and cachet of a mineral water nobody had heard of and fewer still could pronounce.

The Body Shop and Ty Nant changed the conventional relationship in their categories between the packaging and the product to signal to the consumer the arrival of a new kind of brand. Orange went one further: It never showed the product (and therefore the packaging) at all. A prospective new player to the U.K. mobile communications market was faced with the challenge of many of the new telecommunications and software companies: If the product one is selling is invisible—less a concrete, tangible thing than liberation or self-enhancement—what does one show as the product at all? And if the product is not tangible, what is the packaging and how does one present it? Late into the cellular category (and actually a different technology, not that the consumer cared), Orange took the view that if it could not own the cellular category, it would create a new category that it could own. Naming itself after a color, not a corporation, it created the concept of a wireless world—"A wirefree future, in which you call people, not places, and where everyone will benefit from the future of technology." A key signal of this to the consumer was to never show a cellular phone in the advertising, or indeed any part of the mass-market communication to the consumer.

From packaging to provenance. When Absolut Vodka launched in the United States in 1980, the conventions of the category dictated that unless you had a label screaming an authentic Russian pedigree, you were dead. While the company explored potential for wielding the sword of Swedish quality against bulwark of the Russian authenticity, they found it, candidly, a pretty dull sword. They showed the consumer rolling fields of corn and asked them about the meaning of Sweden, and all consumers could think of was cold blondes. And to cap it all, they didn't even have a label on the bottle in the first place. So they had to find another way of communicating vodka quality—breaking with a key category convention was forced on them.

The solution was not to talk about quality but to assume it. Through talking about purity with wit and style, and by breakthrough use of media, it became the most emulated brand in the white spirits market.

Conventions of Medium

Conventions of medium concern the way the brand is delivered, both physically and emotionally. They encompass distribution (perfume, for example, is always sold through pharmacies) and message delivery (lingerie is always advertised in women's print).

People expect individual categories to express themselves in particular kinds of media. The dilemma a Challenger faces is this: Does one play in the same media in order to be seen as a legitimate contender in the category but accept a low share of voice because of the presence of other players there? Or does one leave the beaten path and derive a possible (but perhaps uncertain and short-lived) advantage by appearing in a context the consumer does not associate with the category one is attempting to (re-)enter?

Often the decision is forced on a Challenger; it cannot afford the convention—three flights of television advertising every six months, for instance, rotating five spots at a time. As we have already observed, however, the breakthrough comes not in simply realizing that one has to play in a medium where one can be more visible, but in realizing that there is, by the same token, an opportunity to use the unconventional nature of that new medium to one's own advantage.

Consider Wonderbra, the push-up brassiere whose brand launch ("Hello Boys") we discussed in Chapter 5. This is a famous campaign. At its inception the campaign was based on a strong strategic insight, namely, that there was an opportunity for an underwear brand to capitalize on a change in attitude by women toward their own sexuality. This strategic thought was in turn brought to life in a stronger creative idea, centering around the power over men a Wonderbra gave you (and the consequent pleasure of Behaving Badly).

But the real breakthrough in many ways was not the strategic idea or the creative thought but the choice of medium as an expression of them both. Underwear advertising in the United Kingdom had historically been a discreet, private business between advertiser and prospective buyer, any communication buried from public view within the intimate boundaries of a women's magazine. But if Wonderbra's whole positioning lay in encouraging women to be bolder with their sexuality, then the medium in a very real sense had to be part of the message. To run a deliberately provocative advertisement such as "Hello Boys" in women's magazines was one thing; to run it on posters by the side of commuter traffic on its way into the city was another thing completely. With £500,000 spent on the outdoor campaign, the brand generated news coverage and publicity worth an estimated £50,000,000 over two weeks. (Wonderbra in South Africa also took the concept of unusual media into the store. Once the campaign was running, they placed floor panels in the women's apparel sections of large stores with the proposition, "If you can see your feet, may we recommend a Wonderbra?")

The fashion designer Vera Wang had even less to spend in launching her evening-wear collection. The expected medium for this kind of launch is a high-end fashion show. We are all familiar from the media with such shows—catwalks, supermodels, celebrities, flashbulbs: It seems to be the price of entry for every designer each year. But they are expensive, costing up to $500,000 each, and Wang couldn't afford $500,000. Although she had made something of a name for herself by designing skating outfits for Nancy Kerrigan, in financial terms her company was only just beginning to take off. She had to find another medium in which to launch. So she produced an "image book."

Instead of an invitation to a catwalk, each of the fashion press received a black book the size of a paperback with the words "Vera Wang, Volume 1" in silver on the jacket. Inside were 28 pages of photographs of models wearing two dozen of the dresses in the collection. There were no props, no jewelry, only stylized photographs of the details of the clothes.

The quiet confidence of the book commanded a considerable attention among the 7,500 strong target of fashion press, regular customers, and potential retailers who received it; besides media coverage, she received calls from all of these. But its benefit went further than the admittedly critical one of attention and sales. Its unexpected nature afforded two additional benefits that the conventional medium wouldn't. It allowed her to express her design philosophy—her identity—at a time when she was chiefly known for wedding apparel, and it positioned her as being at the cutting edge of the fashion business. Since then she has opened a New York flagship, along with in-store shops in fashionable department stores such as Barneys Beverly Hills.

At its inception, Gateway 2000 couldn't afford the cost of traditional media to build its identity, so it used a medium it already owned: the boxes the computers were sold in. Using an item historically ignored by computer companies (and indeed all white- and brown-goods companies) for all purposes except model numbers and shipping instructions, Ted Waitt covered the Gateway 2000 boxes in the brand's now-celebrated faux cowhide black-and-white motif. Like Wonderbra, the power of the communication to the consumer came in the interaction between innovative message and unconventional medium: While a surprise to see a computer box used as a medium at all, it was more startling to see a high-tech product wrapped in a farmyard motif (the same design on another medium such as a poster, physically distant from the technology, would have lost the force of the interaction). The values that Gateway 2000 sees as setting itself apart, which it refers to as "Silicon Prairie," were simply and directly communicated to each evangelistic new user.

In 1984, at the Los Angeles Olympics, Nike captured the imagination of the city and the cameras of the television networks with enormous walls on which they had painted Nike-endorsed athletes—huge, dominating figures of competition, desire, and triumph. The world applauded Nike as the official sponsor of the Games, epitomizing as it did everything that was splendid about athletic endeavor. Only Nike wasn't the official sponsor; Converse was. But while Converse paid the money, Nike broke the convention of medium and stole the glory.

Guests for fashion shows by John Galliano, the British designer who is currently creative director of Dior, have received their invitations in forms as unusual as a red-satin ballet shoe, a school report for Miss Suzy Sphinx, a poster advertising an amateur boxing competition, a bullet in sand. Through the unexpected medium of his invitations, Galliano creates standout in a crowded season and heightens anticipation among a generally blasé press audience for the creative content of his shows.

"Conventions of Medium" does not, incidently, refer solely to the medium of communication. Interpreted in the broader sense of "Where you are" (contrasted with Representation's "Who or What you are"), it can also encompass product location—where the consumer finds you.

Gateway 2000 Box

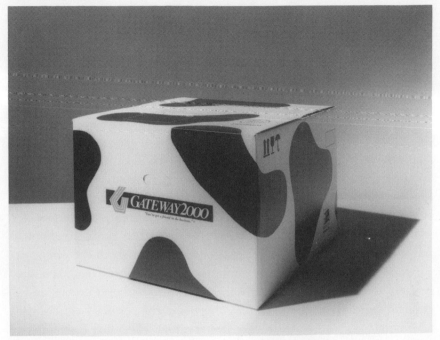

Supplied by Gateway 2000.

PlayStation's launch in the United Kingdom centered around the thought that the new system was the most powerful on the market; seeing this as an opportunity to appeal more directly to an older group of 18- to 30-year-old gamers, PlayStation set up gaming stations in London clubs such as the Ministry of Sound. More commonly associated with the ingestion of other adult mind-expanding substances, be they music or alcohol, such locations offered the opportunity for PlayStation to present itself to, and get sampled by, this older, perhaps cooler target market as offering a recreational experience at a level of sophistication above their little brother's Nintendo.

Conventions of Product Experience

Conventions of product experience have to do with the product offered and the surrounding experience it delivers. At a simple level the original sound of a Ping Putter (or the engine note of a Harley-Davidson) is one way of a Challenger building in experiential difference in a familiar category. At a more sophisticated level, we have seen how Starbucks turned themselves into a destination by changing the conventional coffee-shop experience.

Cirque du Soleil began life in a category you would have said was anachronism. In a society increasingly devoted to adrenaline and the special effect in our entertainment—what Hollywood refers to as "the ride"—circuses were associated with childhood; identical and predictable, we knew the circus routine and dismissed it as a thing of the past. This was surely the age of computer animation and the IMAX theater; had one been a Canadian venture capitalist approached in the early 1980s by a group of stilt walkers looking for backing to start a new circus, one would have dispatched them to the nearest Cineplex to look at the round-the-block lines for *Terminator 2* and thought no more about it. But Cirque du Soleil broke many of the conventions of the circus experience. First, they aimed for an adult circus: sophisticated, androgynous, and with enigmatic show names that one didn't understand— Quidam, Saltimbanco, Allegria. Furthermore, they created a circus with no animals—or rather, a circus where you marvel only at the ability of the most extraordinary animal of all, the human animal. They fused into circus elements of music, dance, and the theater. They made it impossible to become familiar with their routine because they completely reinvented it every two years. Each time they returned to a city they offered a completely different spectacle and mood. Some conventions of the Big Top, of course, remain; there are clowns, acrobats, strong men. But the important ones are shattered.

They did all this because they saw that the secret to success was not competing against other circuses, but competing against every other show in town. The result is that they now have three permanent touring companies and shows in residence in cities as far apart as Las Vegas and Tokyo.

For many years Sainsbury's led the U.K. food retail market. Having opened and maintained a lead over its nearest rival, Tesco, largely through the perceived quality and choice of the food offered (accelerated by the extraordinary broadening and gourmandizing of British food tastes in the 1980s and early 1990s), many thought Sainsbury's position at the beginning of the 1990s unassailable.

Tesco pursued a two-stage business strategy. The first had been the upgrading of its store and product quality; although necessary, this only served to match the brand leader on performance. The question that then faced Tesco was how to win: Sainsbury's had defined food as the battlefield, but to become brand leader, Tesco would have to find another territory it could own.

The place in which Tesco chose to fight was the whole food-shopping experience. Stepping back to look afresh at the consumer's relationship with the whole process of shopping at a food retailer, it realized that while the range and quality of food was certainly an important part of the relationship, there was also a broader level of interacting with any food retailer on which consumers were less happy—the hassle of negotiating yourself (and probably small children) through the shopping process: parking at the wrong end of a large car park, being stuck in a long line at the check-out with two hyperactive infants, packing up the shopping bags yourself while the cashier demands money and the children demand chocolate, and so on. Was this something Tesco could own? The experience? It determined that it would match Sainsbury's in food and store quality and innovate on the shopping experience. Its agency had developed a tag line in the earlier stage of their activity—"Every Little Helps."—which they knew struck a chord in the frazzled consumer, and, retaining this as a central driver for innovation as well as communication, began to launch a series of product improvements that, though not winners in themselves, collectively added up to an improvement in the consumer's shopping experience at Tesco: staff to pack bags for you (still a novelty in the United Kingdom), more cash registers open when there were lines of two people or more, baby changing facilities, privilege parking for those with small children, and many more—one after the other. While other retailers had written off the shopping experience as being a necessary evil, Tesco made it the place to fight.

The result has been the seizure of brand leadership from Sainsbury's. By 1995 Tesco had equalized profit per square foot and went ahead in share. At the time of writing it has been the brand leader for three years.

Back to cars. Saturn is probably one of the two most analyzed new product launches in the last 20 years. One of the primary reasons is that they structured much of their operations simply to break one convention: that of the experience. Much of car purchase is associated by the consumer with hassle and stress; people talk of actually feeling nauseous as they drive off the lot. The convention Saturn broke was that of seeing and presenting the product as the car; they sold instead an *experience*—a new kind of purchase experience on the lot, and a new kind of relationship with car and manufacturer either side of stepping onto the lot. Advertisements talked of people writing to the company before they received their new car and celebrated the owners who drove to the "Homecoming Reunion" in Spring Hill a few years later. The move to experience was at one level forced on them: Having the ambition to fight back against the Japanese imports on the one hand, and a competent but unremarkable physical product on the other, the only way to achieve their objectives was to find a distinction through changing the consumer's relationship with the experience that surrounded the product.

To return to Galliano and his fashion shows, his use of "gateways" of experience is interesting. He has a flair for the big set in his shows (40-foot spruce trees transplanted to a sports stadium to create an "enchanted forest," for example), but also for the entrances to their shows. One year, guests walked through a wardrobe to find themselves, ankle deep in fresh snow, standing on the roofs of a Spanish city. He manages not just the brand experience very carefully, but the *transition* from our world into his.

Increasingly, then, Challengers compete and succeed by being in the experience business: the anticipation and the delivery of an experience that breaks the category convention.

The Role of Price, and Other Misconceptions

It is sometimes argued that while brand leaders tend to sell on quality, second-rank brands attempt to compete on price. But none of these brands have succeeded in the medium term through a price platform. Price may have indeed been a part of the initial positioning and trial, notably for Southwest Airlines and Virgin Atlantic's economy class, but they are no longer the sole reasons these brands are bought; if Freddie Laker taught the minor players in the airline business anything, it is that if one attempts to compete on price alone, the big players can squeeze one's pips at any point. As United steps up the low price war on the West

Coast with Shuttle by United, and British Airways enters the European price segment with a specially designed new service, the insecurity of a Challenger competing on a price platform alone is painfully clear. So while Virgin does have price as a key part of its mix in the airline business (and, indeed, whatever market it enters initially), its current success as an airline has as much to do with entertainment product dimensions and a genuinely superior product as price. (In point of fact, when winning the Japanese route, the Japanese authorities, to protect their national carriers, insisted Virgin charge what amounted to a price *greater than that of British Airways* in order to protect the Japanese airlines.) So, too, MCI had price as a key part of the brand promise, but it made its success through an idea—"Friends and Family"—that took the benefits of price to a much higher emotional level.

Of our other Challengers, Saturn is inexpensive, but it is not advertised as such. Swatch for its part found in initial research that they had more interest in purchase if they *raised* their price from the initial consumer offer. Absolut has never discounted or couponed, even in the teeth of the recession. Tango sells at a 10% price premium to Coca-Cola. Tesco, ironically, had for years operated as a price leader, but they succeeded as a Challenger by changing the nature of the experience (retaining good value as simply part of the mix). Successful challenge is not about price; it's about how one *thinks* and *behaves* as a brand.

A second, natural misconception is that Thought Leadership through unconventional practice may forfeit conventionally desired attributes, notably quality ratings. This is not born out by the quality rating of the Challengers we are looking at. Southwest Airlines, for instance, doesn't talk a lot about quality, doesn't dress its flight attendants in Armani uniforms or offer haute cuisine, yet it has topped U.S. airline quality charts for two years running. Saturn never talked about product quality, never even showed a great deal of its car on screen, yet consumers put it on the same quality level as Ford in four years. Virgin has won airline awards eight years running.

Finally, there is sometimes a confusion between selectively breaking with certain conventions and simply being outrageous. The second of these does indeed have its followers, and there is a school of thought that argues with some justice that if you cannot afford a great deal of paid-for advertising, you should strive to do something provocative in the little you can afford that gets you free coverage in free media. Besides the attention, it offers the considerable benefits of being outside the immediate environment of competitive clutter.

But in talking here about using the medium, experience, or representation in an unconventional way, we are going far beyond advertising aimed at generating publicity. It should be clear that this is not a question of flouting taboos, but of finding competitive advantage. As such, it should be regarded, if done intelligently, not as a high-risk option for wild-eyed entrepreneurs but as a low-risk route to growth for a Challenger who wants to do more with less.

Thought Leadership Is Not the Same as Slash and Burn

Breaking convention has become a hot topic. But it is not whole-sale rule breaking that the Challenger should aspire to. Rather, the Challenger needs to understand which conventions of representation, medium, or experience to break and which to observe.

Lexus, for example, changed some of the conventions of product experience but deliberately decided to keep other conventions of representation. The changes were forced on them; they found in their development research that the five key attributes American luxury buyers wanted were prestige, safety, resale value, performance, and styling, in that order. But they could not compete on prestige or resale value immediately, so they focused on the last of these—performance and styling. By breaking the conventions of the product experience, they redefined luxury. The resulting product, at the resulting price point, redefined what a luxury car should be.

But the Lexus launch team didn't throw every convention out in the process of redefining luxury. There was, for instance, a fierce debate within the team whether to include a grille on the new car. Many of the Lexus design team preferred to leave off the grille—and indeed, the motoring press itself was expecting something more iconoclastic, expressing astonishment at some of the early shows where the grille was revealed on the new car. But the most senior members, including Kunihiro Uchida, the chief designer, mandated it.

In an interview afterwards Uchida was asked why he decided to include a grille—many journalists felt that a car without a grille would have been a more futuristic car; he replied that he was confident that a luxury car should have a grille. He realized that, in effect, a Challenger couldn't break every rule at once; his new car needed to anchor itself in certain conventions of representation in order to allow the conventions of product experience they broke to be of mass interest.

Thought Leadership and Behavior

The third credo, then, is that of assuming Thought Leadership of the category. This is begun through deliberately breaking some of the conventions of the category, while rooting yourself in others.

Thought Leadership is not just about marketing strategy. It's about *behavior*. In most of the cases we have looked at, the breaking of convention was forced on them—usually because they lacked the money (Vera Wang, Gateway 2000) or pedigree (Absolut, Lexus) to go the conventional route. But they turned this into an advantage, by changing the relationship the consumer had come to take for granted between the product and the way it represented itself, or the product and the medium it used, or the product and the experience it offered.

The result has been to define the rules in their favor. The success of Absolut has allowed the spawning a group of small but growing super-premium vodkas, such as Ketel One and Royalty, none of whom are Russians, and all of whom trade (less effectively) on style more than product credentials. The success of Lexus has meant Cadillac rethinking their engineering. Virgin Atlantic's entertainment offering in economy was the catalyst for British Airways to overhaul their own. And so on.

Finally, we have to be aware that such leadership may not always meet with universal acceptance in the beginning. Thought leaders are not always embraced by everyone at the same time. Stepping back a moment into the marketing of music, for instance, consider the early days of Elvis—the original Elvis, that is, rather than the occasional alter ego of the president of Southwest Airlines. While Elvis is now a figure at the center of U.S. music history, in reality, the early years were difficult. The man that broke Elvis, the legendary Sam Phillips, was unashamedly looking for a fusion that would break the musical conventions of the time—a white man with a black sound. The salient images of Elvis may now be of a sedate, middle-aged man playing to blue rinses in Vegas, but what Elvis unleashed in addition to the sound that Sam Phillips sought in the beginning was something very different. His stage act for "Hound Dog" was banned as being too inflammatory. Radio stations received death threats for playing his music; The Parent-Teacher Association called it "vulgar, animalistic noise," and the King a "rock and roll bum," and "a sex maniac." Police filmed his shows, and one-and-a-half years after the release of "It's All Right Mama," he was still being introduced on programs as "The most controversial name in Rock and Roll."

The success of Thought Leadership should be measured initially, then, by a more intense relationship with one's core target, rather than immediate mass market appeal.

7

The Fourth Credo: Create Symbols of Reevaluation

"The big do not always eat the little. The fast always eat the slow."
The chairman of BMW Europe, 1989

Living in what has been called the postliterate society, one does not need to argue the case for the power of icons and symbols in marketing. The most valuable brand in the world is Marlboro, worth some $40 billion, a brand that has been built entirely around a single icon—the cowboy has proved itself the most commercially valuable myth in modern popular culture. Marlboro is, indeed, a remarkably pure example of Mechanical Advantage: one single idea (not an innovation, an idea) repeated essentially unchanged for over 30 years, on the basis of which the most valuable brand in the world has been built.

The second-most valuable brand in the world is Coca-Cola, a company with an original packaging icon so powerful (the contour bottle) that it still lends its graphic representation to the side of the aluminum can that replaced it. A company whose determination to own symbolism as fundamental and powerful as the color red is reflected in the popular (but sadly false) myth that Santa Claus owes his now universal red coat to the chutzpah of a Coca-Cola artist, Haddon Sundblom, who supposedly changed him from a blue-coated elf to a fully grown, red-suited man for the purposes of a 1931 Christmas brand marketing drive.

Commercial value aside, it is not hard to understand the importance marketeers attach to symbolism in brand building. At its most basic, if 70% of human communication is nonverbal, it is reasonable to look for the expression of one's identity to be manifested in some kind of visual form, over and above a graphic treatment of logo or name, simply in order to complete the communication relationship with one's desired consumer. Indeed, as we move to a consumer retreating from the marketing relationship, and the need for a softer and softer verbal "sell," striking visual imagery may remain the strongest way of rapidly advancing our brand's case without turning off the consumer.

But the inherent advantages for a Challenger brand go far beyond a visual cuing of identity, important though that is. First, they have to do with immediacy—an instant cuing of identity, Phil Knight of Nike has remarked of the Air Jordan "Jump Man" icon, which came almost to embody the brand's attitude in the 1980s, that it saved a lot of time—you couldn't explain much in 60 seconds, but if you showed Michael Jordan, you didn't need to.

The second advantage for a Challenger would seem to be the communication of emotion. To continue with the "jump man" example, while the imminence of the dunk the icon portrays is the achievement every amateur basketball player dreams of, the theatrical splay of the legs demonstrates not just achievement, but effortless, flamboyant achievement. The appeal of the image lies in it saying something about the emotions and style of the person, as well as the ability of the player.

So there is indeed an extraordinary compression in this. But it is the *emotions* the icon arouses in such a short time that make it so valuable.

Emotion and speed, of course, are two of a Challenger's key drivers; Challengers are from necessity brands in a hurry. It is not just that life is speeding up that we have become a world of short cuts and quick fixes, of skimmers and scanners, or that the post–MTV generation has become expectant of faster paced communication and brand conversation. It is that both success and survival for Challengers *depend on effecting change fast:* momentum and critical mass are all-important with both trade and consumer. And that change in turn hinges on establishing an emotionally centered appeal.

So when we observe that one of the striking things about the Challengers we are considering is a sharp hunger for symbols and iconography, we are not talking icons in the mold of Tony the Tiger or the Pills-bury doughboy. We are talking about symbols of *change*: Challengers de-ploy icons and symbols specifically to *prompt reevaluation*. They create surprising, striking visual devices and events designed to puncture the consumer's autopilot—that at the same time reflect and communicate who they are.

For our targets are not waiting to change their minds about the brands they see in front of them; in the majority of purchase decisions, they already have a range of brands that happily suit their needs. The purchase decision, in fact, is often not really a decision—it is a habit. It is easy to lose sight of this; like the old Steinberg cartoon of a New Yorker's view of the world, as marketeers we naturally distort our target's world to fit our own preoccupations. Since we spend all our time think-ing of our target's consumption and choices in, say, fish sticks, there is a natural tendency to be a little disappointed in listening to them tell us in focus groups that they don't really think about—or even *want* to think about—fish sticks at all. What they think about is how to get their son to soccer practice while their daughter makes ballet, or how they are going to find the money for college, or why their partner is in such a bad mood, or whether the cat needs putting down, or how to get the car cleaned before dinner with the Bukowskis on Thursday night. That is where their time and energy is devoted. In terms of "consumption" and brand decisions, they are on autopilot.

But autopilot obviously favors the status quo, even the brand leader; and for that reason a Challenger cannot live in an autopilot world and cannot flourish under the status quo. To achieve a Challenger's objectives, therefore, symbols have to jerk the consumer out of *what they expect the world to be like*, with the objectives of generating salience and reevaluation.

Puncturing the Dominant Complacency

What our target expects the world to be like is, within any one market, clearly multidimensional, containing a number of interlocking expecta-tions and what we might call "complacencies." I have called them com-placencies because they are more than simply an attitude; they are settled consumer opinions that have become comfortably embedded in their way of thinking about the brand landscape. Some of these complacencies may be based on truth, some are simply opinions. That high-fat products are bad for you, for example, or that whiskey is my dad's drink. That the French are chic but aloof. (Test for this year's graduate intake: Come up with a marketing strategy for a high-fat French whiskey). That beer drinking is for guys, or that cigar smoking is antisocial. That Brand X is old fashioned, or juvenile, or for yuppies.

Although within each market there is an interrelated collection of such complacencies and habits, one will be the most important, because it will be the central departure point for many other accompanying attitudes. Let us call this the dominant consumer complacency. For a brand that is late to relaunch, for instance, the dominant complacency may be the weak opinion the consumer has of their product (for example, Harley-Davidson or Jack in the Box). It may be the consumer's view of the category that is the dominant complacency that has to be overcome (perhaps cigars, or high-fat categories, or certain luxury categories like fur). Conversely, for a brand launching into markets that are established but successful, the dominant complacency may be how the consumer views the existing establishment player in the market (a nation's view of its own national carrier in the airline market for instance). A Challenger cannot hope to pick all these locks at the same time; instead, it has to identify the dominant consumer complacency that it has to turn. These are the principal barriers to a Challenger achieving momentum, and they must be broken. And at the same time, the Challenger must use the breaking of them to assert who it is: it must build the Lighthouse Identity (our second credo).

As one might expect, a frequent strategic route for a Challenger involves surprise—attacking the dominant complacency head-on. Challengers put things together you wouldn't expect to find together—car hoods and champagne glasses, skyscrapers and watches, power stations and bras, eggs and brains, cows and computers—where the juxtaposition in each case demands you reevaluate your position on one of the pair.

The Dominant Consumer Complacency: How the Consumer Sees You

Several companies, realizing that the dominant complacency is in fact themselves, have resorted to televised dynamite to signify a dramatic break with the consumer's existing perceptions of the brand. In the mid-1980s the British holiday company Butlins blew up one of its own old, prewar camps on screen to begin to woo back a new generation of holiday makers that cheaper package holidays had successfully lured to the sun, sand, and Sangria of Spain. Hill Holliday Cosmopoulos Connors created a commercial for Wang toward the end of the computer company's life that showed the Wang skyscraper descending in slow motion detonation as a voice-over talked of the changes the company was going through to rebuild itself.

Jack in the Box, however, is so far the only company in the world to have successfully blown itself up twice. Faced with a decline in sales and consumer confidence after a tragic incident two years earlier in the U.S. Northwest, shortly after Christmas 1995, it dramatically broke with its own past on-screen—and blew it up its own boardroom on the implied grounds of mismanagement. The commanding figure who pressed the button was ostensibly the new CEO of Jack in the Box, promising change and reform in a pin-stripe suit and a no-nonsense manner, and apparently entirely oblivious of the fact that he had a large plastic clown's head rising above his collar and tie. The new clown was in fact a reincarnation of an old equity the company had used as its original icon—a clown from a child's Jack-in-the-Box toy, which they themselves had blown up on screen some 15 years before to signal a move away from children's food to a more adult-orientated menu.

The advertisement unintentionally triggered controversy, as dynamite sometimes will. The campaign broke first in Phoenix: A local journalist, lean on news after a quiet Christmas, began to accuse the commercial of bad taste, following on from the recent New York subway bombing, and the story quickly went national, even though the campaign had yet to run outside Arizona. *Advertising Age* was quoted on television as saying that it was bad taste and bad business for Jack in the Box.

Consumers didn't think so. Pretesting had given the company confidence that consumers welcomed the radical nature of the promise, and behind the humor of a clown in a suit, they understood that a more serious message of change was being laid down by the company. In response to the press furor, company executives spent two days in the field talking to some 200 consumers, as diverse as bikers and Mormons, to see whether the press was in fact right and that the pretesting had somehow

Jack in the Box: Boardroom

A man in a Brooks Brothers suit walks into frame. We track him down the paneled corridor. He is distinguished by the immaculate cut of his suit and his huge plastic clown head.

Jack: Hello, I'm Jack, founder of Jack in the Box.

Perhaps you remember me—

Cut to historical footage of Jack in the Box clown blowing up.

Jack: Ever since that setback, I vowed to one day regain my rightful place as head of Jack in the Box. I'm happy to say, through the miracle of plastic surgery, that I'm back in charge—and ready to make Jack in the Box better than ever . . .

Jack stops in front of imposing double doors. A brass plaque reads "Jack in the Box Boardroom." Jack takes a detonating device from his pocket, and pushes the red button. An explosion from within the boardroom rattles the corridor and smoke billows out. Jack pokes his smiling head into frame.

Fade to logo: Jack's Back

failed to elicit an underlying consumer unease with the idea. They found nothing. Two days later they ran the campaign in the rest of their trading area—the Western United States and Texas.

I have referred to the business results the new campaign generated elsewhere, but as an interesting aside, the awareness levels were so high after three months that the research company tracking image shifts caused by the advertising was unable to find enough respondents to form a control sample among those who had *not* seen the new advertising: Of the 400 people they interviewed, *only four* claimed to be unaware of it.

(Of course, it does not require dynamite to blow up a brand. You could just launch New Coke instead. The most famous marketing blunder in the world turned into the one marketing decision that did most to turn around the fortunes of Coke: It inadvertently forced a dramatic reappraisal of the consumer's relationship with the brand. Share increased significantly over the following years.)

The only time British Telecom's image attributes have jumped was when it took the single greatest symbol of its own inefficiency—public phone boxes that notoriously seemed almost universally broken, or to stink of urine—and having promised in advertising to fix them within a year, actually did so.

In some ways this kind of communication also acts as a forcible communication of the first credo to the consumer and themselves—Breaking with One's Immediate Past. To succeed, these had to be more than simply an innovation or the launch of a new product. What made them a symbol of reevaluation was the wrapping, the context, rather than the novelty in itself. What made the Dodge Viper, for instance, a powerful symbol of reevaluation for the Dodge brand was not so much its just being a sports car so much as the *kind* of sports car it was, the extremes it represented: the virulent red color, the fat flare of the hood around the engine, the note of the engine. In short, everything about its wild impracticality was the antithesis of the quiet, sensible brand Dodge had come to be known as. And unlike advertising, the indisputable existence of one-and-a-quarter tons of red steel brooks no argument. (Laurel Cutler estimated that the fact of the Viper was worth $300 million in advertising alone for Dodge; it cost them $70 million to build.)

The Prowler took it a stage further for Plymouth. When the car was first shown at the 1993 North American International Auto Show, one magazine described it as having "grabbed the automotive press by the neck." A few months later *Autoweek* wrote: "Kudos to Chrysler for building it. It's already paying off: a neighbor asked what kind of car and when we said Plymouth, she was incredulous. '*Plymouth?* Wow, they've come a long way.' Bob, you may have just sold a Breeze."[1]

It doesn't have to be about a launch. The shock the networks and industry observers felt when Fox bought the rights to the NFL showed that the value to Fox was not just the ratings, but a wake-up call to the industry, analysts, and consumers that they were moving into the mainstream. The single appointment of the dreadlocked British fashion designer Galliano to creative directorship of the traditional French fashion house Givenchy, and later Dior—two of the great French couture houses being given over to a *Briton*—communicated instantly to the fashion world that those companies were about to radically readdress their sagging reputations.

The Dominant Consumer Complacency: How the Consumer Sees the Category

Cigars were given permission to become chic again because the "wrong" people were seen smoking them in the media—that is, people who were a dramatic departure from the long-standing stereotype of cigar smokers. First, urban black rappers started lighting up in MTV videos, then a *Cigar Aficionado* cover showed Demi Moore smoking a cigar. The film star celebrated for her body—portrayed even as sexy when heavily pregnant in the pages of *Vanity Fair* a few years earlier—was apparently smoking with pleasure the pungent phallic symbol previously thought the province of generously covered, self-congratulatory businessmen. More than celebrity endorsement, this was subversion; and the style was picked up on the street. The most celebrated brand that emerged from the cigar boom was not a brand of cigar, but the magazine about the love of cigars whose iconography accelerated this consumer reevaluation in the first place—*Cigar Aficionado*.

Lexus at launch had to change the consumer benchmark of luxury cars from the emotional appeal of prestige to ride quality. So they dressed the rational promise of performance in the visual symbolism of luxury:

Cigar Aficionado: Demi Moore Cover

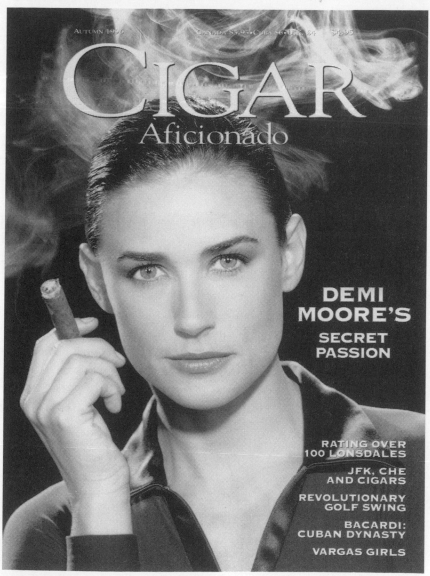

Supplied by Cigar Aficionado.

Instead of side-by-side demos, or the comparative graphs beloved of toothpaste and detergent manufacturers, they balanced a tower of champagne glasses on the hood as the LS 400's rpm counter leapt toward the red—and in doing so changed the gold standard of the category. A luxury car market that had been about engineering heritage and admiring

the gleaming chrome of a legendary badge became instead one with superior ride and performance at the center—at a price below $45,000.
Cadillac's entire marketing and product strategy was overturned—the
horsepower and performance edge of the STS and the development of
the Northstar engine were precipitated in large part by Lexus's redefini-
tion of the market in 1989. Eight years later they were comparing themselves to Mercedes in U.S. television advertising on the basis of engine
power alone. The image of Lexus's champagne glasses became so famous,
in fact, that it was used as a central reference point for the launch positioning of the Nissan Altima; in wanting to establish "luxury" value credentials, the new brand stole a now universally understood reference
point and set it not against the high $30,000s of a Lexus, but against the
price of a $13,000 sedan.

The most widely recalled antidrug campaign in the United States
was that which used the single image of eggs sizzling in a pan—a startling
representation of what drugs did to your brain, more powerful than any
amount of reason, logic, or "just say no's."

Differentiation, marked differentiation, for a Challenger is essential,
and surprising category expectations through reevaluative symbols also
allow opportunity for the challenger to rapidly establish a clearly differentiated positioning for itself. We noted in the last chapter Gateway
2000's careful collision of cows and computers to position itself as the
"uncomputer computer company"—a scion, in a sense, of the reasoning
behind Apple's bitten logo before it. While symbolic *vocabulary* (e.g.,
Chrysler's "cabforward") can be a part of this reevaluative armory, it is
rarely as strong as the single visual.

The Dominant Consumer Complacency: An Established Brand Leader

Some Challengers have to juxtapose themselves with the competition
to subvert the consumers' understanding of the existing order. Volkswagen in the 1960s, of course, innocently pitched itself as the lone
voice of reason in U.S. automobile ownership, and with a highly idiosyncratic product in the context of the U.S. car industry, its symbol became itself.

The Beetle should by rights never have been introduced to the
United States; it would have failed every research group and test market,

running as it did against everything the U.S. car market believed in: fins, ostentation, swimming pools for gas tanks, back seats the size of Kentucky. And instead of hiding this, the company played to it and sold hundreds of thousands of cars. But Volkswagen's shape in the United States was really the shrewd positioning of an accident of birth, to embody a car company hungrily zagging while the rest of the U.S. automotive industry flatulently zigged.

The most celebrated instance in advertising of a Challenger juxtaposing itself directly with Big Brother is Apple's 1984 commercial, which ran once during the Superbowl, but which sent an unforgettable shot across the bows of IBM and the buying public. Confident enough never to even show the product, it was followed by far more informative series of print and television advertisement explaining the advantages of the MacIntosh over the competition.

What we are discussing here, then, is not the clever use of accidents, but something more deliberately and strategically introduced—symbols that have been deliberately created as part of the long-term marketing or remarketing of an entire company. Like Sonic, for instance.

Sega imposed its feet on the video-game category with the introduction of Sonic the hedgehog as a harder, faster icon pitted against Nintendo's amiable but childish plumber. The charactization of Mario had in fact been forced on Nintendo's software developers because of the limitations of technology at the time: He had been created as a cuddly plumber because the pixel definition was so poor he needed to have a moustache under his nose to help distinguish his mouth, and plumber's overalls to help define the movement of his arms. But Sega had no such restrictions; when they created Sonic (and his later alter ego, Knuckles), they had a technological blank slate and used it to make the sharp lines and sharper image of their icon symbolize a new attitude toward video gaming. Sonic was more than simply a game: He and his subsequent incarnations embodied Sega's identity and attitude towards both gaming (no monkeys and bananas here—Sega's Mortal Kombat spurted blood from severed heads) and marketing. Sonic helped Sega change the price of entry in video games from fun to cool.

So, too, the Energizer Bunny subverted the drumming toy device associated with the Establishment brand Duracell. Taking the established icon for battery endurance, but adding sunglasses, flip flops, and attitude of their own, Energizer introduced a new dimension to the category—fun, entertainment, wit. Initally unresponsive, Duracell became increasingly alarmed at the image and sales success Energizer were beginning consequently to enjoy and took their eyes off the ball, to the point of abandoning at one key stage not simply the advertising device of the side-by-side toy demo, but the long-lasting claim that had built their brand and that was in fact the only relevant category benefit in batteries for any brand.

When Branson launched Virgin Atlantic, he opted from the beginning for irreverence and entertainment, poking a symbolic finger in the eye of the airline establishment. While the rest of the business boasted solemn liveries replete with national crests and symbolic animals, Branson created icons of a new, fresh airline on the block in every way that he could. Instead of a crest, he painted an optical illusion on his tailplane—a painter who had not yet finished the job, apparently being caught in the slipstream as the plane took off. He called the first plane not after a chateau in France or a city in Illinois, but a pun on the name of the airline: Scarlet Lady. Everything about the plane symbolically cued the antithesis of the then-matronly British Airways.

The Moon Rocket and Acceleration

What we are talking about now, then, is the use of symbols that surprise in order to propel the Challenger more rapidly in its chosen direction: symbols and icons that prompt consumer reevaluation of their habitual attitudes toward the central issue, not with logic, but emotion. And if these symbols can be infused with a sense of drama, they are used specifically for *acceleration:* to help the brand achieve critical consumer mass faster. It is famously said that a moon rocket uses half of its entire fuel simply to go the first mile—to obtain the critical momentum to leave the earth and reach its desired speed; after that, fuel is used mainly to change direction and to overcome particularly difficult transitions in its journey (re-entry, lunar landing, and so on). Although brands don't have convenient interludes of zero gravity to help them on their way, the analogy is sometimes used that the same is true of getting a brand off the ground—

the real effort and difficulty lies in achieving that initial critical momentum: Half of one's disposable fuel should be set against that task alone, breaking free of the gravitational pull of consumer indifference.

In the case of Challengers, one's proportional media, promotional, and trade budgets are comparatively low. How one divides one's budget is therefore not so much the question, for the fuel one has at one's disposal lies not so much in dollars as in ideas, ingenuity, and passion. It is this context in which the deployment of dramatically executed symbols of reevaluation must be viewed; if they can create rapid momentum for the brand in the eyes of the consumer at the outset of a new marketing campaign given in weeks rather than years, then they must be regarded not as idiosyncratic whims of fancy, but perhaps some of the shrewdest marketing decisions ever made. Look at Swatch's launch in Germany, for example. Constructing a gigantic, fully working, orange Swatch 500 feet high, they suspended it outside the tallest skyscraper in Frankfurt, which happened to be the headquarters of the Commerzbank, one of Germany's leading financial institutions. On the watch were written just three things:

Swatch. Swiss. DM 60.

What at first sight appeared to be just a spectacular publicity stunt in fact was a brilliant piece of repositioning in one simple act. It announced Swatch, it broke the myth that all Swiss watches were luxury products that took themselves overseriously (while still claiming the quality of a Swiss provenance for itself), and it communicated a price that had never been associated with Swiss quality before. And, as Nicholas Hayek, the head of SMH, noted, it signaled immediately the essence of the Swatch brand promise: "It was a big provocation to hang a watch from a huge, grim skyscraper. And it was funny, fanciful, a joke—joy of life. Believe me, when we took it down, everyone we had wanted to reach had received our message."[2] Had they simply pulled off a public relations coup in which they stopped the Frankfurt equivalent of Big Ben, they would have achieved notoriety but not momentum.

Wonderbra had a different reason to create a symbol out of public display. We saw in Chapter 6 that while underwear advertising in the

Swatch on Commerzbank

With permission of Swatch.

United Kingdom had historically been a discreet, private business between advertiser and prospective buyer, Wonderbra's whole positioning meant that the medium in a very real sense had to be part of the message. Not content with outdoor posters, they went one further. In a guerilla expedition Wonderbra beamed a picture of their "Hello Boys" advertisement 150 feet high onto Battersea Power Station from a boat on the Thames, interrupted only by the arrival of a police launch. The riverside traffic jams on the night were followed by newspaper coverage the next day—the cheek of the unprecedented scale of the image dramatically accented the sense of confidence and power that Wonderbra was promising the consumer, and that it was in an altogether different business than lingerie.

In a car launch the surprise is not what's under the cloth. It's giving the buying public something they genuinely don't expect. We have already seen that the newly launched Nissan Altima cheekily suborned the symbolic tests Lexus had become famous for, but at a $13,000 price tag. In doing so it leapfrogged the side-by-side comparisons with other mid-size sedans it competed with and became what *The Wall Street Journal* called "arguably the most successful car launch in U.S. history." Lexus has now given up such public tests on television, presumably concerned not that another luxury manufacturer might be able to mimic them, but that it is simply creating symbols that help the sales of a rival's mid-level sedan.

The creation of *a sense of drama* that we see in the use of such symbols also characterizes Challengers inside their own organization. Steve Jobs at Apple was the master of creating a sense of drama; his adrenaline injection into the artery of Apple in 1983 and 1984 was the loud and public war cry that MacIntosh had only 100 days to make it. Microsofties talked, and still talk, of jihads—*holy wars*—against their competitors: that it *matters*, that it's more than just a job. And if you feel what you have to say really matters, then somehow everything in the world is a potential stage for the brand: walls in Los Angeles for sneakers, power stations in London for bras, skyscrapers in Frankfurt for watches. These are the stages that turn the tired consumer's opinions on their head. They may not be waiting for ads, but they are waiting for news and are always prepared to have their breath taken away by a big idea. By the spectacular.

Although not brands as such, radical changes in attitudes to public issues can serve to reinforce this point. The single, photographed act of Princess Diana shaking hands with an AIDS patient at the Middlesex hospital in London did more to change the British public's perception on AIDS, how it was transmitted, and their relationship with those who had contracted the disease than years of public information, editorial, and advertising. Here was the golden girl of the British royal family, thought to be the epitome of beauty and fortune, touching a person whose disease many in Britain still thought could be caught off toilet seats: a simple but dramatic tackling of the dominant consumer complacency head on.

(Conversely, the introduction of a website by the Catholic church, although receiving a certain press coverage, would not constitute a symbol of reevaluation. While certainly an attempt to make their lines of communication more open and contemporary, it fails to tackle the dominant consumer complacency at the heart of the changing relationship with the church and lacks drama.)

Historical Challengers have, of course, made great play of symbolism to capture the imagination and shape the views of the public—the latter, of course, being closely linked to propaganda once a Challenger gains power. The Russians have always understood the importance of the manufacture of icons, and this reached its height (in quantity, if not quality) in postrevolutionary Russian art. Or think of Gandhi. Simple white robe, shaven head: He understood the power of appearance and clothing long before the spin doctors started on Mrs Thatcher. And on an entirely different level, the hanging of John Brown at Harper's Ferry in 1859 was called by Herman Melville "the meteor of the [U.S. civil] war." This was not wisdom after the event; Longfellow had written in his diary the morning of the execution: "This day will be a great day in our history, the date of a new revolution—quite as much needed as the old one." What aroused the instant sense of it being a turning point was the symbol it represented: a white man dying for the cause of slavery.

But perhaps the most famous—and simple—historical use of an image as a symbol of reevaluation is the Pulitzer Prize–winning photograph of six U.S. marines raising the U.S. flag over Iwo Jima in February 1944. Probably one of the best-known images of the United States this century, it has come to represent a pivotal moment not simply in World War II—the U.S. defeat of the Japanese during a 36-day assault that would give the victors a base from which to neutralize the enemy's air and naval capabilities—but also in the twentieth century. The image seems, in retrospect, to symbolize America as victor in a more general sense: ascending from being merely one of the major players on the world stage, a young Challenger against the aging European powers, to becoming the unrivaled leader of the Free World. The image of struggle and courage and achievement by the ordinary American (none of the men pictured was above the rank of sergeant) was later re-created in bronze as a monument to the dead in Arlington National Cemetery. At that unveiling, President Nixon summed up its power thus:

This statue symbolizes the hopes and dreams of America, and the real purpose of our foreign policy. We realized that to retain freedom for ourselves, we must be concerned when people in other parts of the world may lose theirs. There is no greater challenge to statesmanship than to find a way that such sacrifices as this statue represents are not necessary in the future, and to build the kind of world in which people can be free, in which nations can be independent, and in which people can live together in peace and friendship.

Perhaps the most significant thing about this photograph, however, for all its power, was that it was not actually taken at the time when the hill was originally taken, and the flag originally raised. At that time a smaller flag was raised on an existing steel pole by a lieutenant and three entirely different men, and another photograph taken by a different photographer.

The first turned out to be not a bad photograph, imbuing the actual moment with a certain grim sense of accomplishment. But it has been largely forgotten by history because it possesses nothing like the power of the second image, taken three hours later, by a entirely different photographer, when a second group of men were sent by the Marine commanding officer to raise a *second, larger flag, on a pole they were to raise and plant themselves*, and have another photograph taken.

The point is this: the act is one thing—raising the flag encouraged the Marines as much as it demoralized the defenders—but the way the act is presented takes it to a whole other level. With symbols of reevaluation, the image is the message as much as the act itself. And the Marine commander, even in the middle of a 36-day all-out assault on the Japanese positions, realized that he needed not just *a* flag flying over Iwo Jima, but a **big flag** flying over Iwo Jima. And with the help of Joe Rosenthal, who won the Pulitzer Prize for the new photograph, he created an image of victory that will inspire and define the Marines Corps—and indeed the ascendance of the United States—as long as it exists.

The Different Audiences

Symbols of reevaluation have many consumers. The need to signal dramatic change to the consumer is one reason for the break. As vital is the need to change the thinking within the organization—we noted earlier that many Challenger CEOs claim to regard their employees as their most important audience. This is self-interest, not corporate pseudo-philanthropy: they believe if they can fill their own staff with a sense of what the brand needs to be, and with an utter belief in its superiority and imminent success, everything else will follow.

There are of course, different ways to signal dramatically to your troops that things have to be a little different around here. The British Navy put the recalcitrant Admiral Byng in front of a firing squad in the eighteenth century in order to "encourage the others." Public firing squads and layoffs are one emotionally difficult way of signaling the need for a new direction (one imagines that stories of IBM's layoff of around 100,000 people accompanying Lou Gerstner's arrival, for instance, was among other things a fairly powerful indication of forthcoming organizational and strategic change). Organizational change consultants refer to this kind of motivation as a "burning platform"—the metaphor taken from safety drills on oil rigs at sea, where the only way workers can be persuaded to jump into the sea below is if they genuinely feel the platform is on fire.

But the most powerful symbols are those of inspiration: flags to rally around and an enemy to march against. And this means that we are looking for a little bit more than the introduction of "casual Friday" here. Something a little bit more dramatic as a statement of intent than donning a weekly pair of Dockers. Saturn's birthplace, for example, was in the antithesis of Detroit in order to escape not simply its parent's past but the past of the entire U.S. automotive industry. The reality of Spring Hill, Tennessee, may not quite be the idealized small-town America portrayed in the advertising, but it is close enough to be a powerful statement to employees. Could one have recruited a team of zealots to build an entirely different kind of car if it had simply been produced on another production line in the Motor City?

A third audience for symbols of reevaluation, alongside consumers and one's own staff, is opinion leaders. Fox is a company that has consistently made big, dramatic gestures to announce and confirm its presence as a serious player in each of its worldwide markets. Its audiences here are not simply the consumer, but the press, the competition, and program makers. The first night the new station aired in the United States, for instance, the famous white "Hollywood" sign in the hills above Los Angeles was changed to read "Fox"—the only time in history it has ever changed. People from the advertising agency stood in line timed to turn on a chain of 350 searchlights that ran from the altered sign all the way down to Century City, where the press was being entertained. Fox decided they would throw all their marketing budget and energy at the opening night's ratings—and then rely on the programs to carry them; their key objective was to get the rocket off the ground.

Harley-Davidson, rocked back into retrenchment and a second-rank position and reputation in the early 1980s by the incursions of the Japanese motorcycle manufacturers, created in 1987 on a single piece of paper a potent symbol of reevaluation for both opinion leaders and its own employees. In 1983, deep into rebuilding machine and image the battered motorcycle legend had successfully lobbied the U.S. government to create tariffs on Japanese motorcycles that would shield it from the realities of their superiority while it had time to put its own finances, production design, and image in order; a sympathetic Washington obligingly set these in place until 1988.

But on March 17, 1987, with a year of this protection still to run, the government received a formal request for the tariffs to be rescinded. The request came from not from the Japanese, but from Harley-Davidson itself; it was ready to take on the competition again in an open market. The enormous self-confidence that withdrawing their shield a year early evidenced to owners, opinion leaders, and Harley-Davidson workers themselves, from a company that only a few years earlier was being written about as a piece of history, helped further fuel its continued momentum. Two years later, it had once again regained dominance of the heavy-weight motorcycle market.

As we have observed, then, a symbol of reevaluation doesn't have to be a piece of advertising or marketing; it can be a single piece of headed paper. It is the meaning that is important.

8

The Fifth Credo:
Sacrifice

In the world of clutter and information saturation that consumers are faced with, the greatest danger facing a brand is not rejection, but indifference. Rejection is easily spotted and easily remedied—you make a big change or you pull out—but indifference is a far more insidious and expensive problem. Selective listening allows marketeers to convince themselves that with a little tightening up here and there everything will be all right, and they pour more and more money over more and more time against less and less return.

We have seen in the last few chapters that the solution to indifference for Challengers lies in both a strong identity and, through this, a strong relationship with its consumer base. Inevitably, this means that success for the Challenger brand comes from considering very carefully what it is going to *sacrifice* in order to create this relationship and identity.

Indeed, the ability to sacrifice and concentrate one's focus, voice, and actions more narrowly is one of the few advantages a Challenger has. Having to fight a war on two fronts weakens one's ability to do either really well—Hitler's invasion of Russia in 1941 cost him the ability to hold France three years later—and brand leaders have to fight many fronts at once. Here frequently lies the opening for a Challenger in taking on a brand leader—but only if it is *used* as an opening: which is to say, only if it is prepared to make sacrifices itself.

If you doubt the practicality or profitability of sacrifice, look at Southwest Airlines—a brand of travel that is manifestly not for everyone. Consider in particular Southwest flight attendant Kolette Miller. How does she treat her customers? "We have a lot of little toys like rubber cockroaches," she says with a laugh. "If you see someone being a little ornery, you think, 'Oh, he deserves a cockroach in his drink.' And in goes the rubber cockroach."[1] Now you might be tempted to think Kolette is a little out there, even by Southwest's standards: the lunatic fringe of an amiably eccentric airline. But no; at the time of the interview, Kolette had just received the President's Award for Excellence as a flight attendant, the high point of a 12-year career at Southwest. She is someone the airline is proud to hold up to the rest of the world as a model customer-service representative.

Of course, allowing this level of free rein to one's flight staff involves considerable sacrifice in one's user base; it is easy to see that a passenger such as Warren Buffett, for instance, might be less that thrilled to find a rubber cockroach in his end-of-day Glenfiddich. But that's the beauty of being a second-rank brand rather than Number 1: You are not bound by the need for mass consensus. You can have color and celebrate it. In fact, you have to, in order to stand out. And although sacrifice is something that in practice we often balk at, feeling it is overly purist, a narrowing of potential users and profits, the Southwest story suggests that on the contrary, sacrifice *is precisely what generates profitability*, by generating a greater loyalty among those you attract. Look at the financial performance of Southwest compared to the rest of the business. Between 1990 and 1993 the U.S. airline industry dropped $4 billion. Southwest, conversely, has been profitable every year of its history and in 1994 made $179 million. There's money in sacrifice, because there's loyalty and growth in sacrifice.

And color—even Southwest's brand of color—does not deny you being taken seriously as a quality product: In 1996 Southwest was rated the nation's top airline for the second year running by Airline Quality Ratings, ahead of American, United, and Delta. Ten-minute turnaround, bring your own meals, and rubber cockroaches, and they are voted the highest-quality airline. We all know the concept of the 80:20 rule; Southwest is simply showing us the value of implementing it properly.

Where Are My Cockroaches?

The sacrifices a Challenger makes do not lie in incidentals to the business, like minor line extensions, a research budget, or the assistant public relations manager. They are instead in *fundamentals*—distribution, messages, audiences: The overriding objective is significant impact of the right kind on your core audience. Achieving critical mass for your voice.

The Challengers we are focusing on have made different kinds of sacrifices to create stronger relationships with their core audiences. The most common of these include sacrifice in targeting, sacrifice in reach, sacrifice in message, sacrifice in line extension, sacrifice in distribution, and sacrifice of quality communication.

Sacrifice in Target: Trading Numbers for Loyalty

We have already seen how the personality of Southwest will be off-putting to some and bind others to it; the same may be said of Fox as a television network. The content of Fox's groundbreaking programming (*The Simpsons, The X-Files, Martin, Millennium*) turns off many potential older, more conservative viewers; in return, however, it rewards Fox not simply with clear differentiation against the more amorphous established players, but with two kinds of loyalty among the most fickle of audience segments—the 18–34s. The first kind of loyalty is viewership: Although fourth in overall ratings, Fox consistently enjoys leadership at key periods of the week in the premium 18–34 and 18–49 audiences. This is lucrative for Fox—this is an audience for whom advertisers will pay a significant premium to reach.

The second kind of loyalty is loyalty *within* the individual program— that is, the quality of viewer attention while the program is actually on air. In the measure of "Percent of adult viewers claiming to have watched at full attention selected nationally aired TV shows," Fox takes *five out of the top seven* U.S. shows; even within the individual program, the network is creating a stronger relationship with its chosen audience. One might intuitively hypothesize, in fact, that there is a relationship between these two types of loyalty, and that one may well be a predictor of the other—when attention/involvement within the individual program wanes, loyalty of repeat purchase will start to wane shortly after. (This may also provide an example of how a Challenger can learn from categories other than its own. Most categories measure only one kind of loyalty. Why should attention or involvement loyalty not be a key measure of any Challenger operating in an experience business? Why should this not be an important measure of, for instance, supermarket shopping? Or fast food?)

Sacrifice in Reach or Frequency: Trading Numbers for Identity

Absolut's consistent appropriation of the back covers of magazines to frame its latest advertising execution is expensive—the position commands a premium over an inside full page—and in doing so sacrifices executional frequency and consumer reach. But the visibility and sense of exclusivity from the surrounding clutter that this position affords the brand has reinforced the air of prestige Absolut has cultivated since birth, and it has been a crucial part of making the brand the popular icon it has become. This benefit has come about because this is a *consistent* sacrifice Absolut has made. Were it to be something the brand manager toyed with in some years and abandoned in others, the brand would not have built the same advantageous association with that magazine position in the consumer's mind. Boddingtons Bitter has successfully pursued a similar strategy in the United Kingdom over the last five years.

In an entirely different category and medium, Saturn uses the apparent luxury of 60 seconds in a television commercial strategically. Since its whole positioning centers on selling the experience afforded by a car company with small-town, no-hassle values, its marketeers need the time to create a calm, unhurried feel about the way they approach making and selling cars—a feel that is in sharp contrast to the frenetic "benefit bouillabaisse" that the other U.S. automotive brands find themselves

Absolut Venice

ABSOLUT VENICE.

impelled to boil up in 30 seconds. Although, like Absolut, it sacrifices reach and frequency of message in order to afford a premium format, that sacrifice has bought a distinctive emotional personality to fit a distinctive product benefit. And the benefits of Saturn's sacrifice are heightened by its competitors' inability to do so.

Sacrifice in Distribution: Trading Availability for Desirability

The sacrifice of distribution helps the brand build and maintain the intensity of relationship with the Challenger consumer. Oakley, for example, places an enormous premium on discoverability and authenticity. This means aligning and confining its distribution as it expands to those sporting outlets that represent not just sales potential, but the opinion leaders in their category. If expanding into a town with three bike shops, for instance, all of whom are willing in principle to stock their range of eyewear, Oakley will grant distribution to just one—the most hard-core bike shop of the three. This in turn creates usership among opinion leaders in the area, and the brand's credibility and desirability is seeded among a broader audience for the medium term. Equally, despite Southwest's success, Herb Kelleher has said that he has no plans to ever fly Southwest coast to coast: The scale of the operation involved would expand his staff and operational base to the point where he risks being unable to maintain the staff esprit de corps that (along with price) is at the heart of his brand's relationship with its customer base. So, while both Oakley and Southwest could in principle gain enormous short-term advantages by taking up potential distribution, they would also risk accelerating the medium-term decline of the brand in doing so; both put a strong relationship with consumer and staff before distribution-led growth. The overexpansion and subsequent wipe-out of Ocean Pacific serves as a warning for all Challengers: Although ubiquity is good for establishment brands like Coca-Cola and AT&T, it is dangerous for Challenger brands looking to create a stronger affinity with a more focused target, be they self-styled coffee connoisseurs, surfing wannabes, or weekend mountain bikers.

Sacrifice in Message: Trading Depth for Definition

The abyss between the quantity of different messages a company would like to communicate and the single-minded simplicity that it takes to stand out to the consumer in communication is the one that most marketeers find it hardest to bridge. There appears from our side to be *so much* that needs communicating on our brand's behalf: market motivators, tickets of entry, and inevitably at least two or three key competitive discriminators that the research recommendations will have highlighted.

We feel somehow that if we could only sit each consumer down for half an hour in a room and tell them *all* the reasons our brand is superior, *then* maybe we could turn them into loyal buyers.

But there is no escape: Strong brands are necessarily simple and single-minded in their communication, even if it means sacrificing what might seem to be important secondary messages.

Look at Absolut again. There are many stories that this brand could choose to tell about itself: the story of a date, for instance (1879), or of a man—Lars Olsson Smith—or of a medieval town; the story of the virtues of Swedish wheat, or the rectification process used to create the precious liquid (far superior to the processes held up for consumer admiration by rival liquor manufacturers, such as charcoal filtering). It might even usefully advance the occasional serving suggestion—how to mix Absolut with any number of new and traditional beverages for fun and profit.

All of these might have value; all might be interesting in some measure to the consumer. But in fact Absolut has chosen to sacrifice all these messages—except once. In one press advertisement, on one day in the *New York Times*, it did indeed tell all these stories at the same time. Announcing the end of the understated campaign that had made the brand famous, it put forward its desire to talk more about the product. Close inspection will reveal wheatfields, a photograph of a refreshing mixer, the home of rectification, and a great deal of body copy, all true and all interesting.

Yet while all these details were genuine, the ad wasn't; the date at the top of the page was April 1. Because central to Absolut's success has been sacrifice of message: It has sacrificed all secondary communication, concentrating instead all its resource and ideas against the gaining of critical mass for *one core communication task*—premium sophistication.

Sacrifice in Line Extensions

The most striking illustration of the importance of sacrifice in line extensions is an example of someone who didn't: Timberland.

This was a Challenger who up to 1994 seemed to do everything right. For years a minority player in the footwear market, they had a very clear sense of their own identity, rooted in an overbuild of their footwear that they themselves proudly acknowledged. They had communicated

Absolut April Fools'

THE MOST POPULAR AD CAMPAIGN OF ALL TIME NEED NOT RUN FOR ALL TIME.

*I*t was good advertising. It had a good, long run. But everyone knows what must come to all good things.

Ironically, the old ads were, in a way, too charming. Too engaging, really too much fun. They were diverting consumers' attention from a far more important story.

Don't get us wrong, it was right for the time. It was fun and we'll miss it. Gee, it's been 17 years and hundreds of ads since ABSOLUT PERFECTION first ran, way back in 1980. But times change and so must the way we relate to our customers. We think people deserve more; more information about their favorite vodka.

We all know what's on the outside of the bottle (the old campaign certainly saw to that), but now we think it's high time we got to the heart of the matter – it's time to talk about what's inside the bottle.

You are now reading the first ad in the new Absolut Vodka campaign. The first in a series of messages from a company that has a lot to say about vodka.

SO LET'S TALK WHEAT

That's right, wheat. More specifically, wheat from the fields in and around the medieval town of Ahus, Sweden, the birthplace of every single drop of Absolut Vodka. This grain is key to the character of the world's favorite vodka.

Pour a touch of Absolut Vodka into a snifter and savor the aroma. You are experiencing a distillation of the finest grain on earth – golden Swedish wheat, rich in flavor from the minerals and nutrients found in the soil of the fields of southern Sweden. And so it has been since 1879 when Lars Olsson Smith produced the first bottle of what the world now knows as Absolut Vodka.

But it's not enough to have the fields and grow the wheat. It's important to know what to do with the grain once it's brought in from the harvest.

Absolut Vodka is produced using centuries-old distilling expertise and tradition in combination with modern distillation technique, and an elaborate modern purification process called rectification. It's what makes Absolut *Absolut.*

The best vodka is clean vodka. When the spirit is charcoal filtered, which many vodkas are, impurities generated by fermentation and distillation are left behind, and those can wind up in your Martini. Charcoal filtering is a highly inefficient method of removing unwanted impurities.

Rectification, the process used by Absolut Vodka, may be expensive and painstaking – it involves a sophisticated and rare continuous distillation process which runs the vodka through several apartment building-sized columns – but it produces a product unusually free of impurities, while still maintaining the essence of the golden grain of southern Sweden.

This is the secret to Absolut.

BE IT EVER SO NORDIC, THERE'S NO PLACE LIKE HOME

If your vodka is distilled under license in 30 industrial locations around the world, chances are the quality is uneven.

The entire world supply of Absolut Vodka is produced at the same distillery in southern Sweden, in the town of Ahus. Every single drop of water

comes from the same underground spring that has contributed to the mystique of Absolut Vodka for centuries, and so it continues to this day.

Moreover, it is vital for the producer of a great spirit to have complete control of the entire distillation process from grain to glass. Absolut Vodka is just such a spirit.

A FAMILY OF FLAVORS

It's not as easy as it seems. We've experimented with hundreds of possibilities. After all, we're not just producing a flavored vodka, we're producing flavored Absolut!

And our customers have been glad for our efforts. Lemony Absolut Citron (actually a blend of four citrus fruit flavors) is today the world's most popular flavored premium vodka. Absolut Kurant, flavored with the delicate essence of natural black currant, is equally tasty. And our third flavor, Absolut Peppar, is perhaps the most rewarding and unexpected variety in our family.

IT'S NICE TALKING TO YOU

We believe a dialogue with our customers is critical to the vitality of our company. And a dialogue is exactly what we wish to begin, with this new, more informative approach to advertising. So say goodbye to our old voice and hello to our new, customer-oriented style of communication.

Let's start the dialogue right now. Pick up the phone and give us a call with any questions, comments or ideas at 1.800.324.2224.

And remember, it doesn't really matter what's in the ads, it's what's in the bottle that counts.

And that's Absolut.

ABSOLUT VODKA
Country of Sweden

CALL WITH ANY QUESTIONS, COMMENTS OR IDEAS: 1.800.324.2224.

authenticity and functionality rather than fashion, and thereby they become fashionable. They had doubled their turnover in three years. But in growing they forgot how they came to be in a position to grow in the first place. Diversifying out of footwear, they had expanded into a range of apparel and accessories such as polo and plaid shirts, where they had no credibility other than the temporary one of fashion, and where the authenticity and identity were diluted to a marketing facade. So when success brought new product competition from Nike and Reebok, the consumer saw them as legitimate as Timberland, and the Challenger stumbled, forced to close U.S. plants and write off inventory.

Timberland found itself again, by refocusing quickly on its core identity, and the products that reflected that. They were not the first: Both Harley-Davidson and Nike had extended beyond their identity during the times when they lost their way—Harley into Cafe Racer–style "Japanese beaters," and Nike out of athletic footwear into casual shoes. For both the mistake served as a costly reminder of who they really were and prompted them to refocus with new success on their core identity. Not all brands are equally elastic, and, like distribution, if a Challenger attempts to reap too much of its consumer equity too soon in line extensions, it accelerates its growth-and-decline to a space of two or three years.

Fox has recognized this in the appointment of an executive marketing director position specifically to develop *long-term marketing strategy* for *The X-Files*. The issue is how to both harvest the brand's potential among the broader public (i.e., with feature films, merchandise, and books) and still maintain the loyalty of the hard-core followers. One of the core tasks in the new post is therefore the management of promotional partners, for instance. They don't want to be seen by the hard core to be overcommercializing and, like Timberland, potentially lose equity among both casual and hard-core users in the space of two or three years.

Sacrifice in Communicating Product Quality

Quality has always been a deceptively difficult area for marketeers. Motherhood stuff at the best of times, there is abundant evidence adduced to show the correlation between Quality and marketing success (see Figure 8.1).

How can one argue with this? Quality sells.

Figure 8.1

Market Rank of Brands	Index of Relative Quality
Dominators	+14
Marginal leaders	+6
Number-two brands	+0.3
Number-three brands	−2.7
Brand followers	−3.1

Source: PIMS Database of Performance of 3,500 Businesses, 1989[2]

But for a Challenger in the 1990s, the question of how one communicates quality is highly problematic. Although we have talked about successful Challengers having a sense of identity rooted in overperformance, which aspects of that overperformance one chooses to talk about—and which to sacrifice—is a more difficult decision. There are a number of fundamental questions in our way.

First, what does quality really mean? It is probably the most lazily used concept in modern marketing. One could be forgiven for thinking it means at once nothing, in that its nature differs so completely from category to category, and yet everything, in that within a category the term can often become a catchall for *every aspect* of performance respected by the consumer. Its meaning requires very clear definition to be strategically valuable.

Second, assuming that one can find a tighter definition of what quality actually means in one's own category, should one attempt to compete on the target's *current* definition of quality—almost certainly reflecting the definition the brand leader has been promoting for a number of years—or redefine it to one's own advantage?

Third, how are we to interpret the body of evidence that suggests consumers increasingly feel all products are beginning to perform more or less the same?

Fourth, how are we to react when consumers tell us they don't believe rational claims about quality—along with claims like "tasty" and "healthier"—in paid-for advertising? (Saturn has never talked directly about quality, or its JD Power successes, because it believes that so many companies talk about them in advertising already that it is more powerful for the consumer to hear about them *from other sources*.)

Finally, if Challengers choose to talk only about who they are, rather than what they are made of or how they perform, how is the consumer to know how to regard the product? While a brand leader can afford to communicate a product quality story as *one part* of its total mix, we have to concentrate our message.

Clearly, there are premium Challengers who have succeeded by changing the price/value equation, offering more for less (Lexus or Virgin Upper Class, for example). But the solution for a Challenger more often lies in the communication not of physical quality but emotional quality. They sacrifice a level of rational product-quality information in mass media, but the appeal of their chosen differentiated positioning creates a *projected or inferred quality* in the consumer's mind—it makes the consumer *want* to believe it. Gordon Brown, the cofounder of Millward Brown, put it elegantly in noting that advertising cannot persuade people to believe something; what it can do is put them in a position *where they persuade themselves*.[3]

People have their own mental shortcuts to quality—whether a brand has been around a long time (Nissan's "Dream Garage" commercial), whether it is made by a family business (Warburton's), whether the people who make the product care about or enjoy their work (Saturn, Southwest), the amount of time it takes to make (any number of premium whiskies)—that are more powerful cues to quality in the consumer's mind than any number of rational reasons to believe.

Thus, the sacrifice of a direct product-quality message is not necessarily to sacrifice product quality perceptions or measurable improvements in *ratings*. Providing one's positioning allows the consumer to project or infer quality for themselves.

We saw earlier that Saturn talked at launch about their philosophy toward building cars and their care about what they do, and yet within four years equaled Ford in quality imagery—a more established brand who had been communicating "Quality is Job One" for years. Absolut in turn lacks Russian credentials, yet through consistently communicating a message of pure sophistication it has come to beat Stolichnaya in tracking-study ratings for quality.

The point here, therefore, is that to talk of sacrificing the explicit communication of product quality is in no way to deny the importance of product, or the value of talking about product for a Challenger. (The debate about "Brand versus Product" is a false one—the product has to be seen to deliver what the brand promises; both are intertwined.) There are indeed some Challengers—Lexus or the Nissan Altima, for instance—whose entire positioning centered around redefining the consumer's expectations of product quality.

The observation instead is that many Challengers achieve quality perceptions *indirectly*; they apparently sacrifice explicit product claims, yet still achieve high-quality ratings, because the target *infers* quality indirectly from the way the brand presents itself (Absolut) or because the relationship they generate with the consumer leads that consumer to *want* to believe the product is a good one. And the additional value in either of these situations of the consumers themselves projecting quality onto the brand is that they will tend to project the characteristics *they* value most, rather than the ones *we think* they value most. For not only does quality carry different meanings in different categories, but it denotes different characteristics to different people within the *same* category— even within the same brand's core loyalists. In automotive, for instance, quality in the consumer's eyes can mean a wide variety of product dimensions, from build to drive to reliability to internal comfort, with each individual consumer placing a slightly different premium on each particular dimension. Communicating a value that *infers*—or rather, allows them to infer quality—allows the consumers to interpret it along the dimension they regard as most important to themselves.

And finally, as noted in Chapter 2, the Challenger product has to perform, or even overperform, on the key product dimension of its choice. The consumer has been burnt before; now they want evidence in usage. If Missouri is the "Show Me" state, then in marketing terms customer skepticism is now such that we may be about to enter the Missouri Millennium.

The Strategic Purpose of Sacrifice

Hmm, sacrifice. Isn't this just focus by any other name?

The difference between sacrifice and focus is that the latter allows secondary and tertiary targets. It isn't really focus at all, it is just prioritization by any other name.

Sacrifice's value, therefore is not simply one of concentration of marketing forces externally; it also has the internal value like that of hard pruning a plant. *All* the energy, all the dynamism in the company is devoted to the primary goal. This is true even for brand leaders—Coca-Cola's fortune's took off again when they divested themselves of movie interests and bottling plants to focus on selling soft drinks. Years later, Pepsi followed suit in the strategy behind spinning off their restaurant businesses. And it goes without saying that it is crucial for Challengers to focus their more limited energy and resource in a narrower and more focused jet than does the Establishment brand.

So we can say from what we have seen in the examples above that sacrifice serves three main strategic functions for a Challenger:

1. Sacrifice concentrates the internal and external expressions of identity by eliminating activities that might dilute it.
2. Sacrifice allows the creation of strong points of difference (i.e., cockroaches) by changing the organization's mind-set from pursuing weak universal appeal to a more intense, narrower appeal.
3. Sacrifice generates critical mass for the communication of that identity and those differences by stripping away other secondary marketing activity. This is central to maximizing the Challenger's consumer presence, given its more limited marketing resources.

While the brand leader perceives its currency to be mass appeal, and can afford the dilution of preference that creates because it is compensated for by the convenience of their ubiquity and distribution, Challengers need more extreme actions and gestures—they need to create a greater proportion of "committed" and "enthusiastic" users through real differentiation. Challenger currency is therefore not means but extremes: top box preference scores or nothing. And this in turn means we need to create differences for ourselves that may well be sometimes polarizing (not every consumer likes Saturn's no-haggle pricing, or Wonderbra's brazenness, or Southwest's sense of humor, or Fox's iconoclasm, or the showiness of Las Vegas) but that also strongly attract as many as they deter; better a room divided than a room that doesn't care. And once we have delineated our identity through those points of difference, strip away every marketing activity that does not directly support that identity.

For any brand, positioning is sacrifice; for a Challenger, it is the path to growth. What it chooses *not* to do defines who and what it really is.

There is a story about, I think, Picasso. A visitor to his studio saw a huge block of stone sitting in the middle of the studio, and asked the master what it was to be. A lion, came the reply. And how, Picasso, pressed the visitor, will you make a lion out of this unhewn stone block?

It's easy, said Picasso. I simply get a chisel and chip away anything that doesn't look like a lion.

9

The Sixth Credo:
Overcommit

"It is impossible to be too strong at the decisive point."
Napoleon

I n 1996 the Nissan account team was briefed to review the U.S. automotive market. The Saturn no-haggle fixed-price policy had created a
huge amount of awareness and noise, and considerable popular
support—to the extent that General Motors had rolled out the same
program as part of the sales promise for others of their brands. As part of
the account team's fresh immersion in the market, then, mystery shops
were conducted among several dealerships for each of the various General Motors brands that offered, if not the whole Saturn customer treatment philosophy, then at least the "no dicker sticker."

In the mystery shops, Saturn was everything it promised, and everything the consumers in focus groups had extolled it as being: low pressure, extremely courteous, attentive when required, and invisible when
not. Not a shiny suit or a cheap joke to be had.

Oldsmobile, another division of General Motors, offered the same
no-haggle pricing deal, but the shopping experience proved a little different. The young woman who was to be the mystery shopper walked
into an Oldsmobile dealership in Los Angeles and found only one salesman available. The salesman was at his desk, deep in what appeared to
be an amusing private conversation on the telephone. So the shopper

waited patiently near his desk and tried to make it clear with hand gesticulations that she was looking for some information. When the salesman did not respond, but the phone conversation instead became more protracted and more hilarious, the mystery shopper left the desk and wandered around the showroom models on display.

It made no difference. After a further 10 minutes, with the salesman still on the same call, the mystery shopper abandoned her wait and turned instead to the information desk—a simple affair, with a large poster pinned behind the assistant flagging the fixed prices and the model range. She explained to the assistant behind the desk that she was looking for some information on Oldsmobile's pricing, and the salesman appeared to be a little tied up.

"Oh," said the woman behind the information desk, with a nod at the salesman, "I'm afraid he's not going to be very keen to help you. He doesn't agree with this whole new fixed pricing thing." She pointed to the poster on the wall behind her. "Here," she continued. "We don't have any leaflets with the prices on, but I can photocopy this poster for you, if you like."

And this turned out to be the end of the transaction. While the *offer* was the same in these two cases, the *experience* proved very different; in one instance of the offer—Saturn's—the prospective buyer came away with a sense of respect for the company, an understanding of the pricing offer, and an interest in doing business. In the other—Oldsmobile's—case she came away with a black-and-white photocopy of a poster that had been pinned up behind the information assistant's head; one served to differentiate and attract, the other actually to alienate a prospective purchaser. Now this was an offer that Saturn had already demonstrated was of proven consumer appeal and furthermore, that in both cases was instituted and backed by the same parent company. Yet the resistance to its implementation within one of the two organizations undermined an offer of apparently proven consumer appeal to the point of making it (certainly to this mystery shopper) *counterproductive*—to the point where, perversely, Oldsmobile would have been in a stronger position to attract the customer's business if they had never made the offer at all.

The key failure, then, for any company attempting to effect a gear change in its own performance is not the ability to define its intention, but the inability to translate intention into behavior. The importance of the gap between intention and delivery is highlighted by a 1990 study that suggested that only 14% of all churn in customer-service businesses comes through dissatisfaction with poor treatment or rudeness on the part of a company's employees.[1] Five times that number—68%—switch their loyalty to a different brand because of *indifference* on the part of the service company's employees. Now this indifference did not come because no one at the top of those individual companies was interested in growth, or because they failed to understand the importance of customer service. Even money says 85% of those "indifferent" companies had as part of their mission statement something about a desire to "surprise and delight our customers with the quality of our service." This indifference came because they failed to translate strategic intent into behavior.

Now a brand in Saturn's position has to make its core point of difference succeed; it has no choice. As a Challenger, it had to make a mark, from scratch, on a U.S. car market that already offered its consumer over 250 models to choose from. So it *had* (unlike Oldsmobile) to make those points of difference it intended and promised into genuinely different behavior; selling as it was an acceptable but unremarkable car without any experience of user base behind it, the only way it was going to succeed was by changing the purchase and ownership experience.

What Saturn did was overcommit. They anticipated all the reasons why intent might not translate into behavior and restructured their business to remove them as barriers. So, for instance, as a car dealer (let's say for Pontiac) one of my greatest incentives to discount (and thus break with a no-haggle pricing policy) is not the competitive brand dealer across the block but the other Pontiac dealer down the street; if I refuse to deal, they only have to concede a little more to the customer, and I lose my business. Saturn, therefore, only allowed businesspeople to purchase Saturn dealerships *in groups* by geographical area—the point being that under this new arrangement any one location needs no longer worry about losing sales to a rival same-brand dealer down the street if they fail to discount, because they are now part of that very dealership as well. In the same way, in order to be able to deliver the low-pressure sell at point of purchase, Saturn restructured the salespeople's remuneration so that the traditional system of commission-heavy reward was replaced by a healthy salary with commission on top. Oldsmobile on the other hand did not restructure—and exactly the same brand offer backfired in their consumer's face.

The difference between Oldsmobile's implementation and Saturn's implementation is what we shall call overcommitment. The people at Saturn understood that strategy is less than 50% of the solution: that an organization, left to its own devices, finds ways of diluting even the most compelling strategic intent—through laziness, active resistance, or misunderstanding (budgets, self-interest, and fear being what they are)—and that this dilution weakens what appeared upstream to be the building in of significant differences to the point where for most practical purposes, for instance, consumers cannot really notice the difference between flying one major U.S. airline and another. So because driving differentiation for a Challenger is crucial, what is necessary in implementing strategic intent to ensure that the point of difference will be consistently engaged is not commitment but *overcommitment*: doing more within the organization than should be strictly necessary to make sure the difference is maintained. Challengers will not succeed through a philosophy of "just enough"; they will succeed by the *certainty* of consistent differentiation, and this will require overcommitment from senior management and the organization to implement and maintain.

Put another way, the difference between Oldsmobile and Saturn in the example we have seen above was this: Saturn aimed two feet below the brick.

Aiming Two Feet below the Brick

Let us suppose you have always wanted to put your hand through a brick.

You have seen it done; it fascinates you as an achievement of flesh and will. So you go to seek the instruction of a karate black belt.

What he teaches you is this: If you want to put your hand through a brick, you cannot succeed by aiming at the surface of the brick. To break through, you have to aim two feet the other side. Two feet *below* it; that is the way to ensure you will go through a surface the body will naturally flinch from. In the same way a Challenger brand—and the people behind the Challenger brand—does not succeed through commitment; it succeeds through *overcommitment*. It does not do "just enough" for success at the crucial point; instead, it overcommits to ensure success, and to overcome each identifiable pocket of inertia and resistance it will *inevitably* meet (internally and externally) in attempting to translate Challenger intention and strategy into behavior and results.

Let us start by looking at someone who failed to overcommit, an example of a Challenger who aimed for the surface of the brick. The British Labour Party learned the lesson the hard way in 1992. With electoral day on Thursday, April 9, a battery of opinion polls in every national newspaper predicted a comfortable victory for their party, then in opposition, by the beginning of the election week. The party, over 10 years out of power, stopped campaigning on Tuesday the 7th—two days before the elections itself—and went home to chill the champagne, convinced there was nothing else to be done.

But what they had failed to realize was that the decision-making process of the electorate was a far more fragile one than the opinion polls might give them reason to believe: A large body of voters in an election frequently fail to make their minds up until the very last minute. The electorate's pens in this election literally hovered in the voting booths over the names on the ballot paper, as they were at last forced into really making their decision. And many in the end simply couldn't bring themselves to vote for the party they had been telling pollsters they would elect for weeks. Although many of the British people wanted to believe in the social promise of Labour, they couldn't quite trust that they would be as economically well off as they would under the rule of the Establishment brand, the Conservatives. The momentum Labour had built up through an enormous drive over the previous years had been lost by stopping when the battle *seemed* won, two days before the ballot papers were actually cast. And the consequence was to let the establishment brand, the rival, back in power again for another five years.

The Labour party learned their lesson. For the next five years they overcommitted in everything: They never assumed it was over. Now when they won an issue, they reaffirmed it, kept coming back to it. On key pledges they overcommitted in the sense that they went further than they had to—instead of just making a promise, they invited each person to whom they made that promise to check that they had kept it, and call them on it if they had broken with it. Indeed, they printed wallet-sized cards for party members to carry around with them the promises the party had made to the people and to them on their behalf.

And when it came to the 1997 election itself, even though the polls predicted an even more comfortable victory for the party than they had in 1992, New Labour (as they renamed themselves) campaigned fiercely right up to the end. The result was not just victory, but the most crushing defeat inflicted on any party in power in the United Kingdom this century.

Leaving politics aside, what does overcommitment mean in business practice or behavior? Take the example of Swatch we looked at earlier—the hanging of a 500-foot orange watch on the Commerzbank in Frankfurt. For Swatch, it was one thing to come up with the idea and quite another to make it happen. How lucky, we might be tempted to think, that the president of the Commerzbank allowed them to carry out such a bold concept. Consider instead, we mentally add, the inertia and resistance that would probably have lain within our own company when an idea like that was first suggested. And consider, if we are honest, our own personal reaction had someone within our organization suggested something similar for our brand in our next key market. Would it have been to begin enthusiastically working out how it would need to be done? Or would it have been to admire it as an entertaining idea but mentally write it off as something that would never reach fulfillment within our culture?

It is to overcome such hidden mental inertia, as much as overt resistance, that we need as a Challenger to aim two feet below the brick. In the case of Swatch, overcommitment meant that luck turned out to have very little to do with the success of the outcome. Germany was potentially the largest European market for the new Swiss watch industry; they had to make it succeed. Prior to meeting the bank, then, they anticipated the barriers that the key decision maker—the President of the Commerzbank—would put up, and answered them *before* even the initial approach was made. They approached the local civic authorities and sought and received written permission, so that when, later, they actually met the President of the Commerzbank, and his first reaction proved to be something along the lines of "You're crazy; in the first place, the authorities would never let us do it," their reply was to show him such a permit had in fact already been issued. When later the President expressed worry about the effect it would have on customer's opinions of the bank, Swatch showed him a survey of those very customers suggesting that they liked the bank showing it had a human face through a gesture such as this. By overcommitting, by anticipating the barriers to success and overcoming them before they were raised, Swatch succeeded at the crucial point.

Like New Labour, challengers such as Swatch are also in a sense fighting an election battle; they are campaigning for change, and a change of vote. And in that campaign the balance between success and failure in any endeavor is much narrower than one might imagine, because the consumer's decision-making process is much more precarious than one might imagine. How a particular salesperson speaks to a customer, or how well one convinces a key trade buyer of the quality of distribution needed, or the extent of the news coverage gained at launch—any of these may make the difference between preserval or reversal of the status quo.

The first task in overcommitment, then, is to identify the decisive points on which the Challenger must succeed. Clausewitz commented: "The general must throw his forces at the crucial point where, if he succeeds—even if he fails at all other points—victory will be his." In this, the Pareto effect (the so-called 80:20 rule) governs action as much as targeting; if we had to point to the one or two things we have done that have made most of the difference to our business's success—or even to our own personal success—over the last year, we would not have much difficulty singling them out. What we more often fail to do, however, is *anticipate* in advance the decisive one or two points of difference, on which real differentiation and trial will depend, so that we can overcommit against them.

If, as a Challenger, you are focusing on a few bold sweeps of the brush to paint your marketing picture, rather than a flurry of incremental activities—then it is relatively easy to anticipate and plan for the one or two key points, and the pockets of likely resistance that are hidden behind them. We saw that Swatch broke with the protocol of making an approach to a strategic partner, and Saturn broke with the conventional structure of a car dealership specifically for this purpose.

Equally, however, overcommitment may be measured by how you cope with an *unplanned* decisive point that has been thrust upon you.

When Tesco was successfully fighting its own election battle for the supremacy of the U.K. grocery retailing market, by changing the battlefield from food quality to the whole shopping experience, one of the key competitive thrusts they developed was a customer service offer called "One in Front": a promise to the consumer that they would open another register if there was more than one person in front of them as they waited in line at the checkout. The idea had been greeted internally and externally with enthusiasm, and the company had accordingly filmed a commercial dramatizing the promise and given themselves a month to train staff in preparation for the launch.

But then one Friday Tesco learned that its rival, Sainsbury's, was about to run a commercial in seven days launching essentially the same idea, to coincide with its 125th anniversary. What were they to do? On the one hand, they could not allow their key competition to enjoy the benefit of an idea they knew would be an important and tangible part of their own strategy of improving the Total Shopping Experience. On the other hand, Tesco itself was not yet ready; while it had a finished consumer launch announcement in the form of a commercial, it had yet to announce "One in Front" to—let alone begin training—its staff.

So Tesco overcommitted. It galvanized its training force and ran the commercial four days later, bringing forward the launch by three-and-a-half weeks and relying on the pressure of time and the imminent public statement to ensure that the staff was ready in time. Sainsbury's lead was stolen; it never ran its own commercial. And Tesco took another crucial step ahead of the competition.

Lexus went one further. In November 1989, three months after the launch of the LS 400, Lexus found itself forced to recall 8,000 of its new cars. In principle a deep wound for a company attempting to redefine its category on the basis of performance and luxury, Lexus instead turned it to their advantage. They realized that in order to minimize bad press, they would have to outperform every luxury car brand on this dimension, too. Deliberately exceeding all expectations of service and courtesy, their dealers picked up and redelivered customers' cars once the necessary work was done—unless mechanics were able to go out to customers homes to do the job on the spot—and threw in a tank of fuel and a rental car if necessary. Three years later the industry press was measuring all luxury recalls by the standard set by the recall of the Lexus LS400. By aiming two feet below the brick, they had turned a potential disaster into a source of positive word-of-mouth.

Of course, when the stakes are self-evidently this high or the company is small, motivation runs deep and overcommitment comes naturally. Swatch had the motivation: On the success of the brand's launch hung the success of the Swiss watch industry, and Germany was an enormous and vital market. And if, like Jim Jannard of Oakley, you set up your first business with $300 to your name and a wife who is eight months pregnant, you leave nothing to chance. If, like Cirque du Soleil, opening your first show in Los Angeles you find you have invested so much of your capital in the opening night that you don't have enough money to buy the gas to get the trucks back to Montreal if the show fails, it proves a wonderful incentive for everyone in the company to make it work. Las Vegas in its turn reinvented itself because had to—no other industry would come to the town. Once the advent of legalized gambling in Atlantic City threatened their own monopoly, they tried to diversify into other businesses. But for all their aggressive courting of the aerospace and high-tech industries (Nevada can only support nonpollutant, non-water-intensive categories), the new companies wouldn't come: Was a gambling town any place to raise their children? they asked. So Las Vegas *had* to make gambling work. Forced to go back and look at themselves again, they noticed that one of their hotels was doing a little better and attracting a different kind of audience than the city at large. The anomaly was Circus Circus, a hotel in the shape of a pink-and-white tent with a circus in it. And what they noticed was that Circus Circus picked up a high share of traffic in the city, because although people came primarily to Las Vegas to gamble, they visited Circus Circus primarily to be entertained. So the town started to build fabulous fantasies of hotels—their excess matched only by their success—to the point where Treasure Island became the first of this new generation of hotels to generate more money from non-gambling sources than it does from gambling. Where does overcommitment come in? It is no accident that no other city in the world builds hotels as fantastic as Vegas: It is the only city in the world where the whole community relies on their success. Being threatened as a gambling destination forced Las Vegas to become a Challenger, to take on the rest of the United States as an entertainment destination. There is a saying in Norway: The hungriest wolves hunt best.

This is a critically important point for us, precisely because most of us are not in this situation. We're not that small, our partners are not pregnant, and we still have half a tank of gas in the truck. And maybe that's part of the problem. As would-be Challengers, we have to build in our hunger, in the objectives we set for ourselves and the ways we anticipate and overcome resistance within and without the organization.

Aiming Two Feet below the Brick: Definition of Objectives

We said Challenger is a state of mind. It goes without saying, then, that the leader of a Challenger organization has to first develop that determination to succeed him- or herself. Personal overcommitment sets the tone for those immediately around one, and high stakes readily develop personal overcommitment at the top. When Branson started in music, he operated a mail-order record company. In 1972 the British Postal Union declared a four-month postal strike; faced with a real danger of going out of business, Branson committed himself to his idea still further. He opened a couple of shops and sold his product through there instead. The result was the Virgin Megastore, the Virgin label—and the whole cornerstone of what is now a world megabrand.

Such personal overcommitment is characteristic of the great Challengers in history, even quite late in their success. Consider Alexander the Great, for example—a Macedonian less than 20 years old who defeated the largest army in the Western world (the Persians) as a prelude to creating an empire encompassing all of what is now Turkey, Syria, Egypt, Iraq, Iran, and Northern India. By 325 B.C. with the defeat of the Persians behind him, Alexander and his Macedonians had already conquered Greece to the Punjab, largely on foot. But some of his troops had been fighting for 10 years, and loyalty had begun to waver—while much of the army wanted to turn back, Alexander wanted to go on. The crux came when they laid seige to hill fort of Multan. The defiant Indians inside repelled attack after attack by his increasingly disheartened Macedonians, until Alexander sensed that more than the battle hung on the result of the next attack.

He gambled. Taking a small core of his elite troops, the Companions, he personally led a charge with scaling ladders against the wall of the fort. The attack was largely repulsed but for Alexander and three Companions, who found themselves standing alone on the parapet, with the rest of the Greek troops running back to their own lines. His Companions shouted to Alexander to jump down the outside of the walls—they would cover him until he was in the safety of his own lines; instead, he did the opposite. To the horror of the watching Greeks, he leapt *inside* the walls of the Indian fort into the middle of the enemy, and out of the sight of his own army.

The three Companions on top of the wall jumped down alongside him and put their backs against the wall in a ring around Alexander, attempting to hold off the defenders. Meanwhile a baleful moan ran along the Greek attackers outside, confronted with imminent death of their leader. Desperate, they launched themselves at the walls to rescue Alexander. While some leapt from the shoulders of their fellow soldiers to the top of the wall, others broke the ladders apart and hammered the splintered rungs as footholds into the clay walls.

This time desperation carried them to success. By the time they reached Alexander, two of the three protecting him were dead, and he was wounded, but the fort was taken. Their loyalty was renewed. And Alexander wove Northwest India into his empire before turning back.

Once the business leader, then, has developed a Challenger mindset, the next stage is to drive that same state of mind within the core group around him or her. (This is the primary function of Chapter 15 of the book; for the moment, we shall note this task, but put the nature of its achievement to one side.)

But how one motivates one's staff is an altogether different issue. Motivation of staff also depends on overcommitment, but in terms of a joint overcommitment to a new scale of objectives. Overcommitment in goals can help create overcommitment in implementation.

Let's return to Saturn. Saturn at launch set as its objective customer enthusiasm rather than customer satisfaction. When one phrases the goal in this way—and seriously intends to measure oneself against it—it *necessitates* overcommitment in the car business. Car buyers are so cynical about the car-purchase process that to set out not just to overcome "buying pain" but actively to create pleasure and enthusiasm is to force the team faced with delivering that goal to reappraise *everything* about the process, in an attempt to find a way of meeting this Herculean task. And while it may be too cynical to think that Saturn set itself the objective of customer *enthusiasm* in order to be sure of generating customer *satisfaction*, it is certainly true that other car companies set themselves the goal of customer satisfaction and fail to achieve even customer indifference.

The key point to realize is this: We cannot fool the consumer by talking about good intentions. Every businessperson has read, or pretends to have read, *In Search of Excellence* (in reality they have a book tape rattling around in the back of the car somewhere that they started listening to the week before the new job); the point is, however, that they know about mission statements and customer-satisfaction programs, and the world that they can see doesn't seem to have changed. These wonderful intentions haven't led to a universal quality of service that they can feel or enjoy or relax with. So consumers are not interested in intentions; they are interested in what you are going to do *now*. And now with "claim inflation"—the effective devaluation of the consumers' inclination to believe marketing promises by the gaps they consistently find between promise and delivery—they frequently don't believe you're actually going to do what you say you're going to do (remember the "Missouri Mind-set"). So intention is not enough. And the only way to translate intention into behavior—if everything hangs on the outcome—is to overcommit.

Let us throw this back at ourselves. Assuming for the sake of argument that we have some customer interaction built into our brand's success (be it with end puchaser, trade, or some other audience), let us ask ourselves the following three questions:

1. What are the ambitions of our company's mission statement when it comes to customer service?
2. How close are we to delivering on those ambitions, really?
3. And how much closer have we *really* come to delivering on those objectives over the last three years?

The answers for most companies (particularly after that critical third beer on a Friday night when one starts being honest about the company one works for) will probably be:

1. "To exceed our customer's expectations."
2. "Sort of."
3. "Not really."

Certainly, if we were to then think of ourselves as consumers of the wide variety of categories across which each of us may personally browse, we could count the brands whose service we can remember exceeding our expectations on the fingers of one knee. To generate a different kind of strategy and different kind of behavior, then, our study of Challenger companies suggests that we need to radically reframe the objectives and goals we set our staff—and work through the consequences. Imagine, for instance, ourselves in a more acute Challenger situation, where success is in fact coupled very closely with survival. Or imagine that our goals for next year are suddenly doubled—both the softer goals of customer satisfaction and the harder goals of volume. Next year you are required to achieve *double the return with the same amount of marketing resource* and at the same price point. How do you now approach your strategy? Your customer service objectives? The translation of both of these into a new behavior?

I suggest, if taken seriously, all these will change significantly. (Niall Fitzgerald of Unilever is said to practice a slightly different version of this exercise: When one of his teams is unable to crack the problem, he halves the resource and halves the manpower—and through this greater adversity forces breakthrough.) One is forced to abandon all thoughts of incrementalism, or building on the tactical activities from last year, and throw oneself boldly at a few critical points. Set objectives that demand overcommitment to succeed. Perhaps, like Nike in the early days, aim for "fans," not buyers, and look to create the same kind of results.

Aiming Two Foot below the Brick: Dealing with Resistance Outside the Organization

When Oakley started to move into eyewear, they had a consumer base every bit as vital to them as the trade or their employees—the athletes they were trying to woo to use their product. Without the deep pockets of a Nike or Reebok, they could not pay the major athletes or even minor athletes enough to wear their product unless they genuinely became fans of the new Oakley shades. Because of the unusual appearance of the product, being designed to produce the best possible lens for the application rather than aesthetics alone (they were the first lenses to follow the curving contour of the face, for example, minimizing light distortion), this proved initially difficult. When they invited the triathlete Scott Tinley into the factory to try on the new range of performance eyewear, for instance, Mike Parnell, Oakley's president, noticed a problem. Although Tinley was enthusiastic about the performance of the sunglasses, he seemed uncomfortable with the novel styling. Invited to try them, Tinley looked at the floor and shook his head from side to side, looking for possible distortion or light interference. Yes, they seem great, he said to his toes, and he took them off before looking up again, apparently reluctant even to lift his head up and look at Parnell when wearing them.

Parnell realized Tinley was embarrassed about the appearance of the new line and knew this was a critical obstacle he had to overcome—they needed Tinley, if not actually to flaunt his eyewear, at least to be seen as comfortable wearing them, emotionally as well as physically.

So instead of confronting the issue head on, Parnell encouraged Tinley to walk around the factory wearing the new glasses and see if he felt more comfortable after wearing them for a little while (most of the employees were sports enthusiasts themselves and used to interacting with the athletes in the casual Californian culture of the Oakley factory floor).

So after a coffee, Tinley went for a stroll. "Cool shades, Scott," said an attractive young woman in the reception area. "Really?" said the innocent Tinley, his chin lifting a little.

Two other people commented in the next corridor. And another on the company basketball court. And the girl in the test lab.

By the time he left the building, Tinley was keen to try the new glasses on his friends.

The people who had all spontaneously commented were, of course, plants, briefed by Parnell. Hopeful though he was that experience would make a fan out of the triathlete, he had left nothing to chance. Parnell had aimed two feet below the brick.

Aiming Two Feet below the Brick: Anticipation of Resistance within the Organization

One may be able to buy short-term success through marketing activity. Longer-term success will hinge on the everyday behavior of the company and its employees. To get overcommitment to the delivery of a core strand of marketing strategy at the level of the consumer's experience, we have to first get overcommitment to implementation within the organization.

There are two simple parts of approaching the achievement of this. The first is for us to focus on each of the core tasks or marketing ideas we feel success hinges on, and for each one, to identify *the three reasons it will fail*. The second part, therefore, is to then brainstorm the most effective way of overcoming each of these hidden barriers before we implement it.

These obstacles are not usually hard to see; it is just that they are rarely anticipated as specifically in this way. And, as we saw, a Challenger has ideal circumstances in which to overcome them *before* attempting to implement their core marketing activity.

Take another illustration, this time from politics. Imagine you are a personal adviser to the president of the United States. A prominent national newspaper has uncovered some apparent unpleasantness relating to an old land deal your employer and his wife were involved in; it could damage his already shaky popularity unless carefully contained.

The paper has demanded to see certain documentation relating to this land deal. You and the president have different views about the correct course of action on this. He is all for denial. You, conversely, and the other advisers close to the president are all for compliance: better a couple of snide articles, followed by the burial of the story, than to let it fester and swell.

You decide to commit, to beard the president in his den and put your point across as compellingly as possible.

You do so. You are in irresistible form; after some resistance, and even anger, he seems on the brink of agreeing. He asks, finally, for for a 10-minute private telephone conversation with his wife.

Which, of course, is the point at which you lose. While you have committed, you have failed to *overcommit*. You knew, but had failed to think through, that in any given situation, there are three or four people whose judgment and advice the president seeks—his wife, the vice president, and one or two very close friends. The consequence is that once he calls his wife and she forcibly rejects your proposal, her opinion carries the day—and the story continues to grow and haunt the presidency in changing incarnations for the next six years. What overcommitment would have meant in this situation is the anticipation of what the president's ultimate reaction was likely to be, and then having the conversation with each of those parties in advance *in case* he asked their opinion.

So the first overcommitment exercise we shall call "Whitewater."

Whitewater *vb*: To ask oneself, for each core marketing task, the three irrefutable reasons it will fail (or be diluted into mediocrity). To then brainstorm the most effective way of neutralizing or reversing each of them.

The second exercise we shall call "Jannard," after the founder of Oakley.

Jannard *vb*: To ask oneself the same question in three different ways: (1) How should we ensure this activity succeeds? (2) How would we approach ensuring that success if our career depended on it? And finally (and this is, if you like, why it is called Jannard), (3) How would we approach it if it was our business, we were down to $300 in the bank and our family's livelihood depended on it?

This exercise may be seen by some to be a little flippant, but it is in fact intended to be serious—it helps resolve the lurking tautology here, answering the question: "How can I plan for something to take more than I think it will take? By definition the revised plan will *be* what I think it will take." As one moves down each level, the answer to that question becomes apparent.

Its other real value lies in separating natural "Challenger individuals" from natural "Establishment individuals." When trying the exercise, some do indeed, as the exercise is intended to, become more committed, thinking the task through and developing more imaginative and compelling ways of ensuring success. Others, conversely, do exactly the opposite: As the stakes progressively increase, so they become progressively more conservative, until, with their family's livelihood on the line, they are acting as conventionally as possible.

You clearly have to decide for yourself which of these two types of people that the exercise distinguishes is more likely to help the Challenger company succeed.

Sacrifice and Overcommitment

We saw earlier that central to Challenger marketing is ceasing to think about marketing as "strategy" and "execution" and breaking our actions instead into the Challenger triad of *Attitude-Strategy-Behavior*. Challengers are not somehow unusual in that they have a monopoly on good ideas; they are unusual, however, in that they make good ideas happen. This is to do with three things:

1. Mental preparation, and therefore preparedness to follow through (The First Credo).
2. A clearer sense of how the use of ideas can define identity, create leadership, and accelerate the consumer relationship (the Second, Third, and Fourth Credos).
3. Planning: anticipating resistance and inertia in implementation, and aiming two feet below the brick (The Sixth Credo).

In this respect, sacrifice is the inverse of, and enabler of, overcommitment: Besides sacrifice defining one's identity, it also allows one to overcommit.

10

The Seventh Credo: Use Advertising and Publicity as a High-Leverage Asset

"We have to have a new approach. Today marketing, not product, is king."

Randolph Duke, Halston

Most advertising is poor. Consumers and newspapers are constantly cruising for novelty. The combination of these two offers a huge opportunity to aspiring Challenger Brands.

We saw in Chapter 1 the formidable hurdles we had to overcome in advertising, or indeed any communicated expression of marketing—principally the problems of clutter, "audience" distraction, and claim inflation. The communication problems these posed were summed up in a slightly different context with more color and less political correctness by a former editor of the *New York Post* to a young protégé:

> Lemme tell you something, kid. You gotta grab the reader by the throat. He's on the train. It's hot. He's trying to hit on his secretary; she's not giving him the time of day. His wife is mad at him. His kid needs braces; he doesn't have the money. The guy next to him stinks. It's crowded. You want him to read your story? You better make it interesting.[1]

155

And he was talking, of course, about news, which is something the target pays money to see; the vast majority of advertising, which the target may soon pay money to avoid, perversely fails even the most basic of such requirements. Try this exercise: Sit down and watch an hour and a half of commercial television this evening with a small bag of peanuts. Take as the basic premise that any good piece of communication has to be at least relevant and distinctive. Count the number of ads that fulfill this single basic premise and mark each one with a peanut on the arm of your chair. Eat the other peanuts.

It may be depressing, but at least you don't go hungry.

In terms of the customer conversation, what you have been watching is the equivalent of small talk. Establishment brands and the consumer know each other well; the relationship is comfortable and established to the point where it can survive on a conversational diet that is not exciting and not alienating. It is just a way of stopping uncomfortable silences between the two and reminding the consumer the brand is there. It can even be quite interesting small talk—premium skin-care advertising in print, for instance, operates like a sort of club newsletter, achieving very low recall among nonusers, but high among users. While very few nonusers notice the advertising at all, those who do use that particular brand come to recognize both the house style and the diva who represents them, and they use the advertising to update themselves on the latest club conversation.

But fewer and fewer people are paying any attention to small talk, if Figure 2.2 in Chapter 2 is to be believed. So, at one level we have to accept that the Challenger has no choice about trying to stand out; differentiation is a question of survival. Challengers cannot make small talk, but must demand to be noticed: Salience and change are the watchwords. If our *real* share of voice is not some artificial comparison with the rest of our "category," but our media budget as a proportion of $162 billion (bearing in mind that the Category Isn't), then Challengers need to take a bold position in everything they do, and in advertising, publicity, and design they need breakthrough, rather than acceptability and prompted satisfaction. Whereas Establishment brands can rely on weight of exposure and repetition to drive a message home, for a Challenger who aspires to do more with less, clear communication alone is not enough—reaching through all the reasons not to *capture the target's imagination*, rather than just communication, must be the objective.

At another level this perspective on the marketing challenge also represents a huge opportunity for a Challenger, insofar as this is *one of the very few places where the Establishment brand is at a potential disadvantage*. (The other two principally are an inability as a brand to individualize, and its reliance as an organization on the past.) Trying to protect what they already have gained, and avoid alienating the broad mass market, does not encourage brand leaders into bold advertising or publicity-generating activities. Most brand leaders are by definition change-averse, and this leads to a comfortable culture (within brand leader cultures, one gets promoted to the next level for not making a mess of one's current job) and comfortable advertising. For a Challenger, then, creativity (in advertising and the generation of publicity) is a business tool, to be ruthlessly sought out and deployed as a principal source of competitive advantage against Establishment brands.

In this context advertising doesn't become just a part of the marketing mix. It becomes—potentially at least—a high-leverage asset. We can go further: Advertising and the consistent strategic pursuit of the right publicity can in fact be *the most powerful business tool Challengers have at their disposal*.

Energizer in the United States used unexpected, intrusive advertising and a mildly irreverent icon to raise a number-two brand in a low-interest category into a part of the popular vocabulary—and popular culture. And in doing so, it forced Duracell to change the whole way it marketed itself. Bear in mind that these are batteries; these are not things people want to think about, and when they do think about them it is because of the annoyance of them running out. What the Energizer story demonstrates is that there is no such thing as a low-interest category; there is only low-interest marketing.

But the purpose of this chapter is not to showcase the power of advertising—there are many more formal collections of case histories that are more individually compelling (as, for instance, the Advertising Works series, or some of the other volumes in this Adweek series). Most readers will already be familiar with the advertising success of a brand like Absolut, and at this point I will limit myself to one further dramatic illustration of the potential power of advertising for a Challenger to leverage business success in a static market with a dominant brand leader. We saw in Chapter 7 the new marketing initiative to reverse the declining fortunes of the fast-food brand Jack in the Box. It was spearheaded by a new advertising campaign featuring Jack, the "founder" with a plastic head returning to shake some sense into the company that bore his name (symbolized by the reintroduction of a good "signature burger"—the Jumbo Jack—at a price point reflecting the new market laws). Since the new advertising and marketing began, the sales increase has in turn led to the stock price increasing by 600%; with a scaling back of new product introductions, and no real product changes at store level, the results may be said to derive chiefly from the successful leveraging of "Jack," both in the advertising that invented him and in point of sale and promotional material that played him for all he was worth.

So, accepting the potential and particular power of advertising and publicity for a Challenger, then, the question is this: What does it actually *mean* to regard advertising and publicity as high-leverage assets, in the way we think and behave as a Challenger company?

It means change. Advertising and publicity only become high-leverage assets if the company significantly changes its development and approval policies to reflect the new importance it is attaching to these marketing tools; in terms of internal processes it is still being treated as just another part of the marketing mix. What tends to happen is that most of us will agree about the importance of advertising and publicity to a Challenger brand, yet fail to absorb the implications of this for how an organization must restructure itself and its processes. Our strategic and creative approach fundamentally has to change. Returning to the conclusions we drew from Chapter 1, we saw that most of the assumptions we made about the audience, consumer, and the category were out of date. We saw that Communications Don't; that we have now to be in the Ideas Business.

There are in turn two key implications from all of this for us. First, *creative breakthrough is a strategic necessity*. We need, as Challengers, ideas that seize the target's imagination. Anything else is a strategic as well as creative failure, given the time and resource we have to achieve our goals.

The second, consequent implication is that if creative breakthrough is a strategic necessity, then it follows that *a strategy is only as good as the quality of ideas it produces*.

Acknowledging the Strategic Primacy of the Idea

Acknowledging the strategic primacy of the idea is *not* saying that "any interesting creative idea is the right idea for the brand," *nor* is it an advocacy for beginning to write the idea first (whatever the medium, from advertising or design to publicity and direct mail) and retrofit the strategy afterward.

What it *is* saying is that capturing the imagination of the target is a very different brief from communicating a message, and if one wishes to capture the imagination, then, in the words of Jay Chiat, "Good enough is not enough." In an ideas-dependent business, which is where a Challenger necessarily falls and rises, part of the definition of a good strategy is that it should be fertile ground for one or more strong ideas. It should no longer be possible to say, "We had a great strategy, but the creative people couldn't come up with any good ideas," in this new culture. Assuming you have capable ideas people, that just means it was never a great strategy in the first place. The overall vision for the brand, therefore, needs to have some inherent flexibility in its articulation, and the strategic development process needs to change to allow for such a flexibility. If the identified articulation of the brand strategy *fails* to produce ideas that can break through and seize the retreating target's imagination, we *have to find another expression of the strategy*. The development needs to be organic rather than linear; while not actually developed simultaneously, the strategy needs to be flexible enough to encompass the consideration of big new ideas if they are close enough to the overall direction the brand needs to take.

This will be a difficult concept for some to embrace. Surely, having arrived at the one correct strategy through analysis and research, they will argue, that strategy becomes the rigid railroad that steers the ideas? But the premise here is flawed: While there are still indeed certain types of problems for which there is only one correct strategic solution that can be divined from rigorous deductive thinking, they are increasingly rare.

Most types of strategic problem in the New Business World now require imagination as much as rigorous analysis even at the strategic stage.

A New Kind of Development Team, A New Kind of Strategic Development Process

This in turn suggests that certain refinements in the development process need to be put in place. Returning to our "relevant and distinctive" paradigm, we used to think of this as meaning that separate parts of the team would take on separate jobs along the path to the final product—the strategic team, for example, would analyze and identify the "relevant" bit before handing over the brief to the creative team in five immaculately crafted (and endlessly discussed words) to make it distinctive.

But if we acknowledge the strategic primacy of the idea, we have to involve all disciplines, particularly the creative discipline, in the strategic process from the very beginning—because the strategy and creativity will be much more holistically developed. Under this new model, then, each development team needs to be multidisciplinary from the outset, with each discipline actively involved at each stage. This is no longer the old-fashioned "baton pass" from discipline to discipline at each stage. All disciplines will need to walk around the problem together.

And we will obviously need to look in different kinds of places for insights into consumer problems that will provide fresh departure points for the brand and the ideas that drive it forward. If all one ever does is focus groups and quantitative studies into the market—that is, ask the same questions everyone else in the category is asking, in the same ways—then we are handicapping ourselves before we start. Key to our new strategic approach should be to realize the limitations of conventional research. It is not that conventionally run, centrally located focus groups have no value in gauging the interest in certain kinds of new ideas as they emerge, but rather that they are not always the most strategically fertile points from which to start. Instead, we should look to walk around the problem, simultaneously exploring the consumer's existing and potential relationship with the category from many different sides at once.

In a celebrated Japanese film of the 1950s, *Rashomon*, four characters tell a court the story of what appears to be a rape and murder outside a village in feudal Japan. Each of the four people involved in the incident recount to the court their version of the incidents that have just passed, and yet, while each's version of the truth bears some general relation to what the others have already said, it also *varies significantly* from the others in certain key regards. Each character has distorted the truth through his or her own particular lens so as to look and feel better in what has just passed.[2]

The point the film makes is that there is no absolute truth in human narrative. We obscure some aspects of the truth deliberately, forget others accidently, and are often unaware of other, irrational filters of prejudice or relationship we have in connection with a person or product. (Schools of journalism have an exercise that makes a similar point: Two strangers burst into a classroom of surprised and seated students, exchange heated words, and begin to bustle each other until a fight breaks out. The students are then asked to write an account of what has just transpired. No two accounts are exactly the same: all the more striking if we bear in mind that these are trained observers/narrators with a single series of events fresh in their conscious mind.) In the same way, people or consumers do not have the tidy, unequivocal relationships with brands and products that we would like them to. If one asks different kinds of questions in different kinds of ways, one gets different kinds of pictures as to their relationships with our brand and the competitive set. For instance, suppose you ask a focus group of eight young men about their relationship with their car stereos. They will talk to you about independence—the fact that the car is their first taste of being free to do what they like, the first territory they own and can behave as they will in: smoke, date, sing, make love, be truly on their own. And they will tell you that a key part of this is their relationship with music: that they can play the choice of music they like as loud as they like. They will talk of the throbbing bass, feeling the music in their stomach: a visceral experience inside the car. And all of this is true—it is indeed one version of their relationship with their car stereo.

Suppose you then ride around with a couple of them for a day in their cars. You notice an interesting phenomenon: They get to a red light, and if there is a pretty woman on the other side of the road, they wind down the window and turn up the volume. This is nothing about the experience inside the car, or an intense relationship with music—this is about display, sex, and power. This is about showing everyone *outside* the car what stereo you have.[3]

Now, neither of these two "stories" of their relationships with the category is false. They weren't lying in the groups when they talked about their visceral experience with the music. And their desire to impress the opposite sex does not mean they are not also genuinely interested in music. But they do offer two entirely different and valid ways to position a car stereo brand. And two entirely different sources for potential ideas. Since the consumer is not used to talking about their relationship with the category (however many groups they go to), the closer one can get to their real lives, away from a viewing facility mirror, and the more different perspectives one can get into the same problem, the more chance one has of finding a strategic springboard for strong ideas.

And these, of course, are just two ways of telling the story about the consumer's relationship with the brand. If one were to do a semiotic analysis of competitive advertising, one would get a third view of the opportunities in the market; a sociologist would give fourth perspective. Creatives naturally think in a way that provides a fifth—namely, mentally mapping the category in terms of what areas of expression have been covered in advertising or design in the past (and what remains potentially uncovered, therefore, for us and our future). And so on.

It is interesting to push this concept a little further. In observing the world around us, we become primary-sense dependent—that is, we lean on one sense for most of our information and decision making. For most of us, that means our eyes. If you want to have a different view of the world, see things in a different way, you have to blindfold yourself, stop using your primary sense. When we do so, we are struck by how our other senses tell the story of the world in a different way; their story is no less true, or insightful, but their input is usually eclipsed by the primary sense we are dependent on. But once we have stopped, even briefly, being single-sense dependent, when we return to use that sense, it has a new value, because we are using it in conjunction with a greater awareness of the other senses.

So, too, ourselves, as marketeers with research: We become dependent on seeing the consumer through one kind of lens—the focus group, the tracking study, or possibly the Usage and Attitude study. Other types of research tell the story in a different way and open up fresh ways of perceiving the world our brand lives in and the opportunities it offers. For a Challenger, constantly looking for new sources of ideas to add value and competitive advantage to their brand, a systematic embrace of "multisense" research should perhaps be built into their exploration and re-exploration of the market every year.

Advertising and Publicity: Ripples and Risk

For some Challengers news coverage proves more important to their launch momentum than paid-for advertising. What really made Branson and Virgin Atlantic high profile after the launch of the airline, after all, was not the advertising or marketing per se; what really made him and his brand famous initially was Branson's own attempts to break the transatlantic sea-crossing record in the aptly named Challenger. (The president of Southwest has a similar flair for self publicity; perhaps it is something in the DNA of founders of Challenger airlines.)

New television network brands have profited enormously even from controversy. A housewife named Terry Rakolta launched a preventative campaign against Married with Children early in Fox's network life. Having written letters to 45 advertisers, Mrs. Rakolta was invited to appear on Nightline, Entertainment Tonight, Good Morning, America, and the front page of the New York Times, where she obligingly complained with horror about the program's offensive and exploitative nature, together with its showing of gratuitous sex. In introducing the segment the news stations naturally illustrated it with a clip of the show and then back-filled the story with a history of Fox for those unfamiliar with the new network. The outcome, of course, was that the unfortunate Mrs. Rakolta did more to ensure national interest in watching Married with Children and Fox than any single piece of marketing Diller's group themselves had done or could do; Fox's then head of publicity, Brad Turell, estimated its value to the fledgling channel at $100 million worth of promotion. Longer term, indeed, she also inadvertently pinpointed the way to success to those running the network of the opportunity for future growth: They have successfully sailed close to the wind ever since.

If Fox found controversy valuable by accident, Channel 4, the fourth television channel, which launched in the United Kingdom in 1982, used it more deliberately. The new station made headlines the morning after it launched when one of its programs—*Brookside*—contained both swearing and naked buttocks. The show's creator felt in fact that the characteristics giving offense were entirely in keeping with it being a "social drama," not a soap opera, but it was also an astute marketing card to play on the channel's opening night. As with Fox, early success in grabbing headlines with bold and controversial content encouraged the commissioning of more: Channel 4 went on almost overtly to market controversy with its graphic language and sexual content, to the point that journalists asked to preview Channel 4's programs claimed that the station's publicity department would draw attention to potentially controversial aspects in the forthcoming program. The *Daily Mail*, a conservative national newspaper, acted as an institutional Mrs. Rakolta and was particularly helpful in mounting a long-running vendetta against the channel. Channel 4's innocently helpful response was the introduction of red triangles in the corner of the screen as a warning to viewers who might be disturbed by strong content and came across the program while channel surfing. Viewing figures rose significantly following the introduction of those little red triangles.

What is unusual about Challengers, then, is not that they use PR to their own advantage—every company over a certain size has a public relations department or agency—but that their hunger for it (given the need for salience and identity, coupled with the paucity of conventional marketing resources) leads to the *aggressive and consistent manufacture* of it; and this in turn means that its manufacture occupies a far more central role in the marketing process than in establishment brands. Small companies are not above building in notoriety from the outset—with Death cigarettes, for instance, the whole brand was structured around the generation of such news and word of mouth. Candie's ran an advertisement of Jenny McCarthy sitting on the toilet with her underwear around her ankles. *Time* magazine tut-tutted, magazines refused to run it, and the company instantly achieved the image they desired: the whole point was that your mom wouldn't approve.

Yet if this leaves the impression that the publicity currency and objective of Challengers is the wanton generation of notoriety, that would be wrong. Just as Challenge does not mean in-your-face assault, so Challenger PR does not require shock value or controversy to be a built-in

Sullen Fish

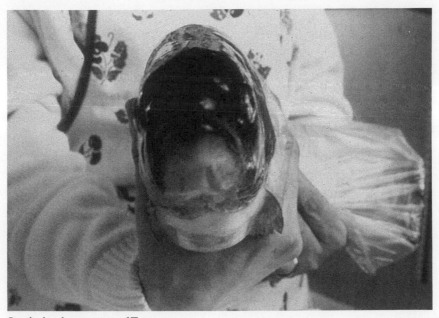

Supplied with permission of Tesco

part of the process. Some of our Challengers focus on producing advertising that generates a ripple of PR in its wake, not just because it is entertaining or controversial, but because it creates or provokes news. Tesco, the U.K. grocery retailer, introduced a customer policy whereby you could return any food product you were not happy with for whatever reason. Their agency, Lowe Howard-Spink, produced a commercial where a woman returned a trout she had bought, not because she questioned the quality, but simply because she didn't like the expression on its face; she felt it was "too sullen." The in-store fishmonger offered her a "nice, cheerful sole" instead, and she went away happy.

This proved an invitation the tabloid press found hard to resist. Journalists all over the country started returning depressed-looking seafood and asking the in-store fishmonger to recommend something "a little happier." The men and women behind the Tesco fish counter duly obliged, and news coverage was born.

Much of Absolut's success has come from using advertising to create a ripple of PR every time. Look at its commissioning of artists to interpret

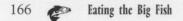

Königstadt-Terrassen: Restaurant

Supplied by Bürhaus Immobilienverwaltungs—KG.

the Absolute bottle, for instance. When Helmut Newton was asked to photograph the designs of seven of the world's leading international fashion designers for Absolut, the resulting photographs displayed around the world attracted a broad range of magazine editorial, shows in art galleries, even television coverage. Although each execution ran once in each magazine, Absolut later estimated Newton produced what it called an "afterwave" that was 10 times larger than the effect of the advertising on its own.

The concept that people are not so much risk-averse as loss-averse explains why it tends to be the smaller Challengers, who have little to lose, we see most boldly seeking publicity. Take the example of an office building in Berlin, the Königstadt-Terrassen. 150 meters from the fashionable—and expensive—area of Mitte, it had a tiny marketing budget with which to persuade potential tenants to desert the Establishment brand and move a short walk down the road to a location offering considerably better value.

Its solution was to create three new media, the first being trash bins. Adhesive stickers appeared overnight on the bins around Mitte; on them were printed the words "You might as well throw your money in here as rent in Mitte," followed by the new office block's telephone

Königstadt-Terrassen: Sidewalk

Supplied by TBWA Berlin.

number and the tag line "Spit on Mitte" (denoting at once the outrageous rents and the short distance to the Challenger alternative). The second medium was condoms. The company printed condom packets with the legend, "Too poor to have children? Perhaps you are paying too much for your office space," followed again by the telephone number. They then distributed these in local restaurants and bars.

While the first two attracted word of mouth, the third lured newspaper coverage. Six chalk outlines like those used by police around "suicides" appeared on the sidewalks around Mitte overnight. Next to them were simply the words, "He jumped because he couldn't afford the rent," and again, the telephone number. In a city with 1.3 million square metres of empty office real estate, within four months they had increased rental income by 52%.

The example brings us back to the difference between publicity stunts and intelligent Challenger marketing. While at one level the objective in all of this for the Königstadt-Terrassen was certainly to generate word of mouth and publicity, it was also a remarkably shrewd and efficient piece of communication. Within its local target market, the company generated salience, clearly communicated the product benefit, invited reappraisal of an ingrained prejudice (the dominant consumer complacency) for the existing player, and created the beginning of a personality for themselves—while implicitly flattering the people who had already decided to move. And all this for an office block—not something one would have historically classified as a high-interest category.

Publicity and Folklore

We have talked above of Challengers that have used advertising intertwined with publicity to enter popular culture, both as a defensive measure, to offset a relatively low share of voice in conventional media, and as a source of competitive advantage, to become a part of the cultural fabric in a way that the Brand leader has not. However, some Challengers have achieved short- or long-term success not by using the two together, but by turning their back on conventional advertising solutions altogether and putting *all* their available marketing budget instead into the direct or indirect generation of publicity.

Lawsuits, for example, seem to be quite potent publicity vehicles for Challenger airlines. Easyjet, a small low-cost airline competing on Western European routes, found itself in familar marketing territory after gaining a new route to Holland: the euphoria of gaining distribution was quickly displaced by the need to rapidly build awareness of itself and its price advantage among its potential target market. At the same time it had proportionately a very small amount of money to go up against its bigger and more established rivals in conventional media.

So instead of spending all their budget on media placement, Easyjet reduced it to a third of their planned spend and invested the rest in lawyers. Initiating a lawsuit in the European Court against KLM (the national Dutch carrier), in which they claimed unfair competitive practice, Easyjet positioned itself as being on the side of the public, rather than just a new player entering the market. The day the court case was announced, Easyjet found itself all over the television, radio, and newspapers. A small-scale radio campaign breaking the same day, in which the captain of "Big Bird Airlines" thanked his passengers as they took off for all the money they had paid for their meal, added fuel to the fire, and in fact was played during coverage in current affairs programs to illustrate Easyjet's case.

After one month, consumer calls to Easyjet had doubled; after two, they had tripled. Critically, seat occupancy (the key to profitability in the low-margin airline business) rose over the same period from 35% to 70%.

And while this is about using publicity to achieve short-term acceleration—Easyjet returned to advertising in Holland once the lawsuit was settled—a small number of Challengers, the Body Shop and Starbucks for instance, have used such word of mouth, and the folklore that has sprung from it, to flourish *without using advertising at all* until quite late in their success. Although both are admittedly unusual in that they control their own retail environment—no threat of delisting here—they still offer interesting lessons for non-retail-based challengers, and their cases merit a little further discussion at this point.

Starbucks is an "experience brand," a cup of coffee that is at the same time a destination. This experience in turn is aspirational—the jazz, the information about the beans that lends one a sense of being a part of the coffee cognoscenti, the pseudo-Italian vocabulary. All these lend one a sense of being "in the know" when standing in line, and a badge of being someone who takes care to seek out the important things in life when putting the cup down in front of one's office colleagues. Starbucks thus originally offered early adopters bragging rights; it then achieved a more general audience through the opportunity for product enthusiasm and aspirational identification. While never creating publicity through "events," the cultish nature of the brand-user relationship they succeeded in developing ensured their word-of-mouth appeal at a grassroots level, if not at the iconic level achieved through advertising by Wonderbra and the Energizer Bunny.

The Body Shop, on the other hand, is an "issue brand." It has deliberately set out to create publicity and news for itself over its stance on particular social issues. A brand for which there is a living founder who has chosen to put a face to it and the company behind it, the Body Shop's Anita Roddick has successfully achieved newspaper coverage not through the courtship of publicity for bravado or anti-establishmentism like Branson, but through taking a strong personal stance on issues as diverse as animal rights, women's physical abuse, and African culture. The commercial brilliance of the Body Shop as a Challenger was to use this—a social ethic—as a key point of differentiation against the big cosmetic players, while not requiring the consumer to make any trade-offs (let alone wear a hair shirt) to identify with the brand. On the contrary, Body Shop products offer an unusual alignment of physical hedonism with spiritual nobility: You can sit in your bubble bath and feel as clean inside as you do out. Classically, these two have been opposites: One could either wave placards at a foreign consulate in the driving rain and do the world good, or recline in a scented, foaming bath and do yourself good. Roddick's brilliance has been to reconcile these, to make virtue luxurious, creating an issue brand that requires no social effort on the part of the purchaser except to make the purchase, and then enjoy its effects.

There are a number of similarities beyond both Starbucks and the Body Shop owning their own retail stores and both having succeeded without using advertising till late in their lives. First, both brands succeeded through offering pleasure: little moments of pleasure in one's everyday life. Second, this pleasure was rooted in each case in a more intense product delivery—the Body Shop with its romancing of the fruit and herb ingredients, Starbucks with its romancing of the beans and process. Third, both in their own way stretched the consumers' sense of who they were, in terms of discernment or social enlightenment; emotionally and functionally, each offered for a time a unique experience to the consumer and used their stores to educate and propagate the emotional and functional underpinnings for this experience and identification. And fourth, at key periods in their growth, both created users who identified with and talked about the brand. They represented not so much a badge as a club.

Now word of mouth has always been a more powerful influence on the consumer than advertising alone. And it is also more efficient, in that it propagates itself: vital if one has a limited conventional marketing resource. One can measure really successful folklore by the semipersonalization of it: Everyone in a focus group will claim to know *someone* to whom something remarkable has happened in connection with the brand. They themselves feel they are no more than two degrees of separation from extraordinary performance. Consider the folklore that surrounded the quality control of Marks and Spencer (another brand that achieved its key growth without using advertising), at the time of the

U.K. retailer's image growth in the 1980s and early 1990s on the back of a high-quality and innovative food policy. A focus group research respondent would relate a story about a friend of theirs who, hosting a dinner party and desperate to buy food before the store closed, found the Marks and Spencer cashier wouldn't sell her the last pack of meat available in the store because it was one hour past the sell-by date. Although this friend begged and begged, it seemed, to the point of summoning the manager, the Marks and Spencer staff held firm, saying they couldn't compromise on their quality standards. Yes, the rest of the group will sagely nod, impressed; they all personally knew someone who had a very similar experience. And the next person would begin with a story that had happened to a friend of theirs.[4]

Brands that consistently create such social currency begin to create a folklore or mythology around themselves. Such folklore is more than brand equity; it lives at a level above brand equity. Because while brand equity may be defined as the perceptions or facts a consumer associates with the brand *when probed*, mythology may be defined as those perceptions or facts a consumer proactively communicates about the brand *unasked*. Thus, while brand equity is passive, personal, and residual—sitting as a collection of perceptions in an individual's mind to be triggered within that individual when the purchase process is again embarked on—folklore is active, social, and self-propagating. It is like a virus of favorable equity that gets passed on among existing and potential user groups. Indeed, it is arguable that at the times of their strongest momentum, Challengers live at *a level above* brand leaders, because while brand leaders enjoy strong equity, Challengers enjoy a strong folklore—either at an iconic level through the brand's advertising and marketing, making it a reference point in popular culture, or through ground-level word of mouth.

To understand how an aspiring challenger brand might attempt to create and exploit such a folklore for itself, first let us look at how folklore occurs. It usually arises because the consumer has found themselves in one of four situations:

1. **Bragging Rights.** They have discovered something valuable; they feel they are one of the first to unearth a new premium brand of beer, for instance, or a new group. I heard this new band on the radio yesterday, out of Seattle; you should check them out—they're going to be

huge. This jacket? Oh, it's a little Italian company called Napapijri; I love their stuff—but it's impossible to buy outside Italy. We discovered them while skiing there last year.

2.　**Product enthusiasm.** They have come across an aspect of product performance about a brand that is startlingly impressive: that a Land Rover is designed to be able to drive 4,000 miles continually off-road, for example; that the airline I flew in on this morning had a masseuse on the plane that gave me a neck massage when I woke up; or that an ice cream that was forced upon me last night contained preposterously large chunks of Toffee Chocolate Fudge.

3.　**Aspirational Identification.** They have found a brand with a strong identity and ethos (perhaps aligning itself to certain social issues, for instance), which they admire or would like to be identified with. If I discover that the board of Ripcurl, an Australian surfing brand, is still required to surf every Saturday morning, even though the age of Ripcurl's commercial director is 53, that suggests to me that here is one rootsy apparel company that has yet to sell out (perceived authenticity is fundamental to the endurance of a challenger). If I find that the outdoor clothing company Patagonia gives 10% of its pretax profits to environmental causes, then in buying that kind of clothing I align myself with a certain philosophy, not just of social conscience, but toward climbing and the great outdoors—that it is about leaving it unspoilt, giving, not taking, and so on.

4.　**News Value.** They have come across a piece of marketing activity that has surprised, strongly entertained, or shocked them sufficiently to prompt conversation with their peer group. That Ben & Jerry's built a 20,000-pound sundae in a town in Vermont just for the hell of it, for instance, or that the same pair is currently driving across America in a "Cowmobile," handing out free cones to anyone who happens to be passing their way.

These are the four key ways a brand creates some kind of conversational, social currency for itself—what some call Water Cooler Conversation. And in order to have this currency, it is not sufficient for the consumer to feel it will have this effect on them alone—they need to feel it will raise the mental eyebrows of their audience as well.

A Challenger looking for aggressive growth without using advertising will look to actively exploit all of these. It will have a product that overperforms, on which it can be confident. Although early bragging rights are valuable to create a group of evangelists, the brand self-evidently cannot rely on this after launch and early growth, so it will need to build into its identity some characteristics that can generate Aspirational Identification and build into its marketing budget people and ideas that can consistently create News Value. Sometimes a Challenger will fan such folklore by replaying it as it occurs to a broader audience in its advertising. During an early Saturn product recall, a dealer flew to a customer in Alaska who was physically unable to return his car. The dealer arrived in a rented twin-engine jet, completed the work in the customer's own garage, and flew out again the same day. Besides the natural PR coverage, Saturn's agency (Hal Riney and Partners) produced a television commercial about the event, gently romancing and repropagating their own mythology through their advertising.

Brand folklore, then, comes from the intersection between identity, overcommitment, and experience. Overcommitment or product over-performance leads to an experience the consumer finds surprising. The consistent occurrence of this in the consumer's relationship with the brand, however tangential, means that the experience is seen to be in some way not a fluke but a reflection of who the brand is and why—particularly if it is accompanied by an awareness of a strongly projected identity from the brand. The consumer talks about it to a couple of friends the next day, and the Challenger has not just an equity that is passive and personal, but the beginnings of a folklore that is self-propagating and social—and a source of competitive business advantage against the brand leader.

11

The Eighth Credo (Part I):
Become Idea-Centered,
Not Consumer-Centered

"Our biggest competitor is ourselves."
> *Manuel J. Cortez, President and CEO, Las Vegas Convention and Visitors Authority*

In 1988 the advertising agency Chiat/Day (now part of the TBWA network) swept the Beldings Awards. An award show local to Los Angeles, which has no real status east of Westwood, the Beldings are nevertheless a source of pride within the Los Angeles advertising community, and Chiat/Day had turned out in force. The agency's work dominated the awards; a small pink Bunny on his own accounted for a small mountain of silverware.

Bob Kuperman, then Creative Director of Chiat/Day, stood at the side with Jay Chiat and looked down at his euphoric creative department, dripping with talent and alcohol, their tables awash with the silver Beldings bowls. "You know," said Kuperman to Chiat, slowly, "This is the kind of thing that could ruin an agency."

Kuperman was prophetic. Chiat/Day, a recent West Coast Challenger to the established and besuited East Coast Advertising houses, found its creative star to begin a steady decline until in the early 1990s it was still being referred to as the "Agency of the Eighties"—though this time dismissively. The agency retrenched and refocused, and success

174

came again out of adversity: Ten years later they again swept a small awards show in Los Angeles and indeed reestablished their reputation on a somewhat wider level as well.

What the story illustrates is that one of the greatest hazards of being a Challenger is success. And success, of course, is a very dangerous thing. Successfully entering or reentering a category is one kind of problem; surviving that success without becoming hamstrung by complacency or overexpansion is quite another. From the big cage rattlers (Apple) to the young fashion pretenders (Mossimo), the marketing battlefields of the West are strewn with wounded challengers who started brightly but found it hard to maintain their momentum. And the process we have committed ourselves to, of defining the strategic "software program" for a successful Challenger, would therefore not be complete if we did not consider as well the question of how we address this problem *before* it occurs—that is, how Challengers sustain momentum, rather than regain it through adversity.

Momentum

Momentum is vital to Challengers for two reasons. *Actual* momentum is the source of the return on investment—and as such, the measure of immediate growth in sales and revenue return. But second, *perceived* momentum—the sense by the consumer that this is the brand making the running in the category, that this is a brand to watch—is the basis of its future equity, the seeds, perhaps of a future return on investment (ROI) that will outstrip today's.

The reason most Challengers lose momentum is that they fail to realize that they have to change in order to remain the same. That is, they have to change not their core identity, but *the way the consumer experiences and is stimulated by that identity*. The basis for a Challenger brand's initial success in a mature category, after all, was that it developed from the beginning a different kind of *relationship* with its user to that of the brand leader. At the time fresh and different, this relationship came from the consumer's response to being presented with a brand that in some way broke the mold of what they were used to in the category (as with Timberland and Saturn).

But the success of one brand means the rest of the category assimilates the foundations of that success, too; one ice beer leads to another, and another, and another, until being an ice beer or an entertaining airline or a user-friendly computer on their own is no longer enough. Ideas, like innovations, are replicated (albeit often in more diluted form) and so in turn dilute the power of the original idea to sustain the original relationship. So Challengers that rely on their original product proposition lose their freshness.

And, of course, as consumers we get easily bored; what excited us yesterday jades us today. (This is a human, rather than twentieth-century phenomenon: When the Roman poet Lucretius commented disparagingly of the Roman people that they desired *semper aliquid novi*—always something new—he was writing over 2000 years ago.) It is not just that we all have a low boredom threshold; it is that our comfort zone expands to include what once seemed startling and fresh. But comfort zones favor only the brand leader—if a Challenger fails to stay just outside that comfort zone, be just a little provocatively different, it becomes an increasingly invisible part of the distribution landscape and slowly dies through consumer indifference. The voracious consumer, hungry for *aliquid novi*, moves on to another newer, more tempting morsel in the category.

Which means that the idea or ideas on which the Challenger launched itself inevitably cannot sustain it. It needs more frequently to feed and refresh the relationship with the consumer, which means in turn that it needs to consistently produce ideas that stimulate and provoke the consumer—not once or twice, but continually. It needs to continually keep the relationship fresh: as fresh as it was when the relationship was new. We must never lose sight of the fact that the underlying driver for a Challenger is *momentum—the sense that our brand is making the running in the category*. Successful Challenger brands can therefore never afford to be static. They constantly add to themselves to keep ahead of the market in their relationship with the consumer; and the fuel for that movement is ideas.

Failure to sustain actual momentum leads to the temptation to grow volume instead by accepting the potentially poisoned chalices of line extension or distribution; with these may come erosion of the core equity, loss of the core users, and an erosion of the shape of the user base leading to a relatively rapid decline. And as we have seen, once the Challenger loses its credibility and core users—well, Ocean Pacific marks the spot. Failure to sustain *perceived* momentum, on the other hand, can lead to the "freeze-drying" of the brand, associated in the consumer's mind with being locked into a particular time or trend in their past when they principally noticed it—and therefore by definition not a brand of the moment. The more successful the brand is, the greater this danger. Swatch in the United States became freeze-dried after its enormous success in the late 1980s—forever associated with a sense of frivolity and unreasonable optimism that characterized a certain period in the 1980s. Evian, too, for a while struggled to shrug off the "aerobics accessory" niche created by its capitalizing so successfully on the exercise boom shortly after its U.S. launch. In 1979 the shoe brand Kickers in Britain became the only boot any self-respecting 15- to 25-year-old wanted to own; by 1980 it was consequently emotional history, fossilized by its lack of evolution. The bigger the success, the bigger the jump it would have needed to have made to survive.

Maintaining Momentum, Part One: The Continual Manufacture of Ideas

To say that a relationship has to be fed by ideas is in no way the same as saying it has to be fed by technical innovation or product news. There are indeed obvious categories that still rely primarily on innovation to drive and renew them (3M, for instance, which takes 30% of its revenue from products it has introduced in the last five years); and of course it is a part of marketing motherhood even outside hi-tech to produce product news at regular intervals for big brands to perk up the advertising's effectiveness. Such news usually takes the form of minor product innovations—20% more lanolin, or dual airbags as standard, or a thicker, crunchier coating—and work well for brand leaders, who by and large simply have to sustain mass. Their place as the Establishment brand is easily confirmed by the updating of their product, reassuring the consumer that their functional credentials are second to none.

But when we look at Challengers, we can see that the ideas they employ are very different from product news. The difference between innovation and an idea is illustrated neatly by recent developments by Audi. To make a car entirely out of aluminium is an Innovation; to then leave it unpainted would make it an Idea—the first pure aluminium car. In the telecommunications business videoconferencing is an innovation, whereas MCI's "Friends and Family" is an idea. In the airline business electronic ticketing is an innovation, but a bar in Upper Class is an idea. Challenger ideas do not tend to come out of the R and D department; they come out of the core marketing team, or an enthusiastic customer, or anyone who happens to be passing the founder's office—and they tend not to be product ideas but marketing ideas. Very ambitious marketing ideas. Hanging a gigantic orange watch off the Commerzbank in Frankfurt, for example; or projecting a bra onto a power station. Provoking and stimulating the consumer's imagination.

At the simplest level, Challengers seem to use communication ideas over and above conventional marketing practices (advertisements, promotions, sponsorships, and so on) because in order to unseat the existing player in the category, they need to *engage the imagination and emotion* of consumers who think their needs already satisfied by the brand leader. Sony PlayStation has been a brand that from launch has seen conventional advertising alone as insufficient to ensure its aim to become not just the brand leader but the generic in the category. For four months preceding the formal launch and availability of product in the United States, for instance, PlayStation seeded what it called a "viral" awareness campaign among gaming opinion leaders, using an icon and the Japanese characters spelling *Hamarido Max* (an expression taken from Japanese gaming magazines indicating the "suck in" factor of any game they reviewed). The icon and words—later evolving to what was to become the launch slogan "You Are Not Ready"—appeared in forms as unexpected as hand stamps at night clubs (to guarantee admission and readmission), embossed on drumsticks thrown in the crowd at the end of rock concerts, and logoless flyers in downtown areas.

By the time the company came to launch in September, such activities had helped fuel prelaunch anticipation for PlayStation to such a pitch that 25,000 people had put down a $25 deposit to guarantee receipt of one of the first shipments of game systems from Japan, and Internet hackers had broken into the official PlayStation website two days before it opened in order to be able to break the news of its contents early (bear in mind, all of this preceded any formal television or print advertising spends). Over the following crucial Christmas period, PlayStation outsold the brand leader's system (the Sega Saturn), launched two months before it, and went on to become the overall brand leader across all systems within two years.

Sony PlayStation's marketing group has persisted in strategic use of ideas, rather than just communications, to engage and reengage the imaginations of their target (not least because they have to—machismo, natural cynicism, and the pressure to be cool makes 15- to 25-year-old male opinion leaders in Western markets the hardest and most marketing-resistant target market in the world). When the time came to launch their own "icon character" game, featuring a bandicoot going under the nom de guerre of Crash, the marketing challenge was how to supplant such well-known and loved characters as Mario the plumber (from Nintendo) and Sonic the hedgehog (Sega).

The executional answers varied from country to country, but the underlying approach—that a conventional communication of the new product's game play was not going to be enough—was always the same. In the United States, a five-and-a-half foot incarnation of Crash Bandicoot in orange-red fur drove to the headquarters of Nintendo USA. Standing outside the front doors, he invited Mario the plumber through a megaphone to step outside and measure up to the challenge of the new kid on the block. Documentary-style film—of what was in fact a clever set up rather than a real incident—including the "forcible" removable of our furry hero by an actor dressed in a uniform of a Nintendo security guard, was cut into a 30-second commercial and used to launch the new game.

In the United Kingdom the view was also taken that advertising would not be enough to unhorse such established favorites as Sonic and Mario. The company created a concept playing out the thought that bandicoots were an unusual species in the British Isles and required special attention. At one level this was reflected in a number of activities aiming to "protect" bandicoots: genuine road signs, randomly placed, indicating "Bandicoots Crossing"; car stickers offering the noble sentiment that "A Bandicoot is for life, not just for Christmas"; a radio hoax that a small group of bandicoots had been discovered living wild in the North of England. (This hoax was actually picked up and reported as genuine by *The Fortean Times*, a monthly magazine chronicling the unusual and paranormal.)

Sony PlayStation: Crash Bandicoot

Open on Crash driving an old pickup
truck past the Nintendo Headquarters.
Cut to Crash getting out of the truck as
he grabs a megaphone.
Crash: Hey, Plumber-boy! Mustache man.
     Your worst nightmare has arrived.

Cut to Crash standing in parking lot.
Crash: Pack up your stuff. I got a little
     surprise for you here. Check it
     out. What do you think about
     that? You got real time, 3-D,
     plush organic environments.
Cut to Crash uncovering the wall of TV
monitors all displaying "Crash Bandicoot"
game footage. Cut to close-up of different
game footage screens.
Crash: How's that make you feel buddy
     . . . feelin' a little like your days
     are numbered?

"Crash Goes to Seattle" with the permission of Sony PlayStation.

And so it goes on. In France, when launching the latest Formula One racing game, PlayStation stuck an airplane sick bag into consumer magazines, in case the realism of the game was such that players might find themselves recontemplating their own breakfast. Systematically, all over the world, Sony PlayStation has used ideas over and above conventional advertising or publicity to gain an edge over the competition. When repeated, even at the level of marketing, the use of such ideas can help sustain a personality as a source of differentiation. Nando's, a South African fast-food chain specializing in peri peri chicken has consistently taken on the bigger spending KFC through an irreverent personality consistently brought to life through the more imaginative deployment of ideas "on the ground." So a fast-food public familiar with Nando's delivery trucks bear-

Sony PlayStation: Crash Bandicoot, (*continued*)

Cut back to see a security guard approaching Crash at his truck. The security guard reaches for Crash's elbow.
S/Guard: I'm going to have to ask you to leave.
Crash: You're hurting my elbow.
Cut to close-up of TV monitors with PlayStation logo being displayed. Cut to one TV monitor flashing up the words U-R-NOT-e. Cut to close-up of the "Crash Bandicoot" game logo.

Cut back to security guard and Crash walking through parking lot.
S/Guard: Is that Italian?
   Crash: No, Bandicoot, it's an Australian name.

ing the sardonic slogan "The X-Fowls" (it is, after all, carrying dead chickens) and apparently grandiose commercials revealing "the secret of how Nando's chicken is made" to be a pair of copulating birds, was introduced to a new marinated line through a group of Nando's vans driving around the major cities with tin cans tied by string to the rear bumper; written in hand across the back of the van was the legend "Just marinaded."

Nando's success comes from its consistency in this regard: To do something like this as a one-time deal would be fun, but essentially pointless; it is the *consistently* larger-than-life and more-spirited performance that makes KFC seem old-fashioned and Nando's engaging and appealing. And it maintains the momentum.

Two of the brands we have already discussed go further to illustrate the difference between repeated innovations and the cumulative use of ideas. One of them, Saturn, is not an innovative car as such; it is, as sheet metal, a fairly sensible and unexciting sedan. But its early success came from its being packaged in a plethora of ideas that caught the imaginations of a significant portion of the buying public. Siting the factory in small-town America rather than Detroit, offering no-haggle pricing, using the calmness of 60-second commercials, the engagingly direct honesty of placing of a car sawed in half in every show room (in order to transparently reveal the car's simple virtues), dreaming up the Homecoming Reunion—these were ideas drawn from the well of its identity that caught the public's imagination because they ran against everything that had been the anchor stone of car marketing to that point.

The second example is Tesco. We saw in Chapter 6 that Tesco realized it could never overtake Sainsbury's on the brand leader's chosen ground; while it certainly had to be able to compete in terms of food (freshness perceptions and choice), it needed to find another ground on which it could fight and win. The riposte when it came, then, had been to step back from food and look at the totality of the shopping experience that surrounded the food. Marketing itself on the platform of The Best Shopping Experience, it had produced a tagline that, while it wasn't a huge promise, was a realistic one, and one they knew to have struck a chord with consumers: "Every little helps." The key thrust of the strategy, however, lay in its being about far more than just being seen to be "on the consumer's side"—a common positioning refuge for the brand that has nothing else really to say ("we understand you better than those other people do"). For Tesco, the strategy was not about being *seen* to be on the consumer's side, but being the first grocery retailer really to translate that understanding into action. The proof of the strategy was in the delivery: in doing things that demonstrated they were improving the total shopping experience—lots of them. Communicating them, then delivering them, and being the first to do either. Behaving as if Tesco believed it could never do enough for the consumer.

The following are examples of the ideas Tesco introduced and promoted over a three-year period, usually with specific commercials devoted to each:

- "One in front"—opening a new line if any customer at the checkout had more than one person in front of them.
- Baby Changing facilities.

- A service warming baby's milk for mothers with small children.
- Privilege Parking close to the entrance for parents with small children.
- Bag packing at checkout (long a staple of the U.S. grocery business; but new to the United Kingdom).
- Club cards, offering a points reward system.
- The ability to return any item of food for whatever reason.
- Calvin Klein underwear, Adidas shoes and Levi's jeans at half the price of high-end stores.
- "Try before you buy"—the opportunity to sample any ready-to-eat food before purchasing.
- A "correct change" promise—if they got a customer's change wrong, they would return double the difference.

Each of these was in its own way a new idea to the U.K. grocery consumer. And each was linked by the common theme: "Every little helps."

One can see that the force of the Tesco promise lay in the multiplicity and consistency of the ideas it put in front of the consumer. There was a Native American tribe that supposedly had no word for three: It counted "One, Two, Many." In the same way the cynical and overpromised consumer, seeing one idea implemented, may feel it is a drop in the ocean; seeing two, that the brand is certainly trying but the jury is still out, and seeing three—well, three starts to become hard to argue with. So for Tesco it was the *insistent* demonstration of the promise through successive new ideas that proved compelling. At the level of Market Leadership, the results of the new marketing drive, together with aggressive new store developments, were that Tesco equalized Sainsbury's profit-per-square-foot and went ahead for the first time in market share. At the level of Thought Leadership, each successive innovation served to create more press interest in the next announcement; by the time, for instance, Tesco began contemplating offering home delivery, it made the front page of every Business section of the British Sunday papers.*

---

*Continuously feeding the relationship with different ideas and, implicitly, different arguments also has the merits argued eloquently by Gordon Brown, founder of the research company Millward Brown International: "An argument either has an effect on someone or it doesn't, and it isn't too much use repeating it. Suppose office workers are discussing Margaret Thatcher at lunchtime, and one is trying to persuade the other that she was a great British Prime Minister. The argument might go: 'Look, all other recent British Prime Ministers swam

Here is one final example of "One, Two, Many." Late one wet evening in April 1998, I flew into Frankfurt airport. I had only recently returned to Europe after four years in Los Angeles, so many of the newer, more dynamic brands in Germany (as well as the whole concept of rain) were new to me. By 11 P.M. I had reached the Holiday Inn; pocketing the receipt for my cab, I pushed open the hotel doors to find an orange Mercedes SLK parked in the center of the lobby between myself and the reception desk. Whoever had put it there had not, it seems, relied merely on its unusual color to catch my attention—I had to physically walk around the front of the car to be able to check in at all—and had written on the side of the Mercedes in black letters one word: "Sixt." Emptying out the day's litter from my pockets onto the bedside table upstairs 10 minutes later, I noticed the same word on the wrapper of a moistened paper towel Lufthansa had given me before landing. I made a mental note.

The combination of both of these was a sufficient prompt to my curiosity to ask a German colleague the next day about (I presumed) a car rental company I had never heard of before. My colleague told me a little more; he told me, for instance, of the advertising they had run offering to rent a Porsche 911 for 99DM (around $55) a day. I expressed surprise: How could Sixt sustain a business renting 911s at $55 a day? They didn't, he said; they only had one for rent. But they certainly got our attention.

At the end of my meeting, I took a cab to the airport. It is not unusual to see rental car companies advertising at the airport, so it was not the fact of the Sixt limousine on display at Departures that surprised me, but the position: 45 feet above me, nose down, supported by chains from huge metal poles. In 24 hours, without seeing a single television commercial or print ad, I had come into contact with four ideas from Sixt. Breaking conventions of representation (an orange Mercedes), medium (an airline paper towel, chains 45 feet above me), and experience (a Porsche, at least in principle, for a sum I could afford), these four ideas had defined

---

with the tide—Wilson, Callaghan, Heath. At least she tried to take a grip on things, to change society.' But if the subject comes up the next day, the supporter of Mrs. Thatcher will *not* go over the same ground! If that argument didn't work yesterday, it won't work today either—and the supporter will instinctively change tack and talk about, say, Margaret Thatcher's dealings with the trade unions. In a prolonged attempt at persuasion, we don't *repeat* arguments, we look for new ones."

very clearly the brand position and attitude toward doing business with me. And they had left me in no doubt as to their momentum: There was a new Thought leader, if not market leader, in the German car rental market—*even though they were at this stage a few years into their challenge*. Yet, as I say, not one of these interactions was a technical innovation or mainstream piece of advertising.

(The concept that ideas are fundamental to economic health, incidently, is not confined to brands, or the microlevel of a particular market. The so-called New Growth Theory, largely made famous by Stanford professor Paul Romer, states that ideas are in fact what drive successful modern national economies. The value of ideas in driving an economy, for Romer, is that they are, like knowledge, abundant, they can build on each other, and they are relatively cheap to develop and reproduce.)

So while brand leaders have historically maintained their mass and consumer trust by the use of product news, updating the satisfaction of rational needs, the objective for Challengers is to maintain actual and perceived momentum, and this is done through the continual deployment of ideas that feed and constantly restimulate the relationship with the target. Inherent in these ideas is their ability to provoke and surprise the target, take them just beyond what they are already familiar and comfortable with. This in turn, as we will come to see, springs from our own ability to anticipate rather than simply reflect the consumer's emotional desires.

Seems simple, doesn't it? It is, after all, no different in essence from how Challengers came to be successful in the first place. But be it complacency or protectiveness, many Challengers, once they have reached a certain level of success, fail to continue feeding the relationship at the same rate as they did at their period of greatest acceleration.

I am not making the facile point that it is important to go on having good ideas. If there seems to be a natural tendency to relax when one is successful (what Claude Bonnange has called "The Warrior's Rest"), and yet the Challenger above all other kinds of brands has the need to sustain momentum—which only occurs through maintaining the freshness of the consumer relationship through provocative ideas—then the real issue here is that we need to be more *systematic* about how we build the production of those ideas into the way our company and marketing lives are structured.

We might go so far as to think about the notion of idea obsolescence, like product obsolescence: an idea becoming obsolescent when it no longer has the ability to provoke the consumer—because it has become devalued through competitive assimilation, or because the consumer is bored with it, or both. We might go further—we might set ourselves the *ambition of making our own ideas obsolescent by replacing them with a better one before the competition does*. Competing against your own product, after all, is how key category leaders sustain their preeminence, and not just in the software business. Gillette as a company has the objective of constantly making its existing product obsolete—the Excel was superseded by the Sensor, which in turn made way for the Sensor 2. And— here's the interesting bit—as they launch each new generation of razor, *work has already begun on its successor*. "In the shaving area, both wet and dry, we have never launched a major new product without having its successor in development," Gillette's chairman has been quoted as saying. "you have to steer the market."[1] The same should be true of our ideas—a Challenger's objective should be to make each one obsolete by improving on it before someone else does.

Proof of the symbiotic relationship between ideas and momentum is borne a curiously poignant testimony in the reminiscences of Andreas Whittam Smith, the founding editor of *The Independent*, a quality U.K. newspaper launched on October 7, 1986, to take on *The Guardian* and *The Times*:

> The essence of doing my job well, I believed, was to come into the editorial meeting every Monday with ten to fifteen ideas for what we should be doing . . . It was one of the jobs of the editorial conference to throw out the ones that wouldn't work, and be left with the good ones; I had no pride about that.
>
> The system worked well for many years, but toward the end of my period as editor the stream of ideas began to dry up. I didn't come into the conference with ten to fifteen ideas, I was beginning to come in with five to ten. I was beginning to find it hard to get to five. And I worried about this.[2]

The launch of *The Independent* was for the first few years an enormous success: It was the first new quality British newspaper to succeed in decades; for a while its circulation came even to equal *The Times*. But by the time Whittam Smith departed, by the time the flow of ideas had started to dry up, *The Times* had opened a considerable lead, and *The Independent* was declining toward an unsuccessful relaunch and a change in ownership.

A striking example of the symbiotic relationship between a fertile ideas culture and growth.

Maintaining Momentum, Part Two: Providing Different Ways to Access the Identity/Experience

We have seen that the currency of Challenger momentum—and therefore success—is ideas. Those Challengers that have started strongly and then run dry of ideas, like Saturn now, or Apple in the late 1980s, peak and start to slide. Those that consistently manufacture, and are seen to manufacture ideas that refresh the relationship, like Tesco, continue to grow.

But there is another kind of challenge that a Challenger faces as it grows, namely the change in the *meaning* of the brand to the consumer. Whereas brand leaders offer the consumer a sense of belonging, being a part of a greater community, Challengers (at least at the outset of their lives) offer the ability to individualize, to be a part of something different, perhaps ahead of the curve. For a Challenger to sustain its own early pace and momentum is difficult, therefore, not just because consumers get bored, but because the brand loses its ability to individualize, to be a piece of communication about the consumer. Its meaning, therefore, begins to fundamentally change: How can it say something of value about the individual consumer if everyone else seems to be using as well?

Successful Challengers, therefore, face a medium-term fork in the road: Does one try to preserve one's early formula for success in order to maintain one's core loyalists, or change the nature of one's appeal in order to maintain growth?

Route 1: The Peter Pan Strategy

Some Challengers attempt to be Peter Pan and sustain success by never growing up (I do not mean this in anyway pejoratively), preserving what worked for them in the early days. Quiksilver spoke of the need to keep the brand authentic—"in the water" as they put it: Once the committed surfers felt that their clothes were available to kids in malls in Chicago, they would stop wearing it. Oakley spoke of the need to keep it "discoverable"—limiting distribution.

Both of these, while viable, naturally put a ceiling on volume and actual momentum, in the interests of longevity.

Route 2: The Reinvention Strategy

Think of Madonna. Madonna has outlasted many of her contemporaries as icons of popular culture not because she has relied on a perennial consumer interest in her musical ability and taste to carry her, but because she has consistently reinvented herself and the point of access into Madonna-the-star and Madonna-the-musician. Virgin, Material Girl, Blonde Ambition, self-published Sex Object, Evita, Mother—she continually presents the public with a renewed face, a new point of access into The Brand. Each face is different, but the same: While it has its own personality, its own set of emotions, in each it is still recognizably the Game-of-Madonna that we are invited to play. (In counterpoint Martha Stewart, the cultural Establishment brand to Madonna's Challenger is always unwaveringly the same.)

One of our Challengers, Cirque du Soleil, pursues much the same strategy to maintain its momentum. Its tours reinvent the product offering sequentially, never playing the same show to the same audience in the same city twice. Each new appearance of the brand offers a different product name (Saltimbanco, Allegria), a different theme, a different mood, a different blend of theater, circus, and dance: a new way to experience the old identity. It changes in order to stay the same.

The reinvention route is relatively easy for entertainment brands, where the content is intangible. More traditional categories tend to rely on the third route, namely Mass Customization.

Route 3: The Mass Customization Strategy

Those Challengers that eschew the Peter Pan option, and attempt instead to grow to brand leadership, have to answer some hard questions:

How do I make a rapid transition from a brand of identity to a brand of belonging—that is, emulate the brand leader's role? And how do I stay exclusive, yet grow big?

The answer to both may lie in mass customization, or "individualized belonging." If we were to stay in the field of popular entertainment, perhaps here our model would be *Seinfeld*. Everyone liked *Seinfeld*—the number-one show in the United States for over five years—so in being consumers of the brand, they all had something in common. But the structure of the show offered four very different, well-defined characters, with the story lines evenly spread between them; so while, if you asked four different consumers of the Seinfeld brand to name their favorite TV program they would all answer Seinfeld, each would offer, when pressed, a *different* character they preferred, and a *different* episode featuring that character that they would take to a desert island. In other words, each consumer in a bar could own an "individual bit" of *Seinfeld*, while sharing in the social glue of common enthusiasm. It offered belonging, but individualized belonging.

Perhaps this is the key difference between how a Challenger survives mass popularity and how a brand leader survives mass popularity: While everyone buys the brand leader for the *same* reason, a mass-market Challenger succeeds by offering the ability to *access the brand from several different points*.

In terms of popular culture, this is not confined to television shows. The Spice Girls were the most recent example of the attempt to do this in music (the latest in a long line of marketing "manufactured" bands since the Monkees); the five characters—Scary, Ginger, Baby, Sporty, and Posh—offered a single message ("girl power") accessible through differentiated characters that appealed to audiences as varied as nine-year-old girls, eighty-year-old grandmothers, and twenty-year-old soccer-playing lads. Everyone could buy into the Spice Girls phenomenon, but everyone could access them from a slightly different point.

At a brand level, one could for a while see something of the same kind operating with Starbucks. While the first life stage of the Challenger is discovery, once Howard Schultz began his distribution expansion and the brand lost its discoverability, consumers of the brand started talking not about Starbucks, but "my Starbucks." By this they meant their own customized coffee, and indeed their own store ("my Starbucks is the one on the corner of Manhattan Beach Boulevard and Highland"). Mass customization, individualized belonging: Everyone is an individual, yet everyone belongs.

Yet while each of the last two strategies has some merits in providing a source of growth for a Challenger, neither on its own is sufficient. While the first offers a continual refreshing of the relationship, reinvention of the total brand every two or three years is impractical and undesirable outside areas of the fashion business; the second, on the other hand, offers the platform for mass appeal without necessarily the means to sustain it once success has been achieved.

The most powerful solution to sustaining Challenger momentum seems to lie in fusing the two. We shall call this the Line Renewal strategy.

Route 4: The Line Renewal Strategy

Some Challengers that do not begin with multiple access points build them in as they grow. While at one level it can be as simple as Absolut's introduction of flavor variants, whose distinct undertones are reflected in their individual ads (for example, Au Kurant's laced bustier, or Peppar's scorched pages), other Challengers have more explicitly sought multiple access points to the brand, each with very clearly defined appeals and personalities.

Consider Tango. While innovating creatively in the development of the Orange Tango campaign, Tango has also innovated conceptually by developing a broader range of access points to the brand through other flavors, each offered not just as a flavor variant, but as an *individual and well-developed personality* of its own, through different evocations of the taste. While Orange offers the taste "smack," Apple apparently offers sex and seduction, Blackcurrant, passion and belligerence, and Lemon, yet another personality again. Had Tango continued with Orange on its own, the campaign and the brand would be tired by now, but by turning each line extension into, if you like, an alter ego for the brand, the relationship stays multidimensional and fresh. As such, they are not just product news, or line extensions, but almost new experiences. And having created these access points, Tango then uses them to maintain the sense of unpredictability that made it the talked-about success it was initially.

We might call this Line Renewal, then, rather than Line Extension. Whereas Line Extension offers the *same* relationship the consumer, expressed in other product forms, Line Renewal attempts to offer a renewal of the relationship, by offering "the same, but different." If, in the case of Tango, the consumer has no interest in drinking anything other than the original flavor, the new versions serve as reassurance that the brand continues to be as surprising and irreverent as when he or she first came into contact with it. For those interested in diversity, the brand offers an ability to progress or individualize a little. In doing so, it represents, if you like, the combination of reinvention and mass customization.

Las Vegas might be another example. For Las Vegas, it is the new themed hotels that restimulate interest in the city as a whole: The opening of a miniature version of the ultimate city transplanted to the middle of the desert (New York) is followed immediately by the reconstruction of the most romantic of European cities (Paris). And while this is still only half-built, the ground is already being struck for an Italian lakeside village (Bellagio—created, of course, in a state notoriously deficient in water). Each new themed hotel provides a new and rich experience, which, besides being lucrative in itself, offers a new access point for the consumer's relationship with the city as a whole. The identity of Las Vegas as a fantasy entertainment destination remains the same, but the consumer can choose and individualize the fantasy through which they access that brand experience. Two couples visit Las Vegas: one prefers Caesar's Palace, the other Paris, but both get to talk about how much they enjoy gambling there. Next time, one will stay at Caesar's, the other will go to the newly opened Bellagio—one likes the fantasy to stay the same, one likes new experiences. (The additional value of new points of access into the brand is that it allows "the enthused" to be ahead of the rest of the pack. Las Vegas's constant creation of new and different ways to access the experience is akin in some ways to Oakley's philosophy of keeping it discoverable—even though Oakley were talking about it as a factor of distribution.)

This route, then, offers the most interesting potential for a Challenger to continually sustain momentum. There are, in summary, four elements to the Line Renewal Strategy:

1. The continual use of ideas rather than simply communication.
2. The construction of new facets or embodiments of the brand offering fresh departure platforms for such ideas, and at the same time differentiated points of access.
3. The creation of fresh ways of thinking about the brand's identity at each of these new points of access.
4. And, in terms of implementation, doing this systematically and consistently.

Growth and Identity

But how do we implement the Line Renewal Strategy without also changing our core identity? Do we not have the terrible example of Harley-Davidson hanging over our heads. Was this not a brand who tried to move with the times and lost sight of who it really was?

The core identity for each of the two brands discussed above doesn't change—Tango remains at core surprising, irreverent, its fruit apparently a precipitator of sensations or moods that take one into a world of altered states that touch on taboos from xenophobia (Blackcurrant) to religious cults (lemon) to exploding old ladies and passing gas (Orange). And Las Vegas consistently offers a different kind of altered state: the fantasy of glamour, of being a high roller with the potential to enjoy permanently the lifestyle whose fantasy surrounds you. This strategy of Line Renewal, in fact, could not work without a strongly defined core identity: Line renewal of a hollow brand is simply product and brand diffusion (brand diffusion also occurs when a brand trespasses into a field in which it has no raison d'etre—as with Timberland and polo shirts).

Alchemy

Establishment brands and establishment-minded players one talks to are eager to disparage Challengers. Take the long view, they will say. And they point out that while Challengers might be interesting models for short-term growth, they are frequently poor examples of steady longer-term growth. And this is, of course, true. Challengers can stumble, stale, plateau after initial promise—and the spotlight thrown by that initial promise makes their weakness all the more noticed when it comes.

I tend to give two answers to this. The first is that to accuse Challengers of failing to sustain growth consistently is not actually the issue—all brands wax and wane. The failure Challengers really face, it seems to me, is the failure to reinvent or re-create themselves once they start waning—that is, the failure to understand that they have to change in order to stay the same.

My second response is that we are not holding up Challengers as perfect paragons of business in every way. That we can learn some valuable lessons from their success in building rapid growth for themselves against the run of market play does not mean we are required to slavishly follow their subsequent ups and downs. Or that we cannot narrow our focus in looking at the longer term. Some Challengers have put in place measures to ensure longer-term success in a way that others didn't.

And in discussing this, the Eighth Credo, we are, of course, on the most speculative ground. This is an extraordinarily difficult and ambitious area to consider—we are looking for the marketing equivalent of the alchemist's stone, or the secret of eternal life. But if we are prepared to venture on, we can see that maintaining momentum will require not just the observation of the marketing attitude, strategy, and behavior outlined above, but an underlying *cultural* change. It is one thing to *say* that it is essential for a Challenger to continually create ideas that seize consumer's imagination, it is quite another to do it: Ideas do not come along with the punctuality and obligingness of a Pop-Tart—announce you are hungry and in three minutes back one comes, hot enough to burn your mouth. Ideas are irregular, rarely arrive on demand and, even when they do arrive, are easily trampled on and lost.

We need, then, to rethink the *whole way we think about supporting the brand and structuring the organization*. We need to move, in other words, from being a consumer-led culture to an ideas-led culture.

12

The Eighth Credo (Part 2): Flying Unstable

"A form of hierarchy exists here, but you have to look hard to find it."

Wilbert Das, chief designer, Diesel[1]

The building of the F-16 fighter plane marked a revolution in warplane design and construction. Up to that point all fighter planes had been built to fly stable—that is to say, if the controls were released for any reason, the plane would continue to fly in a stable flight path. But development engineers realized that a plane's chances of both defense and attack were maximized not by maintaining a stable flight path but by their ability to maneuver—that is, *get out of the path* they were in and into another as fast as possible. And an airframe designed to promote stability hindered the plane's ability to do this.

The breakthrough was to design a plane whose airframe was inherently *unstable*: whose wings and tailplanes would naturally jerk the plane out of its current flight path if the computer in the nose did not compensate for it under the pilot's guidance. The result was a plane that flew stable when it needed to—under the computer-assisted guidance of the computer in the nose—but whose inherent instability allowed it to get onto the tail of an intruder, or out of the path of an attacker—adapt and react, in other words—faster than any other plane on the planet. The greatest danger in an F-16, in fact, is to get a bullet through the computer; the plane will spiral down out of control.

194

I suggest that as we move forward into a market future of flux and uncertainty, the most important and telling difference between one organization and another will be the degree to which it flies stable or unstable. Most organizations we look at—and certainly almost all Establishment companies—are built like the early bomber or fighter planes: to fly stable. The inherent stability is built into their airframe through rigorous processes, review boards, old hands, many layers, and received wisdom—all of which keeps them flying more or less in the same path they always have been. They recruit people in their own image ("she's one of us"), on the basis that that is an inherently good thing. This stability makes progress steady, but it also makes such companies slow to react and adapt to changing category dynamics.

Challenger organizations, on the other hand, who have to be faster in idea generation, implementation, and reaction, tend to be built to fly *unstable*—they have smaller groups of people working under less supervision, making up the process as they go along, relying less on exhaustive research and more on informed instinct. Those people are multidisciplinary and are recruited for talent and attitude as much as being good team players; the conversations and meetings accordingly tend to be higher voltage, more abrasive and intense.

Much depends, of course, on the computer in the nose: It is this that separates superior maneuverability from fast but random motion in flying unstable. In the case of the Challenger organization, the computer means a very small group of people, no more than five and ideally only two or three, that are very closely in touch with what is going on at all levels in the organization. Ideas filter up to them, they rely on themselves to make decisions, everyone understands who they are—and they are in very close two-way communication with a broad representation of their people at all levels.

In many ways, in fact, this small group, completely on the ball, represents the legacy of the garage that was the starting point for so many US. businesses. Henry Ford in his neighbor's shed, Hewlett and Packard in a garage in Palo Alto, Jobs and Wozniak, Mossimo and the West Coast fashion brands, and so on: a couple of people, a room and an idea, with complete control over its success or failure. There is a permissive mentality about garages: They are places where there is very little protocol or rank. They are places where you can change your mind, change the idea, argue, and shout, because the really important thing is not the feelings of the other person, but whether the idea is ever going to get big enough to leave the garage. Garages are rarely full of people in suits; they are places where people know each other very well, personally and professionally. They are places where only success will suffice, and everyone is accountable for it: Muddling along as you are is not an option for success. They are places where, when an idea comes along, you push it as far as it goes and take a decision, because ambition is high and time is limited. They are, in short, the complete antithesis of the big company cultures they often go on to become.

In this chapter, then, we shall go on to look at some of the other building blocks of a Challenger culture; underlying everything will lie this sense of building in instability, managed by the watchful presence of the decisionmaker.

Making the Culture Fit the Brief

So, flying unstable is the way Challengers structure their organization to be flexible and innovative. The culture of the Challenger organization must then be wholly defined in terms of the direction you want to fly in—it must be taken through to setting the new agenda via the whole vocabulary and way of describing the task of idea-centered growth.

When Gary Gersh came into to revolutionize Capitol Records, he found an organization that was still thinking in terms not unlike the historic company that had recorded the Beatles, Sinatra, and the Beach Boys in the landmark Capitol Tower just off Sunset Boulevard in the 1960s. Gersh, an industry wunderkind who had broken grunge with the signing of Sonic Youth and Nirvana to a major label (Geffen), realized he had to shake things up a little: Capitol had a formidable back catalog but had overextended into a huge array of artists, many of whom, like MC Hammer, were past their popular peak. One of the first things he did was set up a hip hop division. Realizing that for this to succeed, he was going to have to flaunt conventional rules, he asked those setting up the marketing function within it to come up with their own name for the division and their own titles and job functions within it.

A week or so later he dropped by to see how it was going. They told Gersh they had decided to call themselves the Fruit Stand. Why? Because their music was on the street, full of color, and freshness was everything. And what are you going to call yourselves? he asked. The "Marketing Director" considered this. They hadn't worked out all the details, he replied, but he was going to be the Director of Kerbside Chuckles.

This unconventionality pervaded the group's marketing thinking. To break new bands, for instance, they would record the new artist through many generations of tape, finally putting it onto a cheap store-bought audiotape with a scribbled title, and hand them out at parties to make it look as though they were pirate tapes that had been less than legally obtained. As such, their value and perceived authenticity was high, and they seeded the artist among a core group of opinion leaders before the album actually hit the streets. The originality of the culture Gersh had encouraged was reflected in the originality of the results.

This sense of creating new titles and cultures to get a new kind of job done may have to be accompanied by unconventional structures and job remits. Central to Jan Carlzon's initial ambitions for turning SAS around in 1981 was improving the basic performance of the airline—without this, any improvement in service was irrelevant. He set the airline the task of becoming not simply more punctual, but the most punctual airline in Europe within a year. Instead of pep talks and change consultants, he picked one person out of the organization and told him he was putting him in absolute charge of delivering this goal. He could have no budget, but *absolute power*. The airline made its goal within four months.

Changing the cultural direction can be cued further in Challenger companies by going beyond task description in terms of changing the basic reference points and changing the *core vocabulary* to describe the task ahead. Internally within Fox during the early days, for instance, Barry Diller wouldn't allow it to be called a new network—they always referred to it as an "idea." In the burgeoning Microsoft, staff didn't talk about "identifying the next marketing task." They asked, "Where's the next jihad?" What a world of difference lies beneath these two phrases: One is a rational statement of a professional responsibility, the other defines one's immediate future as a *holy war*. Which of these two ways of thinking do you think would impact your business more? Which of these two has more passion, commitment? Which will lead to a greater impact on the consumer?

As another pair, consider Jobs's celebrated recruitment gauntlet to John Sculley (the computer entrepreneurs were always good at this): Do you want to sell sugared water for the rest of your life, or do you want to change the world? Compare this to the vocabulary used by the head of a flight crew of a large unionized U.S. airline (just embarking on a program of dramatic change), whose parting words to the 20-odd flight crew at the end of a preflight briefing were: Don't forget to water the cabin. The Establishment brand referred to their all-important customer service (she was talking about offering drinks and refreshments to their passengers) as an impersonal task whose trivial nature might possibly escape their minds, while the Challenger CEO talked about employment in his company as being part of a team about to alter the course of history.

It can also be cued by very simple changes in working practice. A senior manager at Perstorp, a Swedish chemicals company whose consumer brands include Pergo flooring, and which has aggressive expansion plans for Europe, has a policy of answering all e-mails *within two hours*. This means systematically breaking meetings to check and respond to questions or ideas that are live. You are left in little doubt as a colleague or subordinate of this manager as to the value he attaches in his projects to ideas, communication, or speed—and all it takes is one simple rule.

Culture Preceding Behavior

The aim of these directional cues for Challengers is to have a living culture in the Challenger organization, not merely a sequence of learned behaviors. Where behaviors depend on training and grow stale, a culture is self-propagating and finds new ways of staying fresh.

Most models of cultural change have a sequence: Action, Behavior, Culture. One starts a program of change by getting the staff to carry out certain actions; through repetition these actions become behavior; and in time shared behaviors become a culture. What is interesting about

Challenger companies, however, is that in many cases they look to create a culture first and *then* teach behavior. By that I mean they recruit
people for specific characteristics that *can't* be taught and then teach
them the rest.

So Herb Kelleher describes his recruitment brief at Southwest as
being primarily a search for a sense of humor, for the right attititude. His
unarguable premise is that Southwest can subsequently train recruits in
whatever they need to do, but the one thing they cannot change is the
inherent attitudes in people.[2]

Oakley explicitly looks for technical competence, but also something
more—a love of and participation in the outdoor sports for which it produces product. This makes Oakley employees as individuals young and
extremely competitive, personally motivated by the products they make.
It also imbues a basic sense of the value of a *team*—which Oakley then
fosters through daily bike races at lunchtime, a full-size basketball court
in the middle of the office, and winter ski trips.

Renzo Rosso, the founder of Diesel, puts it this way:

> How do you find the right people? I believe there is no easy of guaran-
> teed formula. I can tell you one method I don't use, however, and that is
> microanalyzing thousands of resumes and CVs in search of the most
> qualified job applicants. Diesel has been built by people who possess a
> tremendous amount of energy and enthusiasm—but often very little in
> the way of impressive credentials or previous experience. I have many
> times put my faith in new employees based on nothing more than what
> I've perceived to be the outstanding quality of their character. In most
> cases these individuals have soared with their opportunities.[3]

Establishment brands put their faith in training—the things you can
teach people. Challengers seem more often to put their faith in character traits: the stuff you can't teach people; one cannot fan enthusiasm
unless the flame is already lit in the first place. When Challenger CEOs
are talking about their staff being their most important asset, the unconventional values they look for in choosing them suggest this may not all
be 1990s management speak.

For those wishing to create a Challenger culture when none existed before, the first step in creating such a culture is obviously the remotivation

Oakley Entrance

Photo: Eric Koyama

of individuals, the incentivization and reward of people for being innovative, rather than playing it safe. The question of how one achieves the perfectly motivated employee is clearly the scope of books much larger than this, but at its simplest it is a matter of redefining the expectations from the top and assessing performance against them. If in each annual review one were simply to ask one extra question of each employee—"What two ideas have you originated or championed this year?"—and then make a surprisingly high proportion of their raise or bonus contingent on the way they answered this question, one would soon begin to see a change in the culture. To change the brief in many cases is to change the person.

Oakley has turned its building into a brief. I asked Jim Jannard, who personally codesigned the new southern Californian home for his company, and particularly its entrance and atrium, why he had designed it the way he had. He replied: "I want our people when they walk in to be so stoked that they can hardly stand it. I want them to be dying to come back tomorrow. I want them to be desperate to find a place where they can use their own particular talents to add to us and make us great."

Oakley Atrium

Photo: Eric Koyama

Once one has defined the brief for the individual, the second step is how to combine those individuals to produce the most creative results, and specifically, how one plants and cultivates catalysts.

Cultivating Catalysts

Challenger companies look for more than talent. Passion and drive, certainly, are seen to be important (consider the competitive spirit sought by Mike Parnell in recruiting staff at Oakley), yet some challengers go beyond looking for spirit; they seek a certain obsessiveness or even eccentricity. Jonathan Warburton, who has been one of three cousins breathing new life in the historically conservative Lancashire family baker that bears his name—and in doing so taken it to brand leadership in the United Kingdom (over 100 years after the first loaf was baked)—believes that number-two companies should employ "the unemployable people. The product zealots. The people who would get spat out of the big, establishment companies." In relating the David Henderson story, where the company's product director personally lobbied all 500 members of the Canadian Wheat Board in order to obtain for Warburton's an exclusive contract for the finest grade of wheat available on the market, Warburton noted that this kind of initiative was not "a Warburton thing, but an oddball thing"—that is, it was not something that came out of Warburton's culture, but the individual's personal culture: Henderson's obsessive interest in product quality. It took someone playing by their own rules to make the difference to Warburton's. Skunkworks went so far as to contemplate eliminating their human resources (HR) department altogether, for this very reason, feeling that HR departments look for, and place the greatest priority, on the wrong things—stability, manageability, cultural fit—rather than talent, passion, and the ability to make a difference. Lockheed Martin's young Challenger division felt they were losing a lot of potential talent, even if they were high maintenance (and most of them are); because they might not "fit."

Of course, one cannot have a company consisting entirely of mavericks and oddballs and expect the company to run in a straight line; such individuals need to be the exception, rather than the rule (In the words of a former coach of the Brazilian national soccer team: "Someone has to carry the piano.") But their importance to an organization goes beyond their individual performance; it lies also in their influence as a catalyst on a much broader team—the unusualness of their ideas or approach makes the rest of the team feel a little uncomfortable, off balance. Unstable, even. (To this extent each team leader needs to be a minicomputer, managing the effects of instability on the rest of the team.) This seems important in Challenger organizations not simply for what such people can achieve on their own, but what deliberately diverse pairings can achieve as a team: It is the way such organizations puts people together as much as the individual recruitment policy that is going to make the difference. It is in planting catalysts that you will make the difference: people who not just have ideas themselves, but who can collide with other people. John Cleese has remarked that it is a basic biological principle that it takes two different things to create new life; two males can have sex and two females can have sex, but only from a male and a female does resultant new life come. Nicholas Negroponte of MIT is a little more erudite: "New ideas do not necessarily live within the borders of existing intellectual domains. In fact they are most often at the edges and in curious intersections."[4] MIT's consequent policy of putting different disciplines together in a project team—creating "curious intersections"—to enhance the possibility of breakthrough is echoed in Gerry Hirschberg's systematic use of what he calls "creative abrasion" at Nissan's Design Institute, putting together two people who see the world in very different ways—an eyeglass designer paired with someone born and bred at somewhere more conventional like Ford. (Indeed, this is close to the organizational structure we began to discuss at the end of the second credo, where we looked at the need to have an intelligent collision between knowledge of the brand on one hand and an innocence about category on the other.)

Those who think this concept of diverse pairings is some new-fashioned management gimmick may find it interesting to reflect on the early days of Montgomery Ward. Aaron Montgomery Ward, in founding the initial mail-order store in 1871 and challenging the rules of conventional retailing by offering the purchase of goods sight unseen (strangely prescient of Dell), soon took up a business partner, George R Thorne. It was said of both of them: "Mr. Ward had the characteristics of a setter dog. That is, he was here, there, and everywhere and saw everything and wanted to buy everything. [Mr. Thorne] had the opposite characteristics. He would never have found anything, but he knew what to do with it when he got it. . . . It is doubtful if either one of them could have successfully conducted the business alone, but together their success was great."[5]

The outcome of such differences, then, is not teamwork in the sense of quiet codependence and silent understanding. It is the collision of ideas (what Negroponte elegantly calls "intersections" are more likely to be shouting matches). It is the job of Challenger management to create such intersections, regularly.

The Three Climates of Ideas

We saw that the first step in moving toward an ideas-centered culture is the redirection and motivation of the individual. The second is the way those individuals are combined with catalysts. The third step in creating an ideas-centred culture is in creating the right climate for ideas to flourish. Bill Bernbach's famous dictum that "Creative is not a department" means, surely, two things; first, that a good idea can come from anywhere and second, that ideas are fragile things. It is everybody's job in an organization certainly to generate them, but also to help good ideas flower.

This kind of environment does not occur naturally. Three climates are central to allowing this to happen: a climate of recognition, a climate of growth, and a climate of decision.

A Climate of Recognition

As we will see later, the ability to anticipate the consumer is crucial, not just because such anticipation allows the challenger to be faster to market, but because having a strong sense *now* of the way our target thinks and behaves is fundamental to the confident recognition of a good idea, or the germ of a good idea, when it comes along.

The second essential to a healthy climate of recognition is to ensure that all the core-team members recognize ideas in the same way—that is, begin the process with the same fundamental preconceptions as to what will be the benchmarks for a successful outcome. What is fatal to the process is discovering the underlying differences between the team when you come to the execution of the strategy.

Suppose, for example, you are engaged in developing innovative packaging. The brief goes in, the packaging agency goes away, returning six weeks later with what they believe to be a great idea. They present it. It is received with enormous excitement among two members of your group. Terrific idea, they exclaim—entirely unlike anything else in the category.

But wait. What's this? There is a second group around the table who seem to regard this exact same packaging as the antichrist. They agree that it is unlike anything else in the category, and that is why they are so appalled; that is precisely, they counter, why no category consumer will recognize the product for what it is.

But you have to admire its single-mindedness, the first group persists; it really stands out.

The others shake their heads: the first group has played right into their hands. It is, of course, only telling half the story, they point out;

there are two other basic messages fundamental to the positioning that have been excluded altogether.

And so it goes on: The discussion of the execution serves only to illustrate that nobody has discussed the real implications of the brief. Time is wasted, motivation dampened, a possible idea lost; all criminal in a Challenger organization. Instead, common understanding must be reached as to underlying assumptions of each member of the team *at the outset of each project,* framing what would and would not constitute a successful outcome to the brief. Openmindedness is to be encouraged: It is frequently useful to devote a day right at the beginning of each major initiative in which one's prejudices about the category and what it demands are challenged and opened by reference to categories other than our own. This will be one of the functions of some of the exercises in the Two-Day Off-site.

A Climate of Growth

We have to recognize the rarity of a strong idea. And its survival is frequently as vulnerable as its occurrence is rare; insights and ideas are fragile things—as fragile as the egos of those that produce them and are threatened by them.

The key decision maker is therefore critical; besides setting the demand for an idea-centered culture, and having a strong sense of the consumer in order to be able to recognize the germ of a good idea when it is first seen, the decision maker also has to be closely involved in the process to champion and protect them as they grow. Skunkworks fostered ideas through Management by Walking Around (MBWA)—not so that their people would feel more cared for and connected through MBWA, but because they believed that in order for good ideas to have the best chance of survival and growth, management had to be there "When Stuff Happens." Rather than adopting a Darwinian perspective of survival of the fittest, they took the view that ideas frequently die for the wrong reasons (their real application not being recognized by their creators, for instance) rather than the right reasons (they are weak ideas), and that the senior players needed to be continually and randomly present among the idea creators to identify and hothouse the seedling ideas when they are first seen. If they were sitting in an office three blocks away when stuff happens, stuff may not happen for very long. And after a while stuff stops happening altogether, and you've suddenly lost your idea culture.

Growth doesn't only mean protection, of course. It also means demanding more, pushing back, seeing how far one can ride on an idea as it gathers strength: encouraging the team to "push it until it breaks."

A Climate of Decision

In most companies ideas—be they marketing, design, advertising, or new product ideas—are usually presented up through the ranks first, in order to make the individual layers of the organization feel involved and a contributory part of the marketing process. Each individual regards it as their job to add value, and they interpret this as meaning to suggest change. By the time the idea has reached the key decision maker, it may well have been significantly reshaped by prolonged bursts of friendly fire.

This is insanity for a Challenger. The only conclusion one can draw in a situation like this is that the company does *not* regard ideas as one of the most important tools at their disposal. When one looks at the other two or three key decisions a company makes over the course of a two- or three-year period (the frequent life span of an advertising campaign or pack design), very different rules are followed. Does this process happen to the financial plan, for instance? To the choice of Chief Executive? To the speech to the shareholders?

I think not. These are all rightly regarded as critical issues, too important to be left to junior caprice or inexperience. The production of ideas in whatever sphere must be given the same respect; the most senior skill must be involved at every stage. (This is not to say, incidently, that less experienced marketeers cannot come up with ideas; just that they are not always the best people to judge what should and should not be brought to life.)

Ideas that the key decision maker does not naturally come across by "being there when stuff happens" should be exposed early and relatively undiluted. In young Challenger companies, this occurs naturally because the early structure of the company is so flat; the founder or founders are therefore in a position to recognize ideas because there is frequently a founder involved in the idea-generation process itself. In a larger multi-national company, where there are layers and a hierarchy, ideas should be the one decision given passports instantly to the very top.

The Role of the Consumer in a Challenger Company

But before jumping into ideas and how we build their production into the fabric of our company, let us pause to look harder at what we are apparently moving away from; we have been told for so many years that we need to be consumer-centered that some will find the whole notion of this chapter rather unsettling. If we are talking of moving to an idea-centered company, after all, then what exactly is the role of the consumer?

We are not discarding consumer understanding as unimportant; we are recognizing instead that *consumer understanding in and of itself rarely creates dynamism within a company or for a brand*. While there are occasional exceptions to this, which are touched on below, the consumer cannot, generally speaking, be the driving force behind a Challenger company. Consumer understanding has instead to be a template or springboard for a driving force that *does* create dynamism—that driving force being an ideas-centered culture.

Talking about consumer understanding in this way will polarize readers. Some, on the one hand, will find it a difficult concept to embrace fully, given how much weight has been attached in the past to analysis of the consumer or the competition (think simply of the enormous influence of just three authors: Peter Drucker, Michael Porter, and Kenichi Ohmae). These readers will point to the tremendous advantages that companies like Tesco, Saturn, or Daewoo U.K. have enjoyed by making themselves innocent again, simply by listening more openly to what the consumer really wanted. To dismiss the consumer as having no role to play in shaping the future of all markets is, then, in the eyes of this group, surely a little premature.

Other readers, on the other hand, will cheerfully go much further than I have in dismissing exploration of what the consumers say they want or need: it has become fashionable to say that strong businesses are no longer being led by the consumer, and that one has instead to lead

Figure 12.1 **The three categories**

	Diseased	Contemporary	Unimagined
Example	Automotive, cellular providers	Pasta sauce	Gaming software
Advantage driver	Consumer-led	Idea-centered	Idea-led
Role of research	Can ask, can get answers	Can't ask, can get answers	Can't ask, can't get answers
Core task	Make the familiar desirable	Make the familiar novel	Make the novel familiar

the consumer oneself—as if this were a blanket truth for all categories and all business opportunities. Look at the Sony Walkman, this school will tell you; look at hi-tech. The consumer could never have conceived of a need for such things until someone created them and led the market. Build it and they will come.

One can certainly understand the appeal of this latter way of thinking: In particular, it must come as some relief for all those companies who have yet to drive the concept of being consumer-led lower than the corporate mission statement. ("Hey, the pressure's off, you guys; this book I've been reading says we've missed the boat anyway.") For the admirers of this school of thought, the customer has gone from being king (or queen) to being like the child ruler who has inherited the throne too young to know what he or she really wants, requiring us instead to appoint ourselves regent on their behalf and paternalistically instruct them in what they really need.

But this school of thinking, too, is an oversimplification, manifestly true of some brands and businesses and manifestly untrue of others. Instead, we need to group the categories we work in and market into three types: Diseased, Contemporary, and Unimagined (see Figure 12.1).

In *Diseased* industries there is still an advantage to be gained by simply listening to the consumer. Automotive retailing is perhaps the most well trodden example; manufacturers have little control over their dealers and so are unable to implement what the consumer really wants out of the shopping process except at the luxury end of the market. But disease is not necessarily synonymous with age or anachronism: Some of the newest industries find themselves in this category. Cellular airtime providers, for instance, are a regulated category in which most of the existing players are deriving such high-penetration gains from the natural market growth that there has been, until relatively recently, little further incentive to develop the brand around what the consumer really wants. Computer companies for their part still seem to fail to understand the level of simplicity needing to be built into a computer that would allow a consumer to feel comfortable setting up a personal computer at home.

In Diseased categories everyone who is prepared to ask their consumer the right questions knows what the disease is. The advantage will go to the first one who takes the leap and cures the disease for the consumer; the rest of the market will watch and follow when the flow of business forces them to. In cellular, for instance, every provider knew the consumer resented the rounding of minutes whereby they were not charged the amount of time they actually spoke but that time rounded up to the nearest minute; the advantage went to the first provider who marketed themselves around changing that (such as Orange in the United Kingdom). Virgin Direct is marketing itself on the understanding that people would like some plain talk and adult-to-adult conversations from a financial institution, instead of being patronized or confused by them.

In this category, then, the opportunity for a Challenger is to make the familiar desirable to the consumer: at the very least to alleviate symptoms of the disease and preferably to offer a cure. In this category a close working partnership with the consumer can still be a source of competitive advantage, provided that the understanding is translated into ideas that evidence action. Consumers are long past being engaged by sympathy alone.

In *Contemporary* categories the consumer is apparently content (or bored) with the development of the category (no consumer in the world, for example, is waiting for the next innovation in tire tread design). They do not want to, nor can they, imagine the next jump in category innovation (fast-food companies are experimenting with electronic ways of ordering food developed in conjunction with video-game manufacturers; this is not something that one would expect to be volunteered in focus groups). There may be some basic consumer-suggested temporary advantages still to be gained, but for the most part these are overfished waters: Most of the opportunities within the existing category framework have been exhausted, and consumers themselves may be too close to the category to perceive spontaneously any that are still outstanding. An example of this kind of situation might be the kettle market. If you ask European consumers in groups what kinds of kettle they like, they will respond quickly and strongly to white or stainless steel products. This corresponds to a perception of kettles rooted in turn-of-the-century concerns about kitchen hygiene, when kettles were required primarily to be efficient, pristine tools. Yet in a more sensual era today, where the kitchen is a more focal part of the pleasure of a home, where the pleasure of food is more encouraged and celebrated, the emotional role of the kettle may also have changed without our noticing—being used, for instance, to make something as seductive to the senses as coffee. Designers of the new range of Alessi kettles are accordingly attempting to challenge conceptions of the Victorian functionality of a kettle; through multicolored bodies and decorative spouts they are attempting to celebrate the sensual pleasure of the modern kitchen rather than the cleanliness of one's grandmother's.

In this central category, then, we tend to find that asking direct questions of the mass consumer simply yields table stakes. This may not necessarily trouble the brand leader, for if one has the muscle of a Procter & Gamble, one can invent the next development ("wings," for instance) and bulldoze its importance into the consumer's mind. But as a Challenger we do not have that muscle or that power: We need to find new ground to engage the consumer on, but it needs to be ground that readily excites their interest, even if they did not volunteer it when we asked them. This might come, for instance, from cross-fertilization: taking a breakthrough in another category and applying it to our own. Leadership in these categories will come from redefining the category to our own advantage by learning from *other* categories; the consumer may be able to tell us usefully what they like about these other categories but may not be able to translate one directly into the other.

Useful conversations with the consumer here will consequently be highly diagnostic, exploratory, and interpretative. While consumers may not be able to volunteer what they would like to see as the next development in the category, their reaction or response can offer valuable direction, and indeed, there may still be opportunities for the Challenger

inclined to try less well trodden ways of exploring the relationship between brand and consumer, in the hope that they might offer up fresh
ground (see the discussion of the "Rashomon"-style approach in Chapter 10, for instance).

At the same time, using some of the exercises which will emerge from
the discussion of the previous seven credos, and which are put together
in the off-site, we would to try to develop new ideas that initially perhaps
only leading-edge consumers might appear to envisage or respond favor-
ably to. The use of supergroups—small panels of respondents to whom
one talks regularly and thus become artificially advanced in their ability
to talk and think about the market, might be another useful framework
for consumer feedback in this situation.

The desired endgame for a Challenger in this category, then, is the
creation of an idea that makes the familiar novel, fresh, and provocative,
and thereby assume thought leadership of the category.

The third set of categories, *Unimagined* categories, are those in which
the consumers are not even in a position to imagine conceptually what
they want, or even react to breakthrough ideas in concept form. They
need to experience them and sometimes live with them before their appeal can be gauged. Examples of such categories might be hi-tech companies (U.S. Robotics Pilot), content-driven entertainment categories
(gaming software, television programming), or new experience-driven
retail environments (Starbucks, the Rainforest Cafe).

Howard Schultz, for instance, did not develop the idea behind the
growth of Starbucks by percolating it through a succession of focus
groups. It was from walking the streets of Verona that he came up with
the idea of fusing the devotion to the brewing of quality coffee he found
in the original Starbucks in Seattle with the more passionate and sophisticated atmosphere that the shared drinking of coffee seemed to
arouse in the Italian coffee houses. And then he created a store where
this marriage invented a whole new category. The jazz, the exotic vocabulary, the concept of baristas were born from the head of Schultz, not
the consumer, fusing further the apparently disparate cultures of the Italian streets and the U.S. lifestyle.

It is this leap that makes Unimagined categories the hardest to
compete in: hard in the sense that decision making takes place without

any real recourse to reassurance from the consumer, and hard in the emotional vision and tenacity of belief that the concomitant risk taking demands. Here the marketing challenge, after all, is to root a brand/product that the consumer does not yet think they need, to make the novel familiar. One has no alternative, when attempting to compete in or build one of these categories, but to try new ideas and see.

What one can build on one's side, however, is the power to anticipate.

Anticipate or Die

The management consultants Booz, Allen & Hamilton have benchmarked the use of consumer research across differing marketing and management cultures.[6] They identified three kinds of research in use across companies:

1. **"Monitoring" Research** This is, typically, quantitative research such as a Usage and Attitude study—where the marketeer defines the questions to be asked and requires the consumer to answer them from a coded choice of possible responses. This kind of research is characteristically intermittent—perhaps once every three or four years—commissioned to outside experts, and reported back to senior management through a topline report.

2. **"Interactive" Research** This tends to be qualitative research, usually consisting in exploring proposed answers to identified problems. Stimulus is put in front of the target (a new product, piece of packaging or advertising, for example), and the consumer is asked to respond to it. Less structured and more open ended than Monitoring, it also allows for the consumer to contribute more spontaneously, albeit around a specified topic guide.

3. **"Looking Out" Research** This is research where the consumer sets the agenda. Essentially open-ended research around the issues on the consumer's mind, it can be qualitative, observational research, or ethnography and tends to be more frequently carried out (perhaps every week), with senior management more actively involved.

Booz, Allen & Hamilton found two very different philosophies toward research and the use of the consumer in the companies they benchmarked in this exercise. Large packaged goods companies like Procter & Gamble or Unilever, usually having a predetermined model of strategic development in any market, tended to favor the first two kinds of research. They defined the questions and looked for a statistically significant body of answers to help them make key decisions along the strategic and creative path. (Implicit in this approach is the view that the role of marketing is to respond to established needs.)

On the other hand, the management consultancy also found a second group of more innovative, entrepreneurial cultures, such as BMW, Nike, and Pepsi, who used research in a significantly different way. Among this group, the purpose of the research was not so much to validate decisions as to find insight. To that purpose, they focused more on the second two types of research—less statistically significant but more open-ended interactions—where they let the consumer define the questions and allowed the conversation to be more unstructured and interactive. Research would take the form of a more unstructured, regular dialogue—perhaps every week—with the management of the company actively involved. Nike, for instance, has regular away days with their athletes to keep current with the evolving desires and frustrations of sporting competition at the highest level; the U.K. retailer Tesco has Friday evening in-store meetings where the consumer sets the agenda, attended by some of the most senior players in the organization.

The objective here is less to do with taking decisions and more to do with management getting smarter. In regular dialogue where the consumer sets the agenda, management builds a better sense of the new ripples in the surface, the new trends that are beginning to emerge, and above all, develops the ability to *anticipate* how the consumer would react rather than asking them to respond or judge. Overall, the effect is of building management's confidence in itself to take decisions faster, and in a more entrepreneurial manner, because it is continually allowing the consumers to speak what is on their minds. And in doing so, it sharpens the decision maker's ability to respond to an idea—to recognize a good one when you see it—wherever it comes from.

For a Challenger working in a Contemporary or Unimagined category, then, this describes well the relationship needed between the core team and the consumer: a very strong (and by that I mean both current and profound) *feel* for the consumer in one's stomach, achieved primarily through personal involvement in diagnostic research that replicates people's lives as much as possible, and which is going to be more value in high-speed markets than large quantitative studies in themselves. The decision-maker and the team need a well-informed hypothesis about the consumer, and a firsthand, visceral knowledge of who and how they are needs to be the central filter, a measuring stick against which ideas are judged and assessed. The consumer should be someone we know as well as our own partners.

An anecdote: The Parisian shoe designer Rodolphe Menudier, before designing a collection, puts himself in the life of the consumer by physically dressing *his own flat* the way he thinks *they* live—to the extent of having two supermarket trolleys in his Right Bank apartment stuffed with the imagined personal objects of the target of his next collection. "When I design a collection," he says, "I first imagine where the person who will wear these shoes might live—the environment, the climate, the objects, the style. That's how I inadvertently filled and decorated our apartment. Each season I subconsciously look for objects or furniture that might be used for inspiration, and they always end up in the apartment. So everything we have is somehow related to the shoes."[7]

Now there's an idea for a Challenger marketeer.

Leading an Unstable Organization

What, then, can we learn about leadership from all of this? Understanding the need for a Challenger program on which to run the company and understanding conceptually the eight credos is one thing; leading it on a day-to-day basis, actually being the "computer in the nose" is altogether another. The evidence we have seen so far would suggest that strong leadership of a Challenger company and a Challenger culture lies in the following:

- Having a clear sense of identity, or the journey toward the identity, and focusing the company's every action on that.

- A personal and direct involvement in the selection of people—and in particular to look for the characteristics that cannot be taught: passion, raw talent, the ability to be a catalyst.
- The putting together of those people in pairings or groups most likely to yield fresh thinking, and a continual stream of initiatives and ideas.
- Managing the resultant instability, both personally and through putting together a "computer" or "garage."
- Stripping out vertical layers to allow those ideas to come to the surface rapidly and often.
- Being continually and randomly present at the inception of those ideas oneself (being there "when stuff happens").
- Creating an idea climate for others.
- Creating in oneself the ability to anticipate the consumer, thus allowing recognition of strong ideas as one encounters them and the confidence to rapidly act on them as they arrive.
- Implementing the Challenger program.

Finally, leadership in a Challenger company is about instilling a sense of drama. Remember Jobs's war cry in the corridors of Apple in 1983/1984—that MacIntosh had only 100 days to make it. He galvanized change; he made the internal rocket leave the ground.

Change versus Challenge

The most conservative estimates of the failure of Change programs in organizations is 50%. And this is, surely, exactly that—extremely conservative; personal experience would suggest a much higher figure. Over a five-year career spell at any one company, an individual will hear three to five "State of the Nation" addresses, each promising a renewal of commitment and ideology (and a recommitment to the people, who are, the person on the podium assures us, the company's "real assets").

The positive effect of such speeches on their audience rarely lasts out the afternoon, but the cumulative cost of such failure, conversely, is intangible and immense. It lies not simply in the loss of credibility of the leaders involved, but in the growth of a corrosive cynicism about (and resistance to) organizational change in the future, even if the need for such a change becomes generally recognized as becoming more and more necessary within the company.

The reason for this corrosive failure lies, I would suggest, within the core concept of Change itself. It is fundamentally flawed, and its flaw is this: It has no implicit direction. It is a means, not an end. When we read in the *Harvard Business Review* about "Change and the Change-dazed manage," that daze has surely occurred *precisely because* change per se is not a good thing. Change is alarming, because it has no built-in end point to aim for and measure ourselves against. We're not expecting a detailed road map when we begin the journey, but a compass for everyone at the least would be useful.

So Challenge is not just a powerful conceptual framework for external, consumer marketing, but perhaps the internal journey as well. We must substitute for "Change" the idea of "Challenge" internally as well as externally, because the concept of Challenge inherently provides the compass we need. Challenge, unlike Change, focuses and directs, because it has a defining goal built into it, a central motivating objective, a Big Fish to eat—or it cannot be a Challenge.

This in turn makes the means relatively simple—even self-defining. Understanding the central challenge prescribes the consequent action in any given task—even if management has not spelled it out. In other words, even if I as an unbriefed staffer have no specific instructions of what to do, I can work out, based on my understanding of the common challenge, what course of action to take.

We might summarize the difference between the two as follows:

Change	Challenge
A process	A task
Means-oriented	Goal-oriented
Without focus	Focused
Requiring explanation	Self-explanatory
Many-headed	Single-minded
Rational	Emotional
Confusing/daunting	Rallying
Complex measure	Single measure

Martin Taylor of Barclays Bank reckons that every really strong business is simple—to the point where it could be understood by a five year old. The same needs to hold even more true of a business in flux or transition; and the Challenge, and how the company is going to meet that Challenge, needs to be very simply defined.

What It Means to Move to Being an Idea-Centered Company: Final Thoughts

Brands find it hard to sustain momentum; Challengers are no exception. Looking at the Challengers that have maintained that momentum for long periods of time suggests that for most Challengers, sustaining momentum lies in moving from being a consumer-led to an ideas-led culture. Even though there are still Diseased categories where the consumer is vocally dissatisfied with the current competitive offering, what brands like Tesco demonstrate is that continued success in these categories comes not from understanding the consumer, far less from just showing you understand the consumer. It comes from the consistent deployment of ideas that renew and refresh the relationship of the consumer with the brand. Not innovations—ideas. One final example will demonstrate the scale of the change in mindset this requires.

There is much talk about "support" for a brand in marketing terms. This is usually taken to mean the level of advertising or promotional expenditure that is spent against the consumer on the brand's behalf over a given year. Studies have been done that look at the effect on a brand when this support is withdrawn or drastically reduced; the findings suggest that brands decay logarithmically—short term, they hold up, and then after about a year begin to decline at an accelerating rate.

If one applied Paul Romer's theory to marketing, however, it would suggest that we reframe the whole definition of "support" for a Challenger brand from money to ideas. These ideas would clearly have to be supported by money, but the thinking within the company would not just be in terms of adequate support as meaning adequate financial allocation to the marketing budget, but in terms of an adequate investment in, and bringing to market of, ideas that will keep the brand buoyant and vital. This is an investment not just of money, but of time, working culture, personal habits, and people.

This would not, then, just be a question of a Challenger creating a new stand-alone function, having an Ideas Department or vice president of Ideas in the same way that a brand leader treats new product development. While that would indeed be an interesting place to start, meaning at the very least that the company recognized the importance of the issue and had committed to addressing it systematically, it still wouldn't go far enough: The fundamental orientation, the center of the company, has to change. If ideas are the fuel for a Challenger's growth, and the company has to give primacy to ideas and creative thinking, then the center of gravity of the company must move from being a consumer-centered (or analysis-centered) company to an ideas-centered one. Rather than just creating a new title or department, the creation and application of ideas must replace the consumer at the very center of a Challenger company, and all the structures, processes, and disciplines that flow out of that. The consumer will remain a crucial anticipatory filter but cannot be the driving force itself.

For to run dry of ideas is to begin to lose momentum. As with the studies showing that brands can stand the withdrawal of marketing support for a year or so, and then start to decay, so it is with Challenger momentum and ideas; by the time one starts to notice momentum is slipping, it may be too late to regain it (as, for instance, Saturn's failure to push fresh thinking about the car category over the last three years or so has failed to build on the extraordinary surge its initial wealth of ideas gave). The solution is to create continual abundance: to become an ideas culture. This is the only way a Challenger company can derive and deliver Mechanical Advantage—the consistent creation of a greater return from the same or smaller input.

13

The Relationship Between the Eight Credos

I said at the outset of the book that, having established the nature of the Eight Credos, I would attempt to turn them into the beginnings of a process that we could apply to ourselves. I noted that, although this constituted an enormous postrationalization, in the sense that none of the Challengers discussed *as individuals* had ever formally put themselves through such a process, I was interested in formalizing a way for us to try to follow in the steps of their *collective* marketing intuition. This process follows in more detail in Chapter 15, after we have looked more closely at the ambitions a Challenger should set themselves, and at the cultural nature of a Challenger company. But first, some thoughts from reviewing the Eight Credos together.

Being a Challenger is not a series of actions in and of themselves. It is a mind-set, a way of seeing the world, manifested in those actions. As a mind-set it is innate or emotionally held and committed to: hence the use of the word "credo," as a representation of almost religious faith. While your sense of *what* you have to sacrifice may change, the belief that you have to sacrifice at all cannot.

Reflecting this mind-set, the Eight Credos clearly do not operate in isolation of each other; we will in fact later turn them into a sequence, a four-stage strategic marketing process. In this process, decisions or actions taken in one credo are necessarily reflected or dramatized in another—the first seven credos in particular must all center around the one or two central priorities and actions for the brand. The practice rather than the theory of this has been immediately apparent in the overlap in brand examples used between the chapters so far: The conventions of the category broken will often be used as symbols of reevaluation for the brand, and if the target for this reevaluation is external, they will in turn be expressed through dramatic advertising or a publicity-generating event.

Furthermore, although the credos between them certainly have huge implications for marketing strategy, it is clear that marketing strategy is just one strand in the Challenger Marketing Triad:

1. Attitude and Preparation.
2. Marketing Strategy.
3. Marketing Behavior.

Marketing Behavior is a way of thinking about the expression of one's identity and positioning to the consumer that goes far beyond what has historically been regarded as the template of the marketeer's activity, namely, the Four Ps (Positioning, Product, Promotion, and Price). And the Attitude and Preparation has been necessary not only to open the mind, to reengender innocence, but also to drive marketing strategy into behavior; one of the greatest failings of the marketing company is incompletion. Lee Clow, when asked by a client how he could get breakthrough thinking from his agency, replied: "You have to want it." Incompletion usually occurs because there has been no mental preparation: Those involved do not "want it" badly enough.

So there is in fact a structural (rather than a necessarily chronological) relationship between the Eight Credos.

Not all Challengers fit all Eight Credos, of course: Some have never advertised, for example; Absolut has never offered any dramatic symbols of reevaluation. This is an important counter, because the way to test a hypothesis is after all not to try to prove it, but to try to *disprove* it.

The response to this falls into two parts. The first is that in drawing on so many different Challengers it would be startling to see an absolute uniformity of plan: It is more likely that we would see a fit that usefully describes the majority of them, much like a piece of regression analysis maps a fit of a series of points of data to a line of commonality. Some examples will fall on either side of the overall pattern here or there, but the overall shape and nature of the common thread remains clear.

The second part of the answer is that this book is not supposed to represent an absolute formula to be imposed in blanket fashion with disregard for category, culture, or starting place. It is more usefully viewed as a cluster of activities that, taken together in a structured way, can help overcome a strategic problem or market blind spot that is inhibiting growth.

What is important is that, whatever its application, it is regarded at the very least as a cluster of related activities, rather than an à la carte menu. Because trying to become half a challenger is like trying to become half pregnant—it creates the same amount of mess but is bound to lead to disappointing results.

Paper Tigers: The Dangers of Being Half a Challenger

When Mao Tse Tung wrote "All reactionaries are Paper Tigers," he meant, of course, that there are some who affect to be fierce challengers but who lack the real substance to succeed (being made of paper rather than muscle). In the same way, we cannot cherry pick the two or three most interesting credos, take them for a spin, and sit back to see what happens. In the first place, this sends confusing signals to the external and internal consumer (are we kicking ass and taking names, or not?). In the second, it fails to create a lasting momentum.

Country Life is a magazine for Britain's landed gentry. It has enjoyed a civilized country readership throughout the twentieth century. It has covered social events, country matters, and so on, and was perhaps best characterized each month by a black-and-white portrait of a nice young girl, decked in her finest jewels, who was coming out that year. It was a feature known fondly to its readers as "girls in pearls."

In 1997 the long slow decline in *Country Life's* circulation necessitated renewal; it needed an overhaul if it was to keep pace with a younger target with a taste for something a little snappier.

The editor decided to take the "girls in pearls" and spice it up as a symbol of reevaluation. Instead of a Sloane Ranger portrait in a striped shirt with pearls round her neck, they commissioned John Swannell to shoot a pictorial of naked women with the pearls draped elegantly over their unclad forms. All very tasteful—nothing that would pass muster in *Playboy*—but it caused a sensation. Dame Barbara Cartland, the English romance novelist and a reader of the magazine for some 80 years, was widely quoted by the British press as saying: "It's so very, very sad how everything has become sordid these days. All this business of sex; why can't people just leave it alone and behave like ladies and gentlemen?"

Her reaction was precisely the point. *Country Life* chose to sacrifice some of their dying past in order to gain reappraisal from the target their future depended on. But having created a symbol of reevaluation, they failed to carry through. The magazine today is substantially the same as it was 5, 10, 20 years ago. The promise of the act has not been delivered on. And the sales performance, consequently, has shown no dramatic change.

Ty Nant, the Welsh mineral water brand discussed in Chapter 6, attracted huge attention from the restaurant trade as far from the Welsh vallies as Los Angeles for its cobalt blue bottle. In a world of mineral waters where convention dictated that the stuff inside the bottle was the most important thing—and that one must therefore be able to see it—they had produced a bottle whose deep blue color made the contents invisible. But Ty Nant failed to capitalize on the success of the bottle by giving the contents any legitimacy. Having established momentum through breaking a convention of the category, it had to go one of two ways: either root itself in something more substantial, and define an identity rooted in overperformance or, having identified its core equity to be the bottle, and recognized that the bottle as a fashion, realize it was in the fashion business (rather than the water business) and reinvent itself regularly in line with the rules of the market it found itself in (becoming ideas-centered, using advertising and publicity as a high-leverage asset).

So, while some success can be achieved through following one or two of the credos, benefit derived from being half a Challenger is short-lived at best. It may give you a financially advantageous new place in the brand landscape initially, but it will not sustain growth.

As a final example, put yourself the position of the young woman who was Hugh Grant's girlfriend in 1993. Your partner becomes, overnight, one of the world's most eligible men, Oscar-nominated to boot, on the back of a sleeper called *Four Weddings and a Funeral*. As an aspiring actress, and self-respecting individual, you are increasingly dispirited by the prospect of being forever labeled as "Hugh Grant's girlfriend." What do you do?

What you do is realize that you have to take a world event, when press of the world will have their eyes on your partner, and create a symbol of reevaluation of your own. You arrive clad in a tight Versace dress whose generous side-openings suggest that all you have on underneath is a small quantity of perfume, and whose front is structured in such a way that there is a very real possibility if the cameras dwell on you long enough there may be an accident that will confirm or deny that suspicion. The result? You arrive as Hugh Grant's girlfriend and you wake up the next morning in every newspaper in the Western world as Liz Hurley (a handsome contract from Estee Lauder shortly follows).

The exercise certainly propelled Elizabeth Hurley into the spotlight, but it did not make her a real Challenger because nothing else followed. It gave her the opportunity, had she chosen, to redefine the nature of being a model or fashion muse, but she chose no attempt at further leadership of the category (as Isabella Rosselini, for instance, at one point Lancome's muse, had broken conventions of the modeling category with her more womanly figure, her age, and by refusing to make "perfect" the gap between her teeth). Miss Hurley's other half, of course, the previously squeaky clean Hugh Grant, inadvertently created a symbol of reevaluation of his own in a white BMW one night on Sunset Boulevard. This has yet to be followed by any consistent Challenger behavior either.

What Should a Challenger's Ambitions Be?

"I'm going to upset the whole world."
Muhammed Ali, 1964

While all Challengers are necessarily hungry for growth, the specific goals they have set themselves have been of widely varying levels. Tesco, Warburton's, and New Labour all wanted to be—and became—number one. Virgin Cola, on the other hand, "only" desired to be number two to Coca-Cola, displacing Pepsi-Cola. Southwest has declared it will never fly coast to coast, Oakley sells only seven kinds of frames, and Saturn sells one model of car (albeit in three different forms): Even if they desired it, all of these limitations necessarily preclude a position in even the top three of their category as a realistic goal. Fox for its part, although the fourth-ranked network as a totality, has become the brand leader in *certain audience segments,* ones that are both influential and lucrative to boot. It has also created programming with *The X-Files* and *The Simpsons* that are strong international brands in their own right and can live outside the network's aegis.

So being a Challenger is not necessarily about aspiring to be number one, or even upsetting the whole world. Other objectives are as important, objectives that are to do with the shape of the wave, not the size (it being the shape that will determine whether one can ride it all the way to the beach). But whatever our targets and ambitions within the category in terms of market position, if we use our understanding of the Eight Credos to reframe the underlying conversation, to look instead at the *indicators* of a successful Challenger brand, we can see certain characteristics emerge that may in turn offer important complementary goals for new Challengers to set themselves as they start out. These are not exclusive—they do not touch on such fundamentals as loyalty for instance: They serve instead to highlight some of the additional priorities a Challenger marketeer might wish to overlay on his or her marketing plans.

Vertical and Horizontal Salience

You notice a Challenger, even if you are not shopping the category. It intrudes on your consciousness. It has a disproportionately high awareness. This is important because it has to overcome the quasi-exponential relationship shown in Chapter 1 between general spontaneous awareness and top-of-mind awareness (Figure 1.1). A secondary finding from the same research is of equal importance to us—namely, that there are two types of brands one needs to keep an eye on, which display different kinds of movement. The first type is one whose top-of-mind awareness is less than you would expect given its level of spontaneous awareness (i.e., it falls below the curved line on the graph in Figure 1.1); this is a brand in decline—if it is not losing brand share, it will shortly begin to do so. The second is a brand whose top-of-mind awareness is *greater than you would expect given its level of spontaneous awareness* (i.e., it falls above the curve on the graph). This is a brand that is about to gain share—it has attracted attention and curiosity—and provided that it is not overly niche in its product appeal, it will begin to make inroads into the share of other players in the near future.

This suggests that brand salience is the first indicator of a Challenger or potential Challenger brand. Besides salience being important in itself, there are indications that it is a predictor of immediate trial and growth.

This is the conventional meaning of salience. But there is also a secondary type of salience for Challengers—a social salience: One is aware of a Challenger *being talked about*. It is thus not just salient vertically (i.e., within a single individual's knowledge of brands) but salient horizontally (i.e., *between* individuals). Curiosity, excitement, or even the temporary inability to resolve one's feelings about the identity or position of a Challenger, lead an individual to talk about it with someone else.

A Challenger should be looking to create both personal salience and social salience.

Sensed Momentum

Salience needs to be accompanied by a sense that this brand that they are aware of is a brand that is on the rise, a brand making waves. We can call this *sensed momentum*—a sense by the consumer not simply that the brand exists, but that it is beginning to make waves. It is a brand to watch. (This in turn increases its ability to drive its own salience, of course.)

We have seen that a sense of momentum (among all audiences, not simply the end customer) is almost more important for a Challenger than a sense of mass. Momentum not only captures the early adopters but accelerates adoption by the early majority because they have their eye on it. Look at Virgin in the United Kingdom's financial market, for instance; although currently relatively small in share, it has an unusually high proportion of financial services sector consumers thinking of it as "a brand to watch"—and therefore a high consideration set in terms of next purchase. As a surfing professor from Stanford put it, the shape of the wave is more important than the size in assessing whether it will take you all the way in.

The power of sensed momentum comes not just from a desire by early adopters to be in on something before it becomes big, but a more general belief among the broader audience that if a brand is growing in popularity it is probably good. When conducting a "Brand Vault" exercise (see Chapter 15) with consumers on Nissan, one of the pieces of information the Project Team put up on the walls was a headline from *The Wall Street Journal* that read:

Nissan Overtakes Honda, Threatens Toyota

Namely, that in the United States Nissan had overtaken Honda in sales in 1995 for the first time. This was a considerable shock to the consumer, who had a perception that Honda was vastly bigger than Nissan, and it had a very interesting effect on their perceptions of the brand. It turns out that they did not simply think it was a brand they should start checking out; they immediately thought it must be a better product than they had assumed. The consumer, it seems, feels that you cannot fool all the people all the time: If a lot of people are buying it, there must be something good to it.

The point of this is that sensed momentum can be absolute or relative—I can simply have noticed the brand on the fringe of my consciousness a great deal, or I can discover it has passed a benchmark I respect. Passing a respected benchmark clearly has an additional spin. At a category level, if I tell you that salsa overtook ketchup as the United States' leading condiment in 1996, or that personal computers outsold televisions for the first time in 1995, it makes you reevaluate the future of each of them (and your position relative to both winner and loser). So, too, a brand: If I tell you that a single new credit card now accounts for 20% of all gold Visa applications in Europe, it is difficult to remain entirely uninterested in that brand.

Sensed momentum and social salience can provide some kind of alternative purchase justification for a Challenger purchaser, in that it offers the reassurance of a social acceptability of a different kind to that provided by the brand leader. Whereas the brand leader or Establishment brand can offer the reassurance of an unreproachable choice when called on to justify one's purchase to one's peer group, sensed momentum is one of the few ways in which a Challenger can offer reassurance to the purchaser. Daewoo purchasers in the United Kingdom lacked the reassurance of buying a tried and proven brand; instead, they liked the fact that they were buying a car from a company that *everyone was talking about.*

Become Part of the Cultural Landscape

The Energizer Bunny has been appropriated by many cartoonists in the U.S. press since his birth, most of them political. Ross Perot seems to have been a favorite subject, but even Sadaam Hussein has appeared in the press with ears and a drum, as indeed has an embodiment of the Iran-contra deal. What is more startling, however, is that within a year of the same campaign beginning to run in Russia several years later, the Bunny found himself being used in exactly the same way about Boris Yeltsin in a cartoon in the Russian daily *Izvestia*. The joke made in each country is exactly the same, and the icon used to make the joke is exactly the same—because the Bunny has become very quickly in both countries a by-word for the only relevant category benefit: long-lasting (and this is, we should remind ourselves, a category usually thought of as low interest). Since creating word of mouth has to be a key goal for a Challenger brand, in that it is marketing that propagates itself, you know you have an unmeasurable measure of success when you see your brand being used as a commonly understood reference point in popular culture.

Becoming part of popular culture can be a two-edged sword; if the brand fails to maintain momentum, it can mean becoming part of a *temporary* popular culture. Unless the brand can stay a part of popular culture, this can "freeze dry" a brand, where is becomes associated forever with a particular time and place. So, for example, Laura Ashley's floral print clothing seems now almost anachronistic, regardless of the style in which it is cut. The founder's vision for the brand, that it was for women who wanted to feel "sweet," found considerable public favor during a certain period 20 years ago, when a certain faux naïveté was fashionable, and the brand became an icon of a sort. But failure to evolve has

seen it consigned not to the popular landscape, but the landscape of social history, and as such, a clothing brand perceived fit only for children
and ingenues.

Intensity of Identification

For Challengers, the relative strength of identification among the user
base is particularly important. For a Challenger, then, while the *size* of
the user group clearly has some importance, given the requirements of
payback and maintenance of distribution, a principal object should also
be the *shape* of the group in terms of their strength of attachment. We
want strong identification, stronger preference for brand and product,
top box scores. Weak preference will not give us the growth we need. We
will want to build such measures into our Tracking study.

Vibrancy

A further measure of a Challenger brand enjoying momentum is the apparently simple one of *vibrancy*—the degree to which, once they are
aware of it, it resonates within the consumers' imagination. It can be
measured, very simply, in terms of the quantity and variety of imagery or
attributes consumers spontaneously offer when asked about the brand. If
they come to a stumbling halt after two words, the brand is commoditiz-
ing, niche, or dead. If, conversely, even though they are not users, they
are able to talk with interest, variety, and length about our brand, then
we have another indicator that we may be making a brand capable of
taking on the brand leader.[1]

Effect on the Rest of the Market

Later in their lives, an indicator of success is the degree to which Challengers redefine the rules of the market for the other players. Later in
their lives, Challenger brands leave a wake—they open up markets for
others to follow. When Fox launched, for example, it was only the second time in 50 years that a fourth network had been attempted in the

United States (1946–1955 saw the ill-fated attempt by the Allen B. Dumont Laboratories). Now, of course, everyone wants in.

This is not something we want to create, but it will be to our benefit if it occurs—changing the rules of the category in their favor forever. Lexus redefined the price point of a luxury car, and Mercedes soon followed. The superiority of Virgin Atlantic's entertainment offering forced British Airways (and the rest of the transatlantic airline business) to radically overhaul its entertainment offering.

PART **III**

Using the Challenger Strategic Program

14

Challenger as a State of Mind: Staying Number One Means Thinking Like a Number Two

"The day we think we've got it made, that's the day we'd better start worrying about going out of business."

Rich Teerlink, President, CEO, Harley-Davidson[1]

The Broader Relevance

The premise so far has been that Challengers need their own models of strategy and behavior; that we are entirely unlike the brand leader in position and resource and, consequently, need to find an entirely different set of rules of engagement.

It is possible, however, that certain other kinds of brands in certain other kinds of situations may also find the Challenger model of value. While the focus of this book is naturally on Challengers themselves, this chapter will briefly dwell on two other applications of Challenger thinking: brands facing a kind of "Big Fish" other than a larger competitive player, and Brand Leaders.

233

What Is The Big Fish?

The premise throughout the first seven credos was that The Big Fish was the brand leader. In fact, as the eighth credo started to indicate, The Big Fish is in fact *the central issue* facing the growth, transformation, or survival of any given brand: the one critical point of focus that needs to be identified before any useful strategic conversation can be had. Insofar as there are six basic marketing challenges that marketeers can find themselves up against, a larger competitive player only represents one of these threats, although it is usually the most compelling one for a Challenger brand.

The six basic marketing challenges in total are:

1.   A Brand threatened by the superior competitive position or overt aggression of a larger, better placed competitor (for example, Pepsi or Virgin Atlantic).

2.   An Established Brand facing a situation where the social context or popular opinion has moved against it. (Examples of social context moving against it would be, for instance, whiskey in a white spirit world, high-fat products such as cheese in a low-fat world, or fur. An example of a brand where popular opinion has moved against it might be Laura Ashley, or a utility with negative equity, such as a gas or telephone provider, which the consumer perceives to hold a monopolistic grip on the market.)

3.   A Brand in a category where the rules of that category are capable of constant and rapid change, or are about to rapidly change. (Examples of this kind of challenge might include certain hi-tech markets such as computers, and the newer branches of telecommunications, together with certain youth-orientated fashion or entertainment categories such as video games. We might also include brands facing the consumer and business implications of a recession here.)

4.   A Brand threatened with new kinds of competition. (For example, Kodak, an analog company, facing competition from digital technology. Other examples might include traditional leisure shoe manufacturers coming to terms with the explosion of the sport sneaker, or the U.K. gas retailers losing share to the multiple grocers.)

5.   A Brand faced with a declining retail role for traditional brands, either through category commoditization (i.e., consumer indifference) or aggressive pursuit of private label by the retailer.

6.   A Brand whose apparent dominance has caused it to relax.

These are, strictly speaking, brands with challenges, rather than Challenger brands, at a key transitional moment in their lives. As such, though, they may need to consider some or all of thinking and behavior normally associated with a Challenger (for instance, Assuming Thought Leadership, or Creating Symbols of Reevaluation) for defensive as much as offensive reasons: that is to say that the instant goal may be as much about staying in the game, neutralizing the single dominant threat, as generating rapid growth. In the new marketing era, the Challenger brand—and the underlying strategic approach it embodies—may in fact prove an infinitely more powerful, and more far reaching, model than the historical model of the Brand Leader.

Brand Leaders and the Big Fish

The confidence, the arrogance of the brand leader, walking the market-place as if there was no other, no longer applies. Today, to stay Number One you have to think like a Number Two. While the purpose of this book is not primarily to address the needs of Brand Leaders, this chapter looks briefly at how and why three brands—Nike, Microsoft, and Intel—have redefined what it means to be a brand leader entering the next century, principally because they for many years continued to think and behave like the Challengers they recently were.

If we are the Number One brand, the Big Fish that threatens to eat us is ourselves—our own success. The apparent security and real profitability lent by being number one in the market makes us loss-averse and protec-tive: We cease to behave in the way that made us successful and took our brand to leadership in the first place. Walk tall, the old codes for brand leadership read. Never acknowledge the number two. Be confident.

Yet, until recently, the reason Nike has up to now continued to dom-inate the footwear market is that it reinvents its advertising imagery every year in order to stay ahead; it always surprises. Although now the Establishment Brand in terms of brand share, Nike has until recently continued to act like the hungriest and most subversive brand in the shoe market—and it is through this Challenger state of mind that it has so far resisted the assaults of everyone from Reebok to Adidas. As one example, consider the 1996 Olympics: When Reebok pulled themselves together for the Games, producing advertising that they felt finally matched that of Nike in its celebration of athleticism, Nike in turn produced a campaign that debunked their own historical glossy pictures of triumph: They showed a marathon runner vomiting at the end of a race over his shoes—the icon soiled. Like the perverse appeal the wasted antiheroes of heroin advertising have for its users, these images publicly reinvented what it meant to really understand hard-core athletes. And Nike, the brand that had held up that torch of athletic heroism, was the first one to turn it upside down.

What Does It Mean to Be Brand Leader?
The Three Locations of Challenger Behavior

We talked in the third credo about there being two kinds of brand leaders—the Market Leader and the Thought Leader—and noted that these two were not often the same. We might consider two further distinctions between market leadership and brand leadership. The first is that some market leaders are physically market leaders not through strength of consumer preference but through strength of distribution; other brands in the marketplace may be more strongly preferred on a side-by-side basis but lack the distribution muscle. The beer market is a good example of this: Carling Black Label was long the national brand leader lager in the United Kingdom, while being derided by consumers in the southern half of the country and performing relatively poorly there in branded product tests. To look at the share data, awareness, and even profitability of Carling, all would have seemed well—they were those of a brand leader. Yet it owed leadership to the distribution muscle of its owner, Bass. The key test of leadership is thus not volume per se, but rate of sale per outlet.[2]

The second distinction is that in these days of accelerated category blurring, deregulation, and convergence, where grocery retailers are successfully moving into banking and gas (Sainsbury's), clothes designers selling paint (Ralph Lauren), and music labels putting their name on vodka (Virgin), many market leaders are increasingly *both market leaders and challengers simultaneously.* Calvin Klein is an example of a large masterbrand that nevertheless launches challenger sub-brands within categories: cKone, for example. From the consumer point of view the category isn't, and from the market leader's point of view the less the category "Is," the better. The first definitions of a Challenger in the Preface were thus a little ingenuous—precisely because the category isn't: Most brands in the current world are at once brand leader and challenger; BMW, for instance, is brand leader in sports saloons, but a challenger in the luxury cars.

What does this suggest? That everyone is suddenly a Challenger? Clearly not. But it does suggest four things:

1.   Challenger thinking may have an important role even within companies who at face value appear to be comfortable brand leaders.

2.   A key value of Challenger is, therefore, to think of it as a mindset. This does not mean, as already noted, aggression per se. It means an active dissatisfaction with your existing position, having ambitions that outstrip your current resource, and the preparedness to embrace the marketing implications of that gap.

3.   This in turn suggests that perhaps the most useful way to define and differentiate brands is not so much by market position but by their emotional and mental status: Are they Establishment brands and companies or Challenger brands and companies by nature?

4.   And the fourth implication is surely this: that the volatility and speed of the current business and marketing environment demands that a brand leader needs to think—and even behave—like a number two to remain number one. The old models, the number-one brands and how they sustain brand leadership, may have to be replaced by the model of the number two, the Challenger, *regardless of your position in the marketplace.*

Let us look at the three most influential brands of the last 20 years. Each has come to dominate and define the category they are in, but you will find none of them in the famous chart of unchanging brand leaders. The recency of their becoming brand leader is only matched by the recency of their category. As such, they offer interesting and varying lessons; their drivers—Bill Gates at Microsoft, Andrew Grove at Intel, and Phil Knight at Nike—have between them redefined what it takes to maintain brand leadership. And the reason that they have done so is that each, in one important regard—a "Challenger location," if you like—*still thinks or acts like the number-two he once was*.

Andrew Grove, for instance, is haunted: His lesson is one of *an internal mind-set*. There is much evidence in the life cycle of the Challenger to warn that comfort and protection lead to stagnation; that restlessness is the friend of successful business. Not inconsistency—that's different—but a creative restlessness. Leaders who walk around feeding off ideas like a Pacman, planting catalysts to throw those ideas up. But Grove has taken it to a whole new level: If not actually paranoid, as Grove's famous aphorism instructs us to be, then brand leaders and the people managing them must at least be constantly looking over their shoulder. The first location, therefore, is in our head.

Knight and Gates exemplify a different lesson: that it is important to understand the difference between "onstage" and "behind the scenes" in the way you think and act. And the interesting thing is that they both exemplify the same thing in opposite ways—illustrating the second and third locations of Challenger behavior.

Being Smaller on the Inside Than You Are on the Outside

Gates's lesson is one of internal behavior. Microsoft's consumer success in recent years has come in large part from its perceived critical mass. It is Big; and in a market where compatibility, convenience, and transportability of information are key, the consumer perceives it to be the software "everyone" using a personal computer seems to have—which in turn has meant a standardized adoption by computer and printer manufacturers, and preference among consumers.

Yet while it is important to its success on the outside, Microsoft still place enormous emphasis on thinking small inside. This arises partly from a sense of still being the underdog—it still saw itself as such long after becoming brand leader. And as it expands into certain new markets, of course, it remains the Challenger—against Oracle in databases, Unix in servers, Netscape in browsers.

But it is more than mind-set, for it is actively taken a stage further in terms of the way Microsoft apparently structures its organization relative to the competition: the organization is broken down into units smaller than the competitors each is fighting. They turn themselves into the smaller fish. The team attempting to kill Netscape, for instance, is said to be deliberately designed to be smaller than the Netscape team itself. (Skunkworks, in fact, wrote this idea into its operating principles, believing that to reach breakthrough quickly, "The number of people connected to any Project must be restricted in an almost vicious manner.")

The advantages of the hunger and attitude this engenders are further streamlined by the company's internal structure. On one side they reorganize individuals from department to department every 12 to 14 months to prevent stagnation; on the other, they centralized at a time when the rest of IT was decentralizing. The result of these two things taken together is that Microsoft flies unstable, with Gates and Bauman acting as the computer in the nose; through e-mail, they are able directly to listen to and talk with, almost in live time, the entire workforce of their company. This serves not merely to produce a highly experimental culture, but also the ability of the organization to turn on a dime—most strikingly the celebrated instance in December 1995 when Microsoft changed its entire business strategy in 24 hours. In that famous Damascene moment of clarity, Gates realized he had misunderstood the future power of the Internet. The next day, he e-mailed 24,000 Microsoft employees worldwide, telling them of the nature of the mistake, and giving directional instructions as to how the company was going to put it right. As remarkable as Gates's ability to reformulate and redirect in a day was the ability of the organization to respond quickly—through its small unit size and its familiarity with flux.

Now some large multinationals employ aspects of thinking themselves small in extremis: We saw that the chairman of Unilever, faced with a brand team that has reached a strategic impasse, halves both the manpower and the budget at their disposal and asks them to look at the problem all over again. In doing so, he forces the necessity for sharper thinking and more radical strategic reinvention. But the Microsoft example suggests that a brand leader that seeks to aggressively maintain or even increase its brand leadership (Gates is forever on offense, not defence) needs to build this into the *fabric* of its internal organization, the structure of everything it does. This, then, is the second location of Challenger behavior.

Being Smaller on the Outside Than You Are on the Inside

Phil Knight's lesson, conversely, is one of *external behavior*: how one presents one's outside face to the consumer and being smaller, in one vital dimension, on the outside than he is on the inside. He has been quoted as saying that although in fact Nike is the Goliath of the industry, it will always *behave* like the David.

This is important for Nike because it faces two problems of critical mass—an internal and an external one. Having stepped up the fashion "seasons" it launches in any one year from two to eight, spread across multiple product lines and every major sport, the management of product development, introduction, and sell-in has become an enormously complicated logistical exercise. They have had, as a consequence, to become more process-driven: to cope with its expanded operations Nike runs its internal affairs with the precision of the U.S. Marines.

On the other hand, to cope with the threats of Reebok and Adidas and, more important, the increasing consumer sense that Nike itself is becoming an all-pervasive part of the establishment, the face Nike presents to the outside world is still that of Steve Prefontaine, the hungry talent that defies convention, the ability to startle and surprise. Athletes vomiting on their own shoes.

Being smaller on the outside than one is on the inside allows Nike to balance its persona across each of its key audiences:

- The consumer needs to see Nike if not as number two, at least the anti-establishment brand.
- The trade needs to see Nike as *the* player in the market, the definer and dominator, the "must stock" in all its apparel forms.

- The athletes that choose whose endorsement money to accept need to see Nike as offering more star potential than any other athletic shoe company.

However, for all its brilliance even Nike is now reaching a position where it is so dominant and so all-pervasive, even the most masterful marketing illusions make it hard to disguise its establishment nature.

Summary

Three brands, and their three drivers, have redefined the meaning of brand leadership over the last 20 years. Whereas we used to talk of the confidence of the brand leader, of authority and gravitas, the new brand leaders act in very different ways. They are paranoid, they think of themselves as the underdog, they remain number one as long as they can think like a number two, and they translate this mind-set into the physical structure of who they are and how they behave. Gorilla within, guerilla without (or vice versa), they perpetuate their reign by acting as the Challengers they once were in one or more of three locations of Challenger behavior, even if this means artificially rearranging the fabric of their organization to do so.

15

Writing the Challenger Program: The Two-Day Off-Site

We are moving from a hardware society to a software society. From a business perspective, this means we are moving from companies that succeed through physical product to companies that succeed through the consumer experience they offer. And just as it's not the size of the box that is important anymore, but what the contents of the box do for us, so it's not the amount of people or even the talent of our workforce, but the way they think about the task and the behavior that they adopt that will be the key discriminator in the future. And that has to start with the behavior and example of the core group at the top. The key figures in our company need to run on a Challenger Program. We don't need soldiers; we need apostles.

Architects talk about "programming the building"—working out how the building needs to interact with the people who will be working there. In the same way, since Challenger is not really a series of actions but an underlying way of thinking about the problem, the key will be not you or me "getting" that way of thinking, but programming that core group so that they get it—or rather getting the group to program themselves. Our programming them is not simply a distasteful idea, but it is an impractical, distasteful idea. They have to program themselves; they have to turn themselves into Challengers.

This off-site, then, is about getting a small group of key figures in the company to run a Challenger Program, by getting them to program themselves. Like a piece of software the two-day program (and the much longer strategic process of which it is only a taste) will be improved and updated in two years time; in the spirit of Gillette, development of the replacement ideas must be underway even as the first product is launched.

Preparation

Our Own

First, there must be overcommitment. It may seem obvious, but we, as leaders of this initiative, cannot do an exercise like this as a "toe in the water." It has to be viewed by ourselves and others as a watershed, a catalyst for change in attitude.

One practical reason for wholeheartedly attacking the exercise in this way is that the people you will want to be part of the two days will have other important issues and conflicting priorities coming up; within a week of scheduling there will always be one prospective member of the group who will have one excellent excuse for not being able to attend. We have to decide what we are prepared to demand in order to be assured that everybody will be there, will be a part of the opening of the group's frame of thinking. What kind of example are we prepared to set that will in turn communicate our expectations of the importance of these two days to them?

Second, there is sacrifice. This group will need to be a small one—no more than eight people initially, and preferably four or five. Again, this will send a signal; we need to determine carefully our own personal objectives for the session. Who are going to be the core figures that will really make the difference—in this meeting and, by implication, thereafter? Who will be excluded and what message will that send to them and the world? What will be the public message the fact of this group sends, and how can we make that message as beneficial as possible?

Theirs

They should read at the very least a 10-page outline of *Eating the Big Fish*, preferably the book itself. (A 10-page outline can be requested by contacting eatbigfish@aol.com.) It is important that they each have some basic knowledge of the benefits of looking at case histories outside their own categories before coming to the day.

An optional piece of preparation to consider in addition might be this. Imagine you have replaced your existing board of directors, or VP group; replaced not the people, but their titles and job responsibilities. Instead of VP of Sales, or Marketing, or Finance, or Customer Service, choose a title instead that reflects some of the ideas we have been talking about, as for instance:

VP of Ideas.
VP of Momentum.
VP of Consumer Mythology.
VP of The Big Fish.
VP of Identity.

Give each attendee one of these new titles. Each is required to prepare and report to the group on the performance of the company over the past year with respect to each of these issues. For example, the VP of Ideas might be required to report on the degree to which the company is an idea culture, the three or four most important ideas that emerged last year and how they were developed, the effect of those ideas internally and externally, and so on.

The VP of The Big Fish would have the responsibility of ensuring the company has correctly identified, and is collectively focused on overcoming, the one central issue that poses the greatest challenge to a healthy and growing future for it. This report would focus on whether this was the case last year, whether there was perceived to be explicit agreement on the central challenge, the nature of the Big Fish, and whether the entire company or Marketing Group was putting its individual and collective energies toward meeting that Challenge.

The VP of Momentum would have the responsibility of looking at the actual (sales) and perceived (consumer impression) momentum of the company over the last 5 to 10 years. What had been the contributors at times of greatest acceleration or slowing of each? Each of the other titles can be allocated and described in the same way.

Why is this optional? Because the response to it will depend on the kind of people you invite. You may decide your group is naturally imaginative and will embrace the lateralness required by an exercise of this type. Conversely, you may feel that one of the issues you face is that your group is highly rational in their approach and not imaginative enough yet. In the latter case you may want to withhold such an exercise until some of the effects of the off-site had take place.

Regardless, ask everyone to bring to the meeting *their sense of the Big Fish*: What is the single greatest challenge facing the brand, the company, or the business?

Collectively

On the day, some basic rules of this kind of exploratory thinking will need to be observed:

1. Nobody is allowed to say, "but my category is different." Each has instead to work out what the parallel in their own category would be. How one gets from coffee to cars in the Starbucks study might serve as a reminder for those prone to forget the way this is done.
2. All challenge should be positive ("Interesting idea, but does that go far enough, Cindy?"), rather than negative ("What exactly have you been smoking, Ron?").

Location

Ever since Henry Ford, garages have been the birthplace of many of the most successful companies and Challengers in the world: Hewlett-Packard, Apple, the Clash. Two or three people and a room, hungrily beating an idea into life.[1] Echoing this, the two-day workshop will take place in a "Garage." It will be a relatively intimate room, where the walls to begin with are covered with blank paper—to be gradually filled in as each stage is completed. This room will be away from the office: Besides the symbolism of a new beginning, we will need focused attention.

Over the course of the two days, the purpose is not just to develop a number of different approaches to developing the company, or brand,

and its business. In the spirit of the Garage, it is to create something altogether new; a new company, a new idea for the brand, a new place to start for the future. (You may wish to leave a version of this room, translated back to the office, in existence once the two days are over, to remain your garage or war room, in which the core group can meet and implement the agreements reached after the initial meeting.)

We should note, finally, that these two days are not supposed to be either a "quick fix" or a substitute for a much longer process of marketing and cultural change. Put formally, their objectives may be said to be these:

1. To develop *innovative strategic approaches* that have the potential to radically transform a company's business.
2. To create the beginning of a *new way of seeing the market and its possibilities* for the core marketing, production, and sales team of the company.
3. To help generate a new, more aggressive *attitude* toward business development by and between all those present at the program.

They are intended, in short, to be a *beginning*, an acceleration, the first steps of the journey that a prospective Challenger needs to make. Starting to get the rocket off the ground.

The First Day

Stage One: Attitude and Preparation

At the back end of everything we plan, we will need to drive behavior—completion is a major differentiator between companies. Many companies dream, many companies contain people who come up with potent ideas, but very few companies complete. This is because they never get the attitude right. Beginning to get the attitude right, then, is the first purpose of the Challenger Program. So while this is the stage that people are most inclined to shortchange, it is probably the most important stage of all in the process.

Breaking with the Immediate Past (Credo #1)

Premise: Everything needs to be reconsidered. Every assumption put in play—including the currently valued brand and advertising equities, and rules of the category.

There is an important distinction to be made here between reconsideration and rejection. We are at the beginning of the two days going to Break with Our Immediate Past in order to clear our minds, to be able to see clearly the real challenges, possibilities, and assets in front of us. As the two days pass, some of the values and assets we originally sink may float to the surface again. Others will be replaced. But unless everything is put aside, genuinely, right at the beginning, we will never be able to see the possibilities that present themselves.

Exercise: "Grove"

Fire ourselves. Leave the building and offices we have worked in. Come into our new room as an entirely new team coming in. And not just any new team—let us define our cultural set. We are practical but imaginative entrepreneurs: Branson, Huizenga, Grove. Ambitious and in a hurry.

Imagine that we are looking at everything afresh. Instinctively, what is the first thing that each of us would do with the fresh, realistic, and ambitious eyes of our own successor?

Like the man who gave this exercise its name, we may wish to divide this into two parts. First, identify the one thing we would stop doing (in Grove's case, this was staying in the memory business), and then establish what is the one thing we would do instead (e.g., focus on microprocessors). This is the first phase of Breaking with Our Immediate Past.

The second phase is to write up the five rules of the category on the wall in front of us. Each member of the team then has to give a cogent reason why each individual rule is no longer true.

Third, do the same for our brand. What are the five anchor stones of our marketing strategy? These will probably comprise:

Category definition.
Target definition.
The key brand equities.
Brand promise.
Advertising equities.

Again, ask the team put next to each definition at least one reason why it is no longer relevant. Write this counterpoint on the wall. Remember, at this stage *nothing is to be sacrosanct.* Everything is in play.

What Is Our Big Fish?

Premise: We get too involved in the day-to-day details, become snow-blind to the bigger issues and opportunities. Enmeshed in the logistics and the tactics of how to fight yesterday's targets, we sometimes lose sight of the central issue we have to overcome now, the Big Fish we are up against today.

Exercise: "Big Fish"

This session is about identifying the Big Fish. This will already have occurred (at least implicitly) in the reasoning behind the group's answers during the previous exercise. This session serves to make that more explicit.

The Big Fish can be one of the following:

- A competitive player, in or perhaps currently outside your category (e.g., Kodak and Hewlett-Packard).
- An issue (e.g., the forthcoming ban on cigarette advertising).
- A trend (e.g., Low fat).
- A technological breakthrough (e.g., digital, the Web).
- Ourselves (e.g., attitude, conservatism, structure).

Even if it seems that the team has already arrived at the answer, the group should go through each of these, identifying the central threat in each area (bear in mind they were asked to do a form of this exercise before they came). Once all five areas have been discussed, agree on The Big Fish.

Write it on a central chart that dominates the room. (Remember, Clinton's war room in his election campaign was dominated by the words "It's the economy, stupid.") You may find as you progress through the two days that your collective view of the Big Fish changes, but the group always needs to have a commonly agreed upon, primary challenge in front of them. And the nature of that challenge always needs to be a dominant presence in the conversation.

Stage Two: Challenger Strategy

Building a Lighthouse Identity (Credo #2)

Premise: Fundamental to a Challenger's success is a very clear sense of who you are, and the insistent and salient communication of that identity.

Furthermore, since a Challenger has less resources at its disposal than the brand leader it is at least indirectly taking on, it needs to make sure *everything it does* is communicating that identity as strongly as possible; for a Challenger, everything communicates.

For an Existing Brand: Rediscovering Your Core Identity

Exercise: The Brand Vault

Who are we? The underlying premise here is that the identity of the company already exists—that is, there's a lot of potentially valuable components of the brand's past stored away in a metaphorical vault—we just need to find the most relevant dimensions of those facts, equities, or ideas to the current challenge and amplify them. In this, we are attempting to extract (and reapply) value, rather than add value.

The stimulus for this exercise is listening to *others* talk about the identity: consumers of the brand inside and outside the company who have lived with it over a period of time. In particular:

- Heavy consumers.
- Long-standing employees ("it's the engineers who really understand the brand").

In the normal course of events, this would take the form of a research project, debriefed on the day itself. The two groups would either simply be the last two groups of the project, or what were effectively "super-groups"—a selection of the most articulate respondents from the previous groups recalled for the purpose of the day.

The two groups would take place within a viewing facility. Each would be watched by the offsite team. Should a viewing facility be impractical, then a television monitor is possible.

The room the research is to take place in would have its walls covered in material that represented the brand at every stage of its life since

(continued)

(continued)

birth—facts of birth, early trading philosophies, advertising, packaging graphics, packaging types, product manifestations, news articles, endorsers used, sponsorships, and so on. Each group is invited to spend 20 to 30 minutes reviewing this material in their own time, before being asked to sit down and discuss those elements of the brand's historical identity that seem to strike a particular chord, because they:

- Seem to embody particularly powerfully or clearly what is special about the brand, or
- Are moments from the brand's past that seem to embody a time when their relationship with the brand was most intense, and the brand seemed to have the clearest sense of its role and value in their lives, or
- Represent altogether new information that seems in some way intriguing or potentially relevant to the present day.

These findings will provide a clear view as to what from the brand's overgrown past may provide an authentic and motivating bedrock for the future.

For a New Launch, or a Brand That Always Has Been Weakly Defined
Premise: The traditional way to talk about identity assumes a purposeful, top-down approach: One works out who one wants to be and then just goes and acts that way. In practice, the emergence of their full identity for most challengers is a journey, where aspects are refined and developed as the brand matures. The journey in Fox's case was a discovered identity, one of four stages:

1. **Stage one: Differentiation.** Fox noticed they were getting a much better response to certain kinds of programming than others—younger skewed—and dealing with material that the other channels wouldn't touch. They decided actively to pursue further programming that created and perpetuated this kind of difference.

2. **Stage two: Concept.** The group came up with a verbal concept that summed up the key strands of their most successful night of programming (Sunday)—as "The comedy alternative." While a straightforward, relatively one-dimensional description of their product acting as a

placeholder of positioning, it did start to crystallize a consumer role for the new network, delineating a place to live and a reason for being that had at the same time a certain kind of target market in mind.

3. Stage three: Personality. Fox's first advertising campaign, including an execution taking on Jim and Tammy Faye Bakker, came out fighting. It was irreverent and had an attitude. Most important, it had enormous confidence: This was a network that wasn't going to answer to anyone. It laid a personality on top of the brand's role for the consumer and the network itself.

4. Stage four: Fully fledged Identity. By the mid-1990s the identity of Fox had become very clear. Not limited to comedy (e.g., *Melrose Place, Beverly Hills 90210, Party of Five*), it was defined as much by personality and the nature of its content—and the mind-set of the audience it appealed to: risk-taking, irreverent, young, hip.

While such a journey appears in a sense bottom up, it is, perversely, more likely to endure than one that springs fully formed from the mind of the marketing team, because each aspect of refining and tuning is prompted by observing reasons for success or failure in-market.

The corresponding exercise, then, might look something like this.

Exercise: "Diller and the Journey"—Four stages toward an identity

1. Differentiation. What individual things are you doing that define you as different in the eyes of the consumer? Or what are you contemplating doing that would genuinely differentiate you in the eyes of the consumer?

2. Concept. Is there a concept that unifies the key elements of this differentiation? What role would it create for us in the marketplace?

3. Personality. What personality should we wrap the concept in to differentiate further? What about this personality demonstrates confidence, both to the consumer and ourselves?

4. Identity. So who are you? How could you describe yourself in a way that is completely distinct and defined, yet makes no reference to anyone or anything else?

(*continued*)

(*continued*)

Go through each stage. Create the journey. Accept that the nature of each stage might be refined by time or the stage that succeeds it, but that one has to start somewhere. The key thing we have to accept that it is something we are committed to moving toward. If we don't have the exact answers to each of these stages, we have to put mechanisms in place involving the consumer or ourselves that will allow us to answer them.

Exercise: Saturn

Saturn used the Competition's Weaknesses to define their own identity. Pinpointing everything that was wrong with the car business, they made themselves the counterpoint to the Motor City.

Traditional U.S. Automotive Company	Saturn's Identity
City of Industry	Small-Town America
Hard Sell	Soft Sell
Law unto Itself (e.g., price negotiable)	Consumer category like any other (e.g., one price, no negotiation)
Selling Sheet Metal	Offering an Experience
Consumer suspicion	Consumer enthusiasm
Businesspeople	"Friends"
The One-Off Deal	The Relationship

This exercise works most strongly for Diseased categories—banks, for example. It consists in formally identifying the negatives of the category and exploring one's identity as if a photographic negative.

The one area to avoid in this exercise is the trap of putting as part of one's identity "Being on the consumer's side" or "Understanding the consumer": This is too superficial, motherhood stuff. While there may be an opportunity in genuinely giving the consumer a service or relationship that would benefit them, the nature of this service or benefit needs to be made as specific as possible.

Exercise: "Picasso"

Put on the wall every piece of marketing activity from the last two years, together with what is proposed for the next year, if available.

Cut away from your marketing behavior everything that doesn't look like what you are really about.

Divide the activity into three groups:

1. What activity strongly communicates the identity?
2. What activity is consistent with the identity (even if it doesn't strongly promote it)?
3. What activity is not consistent with the identity?

Discard anything that falls into categories 2 and 3. What would we have to do to our discarded material to make them fall into the category of activities that strongly communicate our core identity?

Assuming Thought Leadership of the Category (Credo # 3)

Premise: In order to achieve rapid growth, a Challenger must develop a new kind of relationship with the consumer for the category. This is done through the selective breaking of the conventions of representation, medium, and experience.

There is a choice of exercises in this section, which offer practical and substantive ways of thinking about convention breaking. How many you try in the time you have set aside depends on how they work and how much time you have available. If one proves unrewarding for your brand, in your situation, then move on.

Exercise: "Branson"

How would we change the way the nation feels about our core product (i.e., when reduced to its simplest—money, or soup, or vodka)?

The brand leader's strength is that it often defines and replays the way the consumer thinks about the marketplace. But asking this ambitious and intelligently naive question forces the group to look beyond incrementalism, for sources both of dramatic change, and an Achilles heel in the category (e.g., toilet tissue is embarassing), which may also be a potential Achilles heel of the brand leader.

Exercise: "Schrager"

This is best done by breakout sessions in pairs. First, pick four other Challenger brands that the group admires and that have no immediate relationship to our own category. These might be, for instance

Lexus in the luxury car market
Microsoft in the software market
Southwest in the airline market
Goldfish in the financial services market

Approach, then, the developing and marketing of your own brand as if were in their category. Some may find it easier to think through the eyes of the founder of this other brand: How would the founder or marketing director of these brands market our brand, treating it as if it (or some aspect of it) were the category they had come from?

Exercise: "Roddick"

Select a critical ticket of entry into the category (such as high-quality packaging, or general grocery distribution) and assume it is *no longer available to you*. What else would you have to do to compensate for it?

It is particularly valuable in this exercise to think in terms of compensation through displacement into elements of the brand or product mix that sit either side of the weakness. Think back to Roddick: Being unable to produce glossy, high-quality packaging encouraged her to focus on romancing what was inside the bottle (the product), and using what the bottle appeared in—the shop itself—as an opportunity to put across a statement of what she believed in. How would this kind of displacement force enhancements in the marketing and behavior of your own brand?

Exercise: "Waitt" (i.e., Ted Waitt, of Gateway 2000)

Imagine your traditional media is denied you.

You can use anything else at your disposal, including retail outlets, boxes, nontraditional media. How could you forcefully communicate your identity, and your message, through a nontraditional medium?

It may be of value to add impetus to this exercise through "doubling and denying": How would you communicate to twice your current audience if denied your current dominant medium?

Exercise: "Schultz"

Howard Schultz of Starbucks turned waiting in line for a cup of coffee into a moment of education and feeling of sophistication in an otherwise humdrum day.

This exercise, then, is to explore how one would take the part of the purchase/consumption process the consumer *likes least* and look at how we would turn it into their favorite part.

(Some prompts to use: What gives our target pleasure, or a sense of reward? Learning? Playing? Doing other things while they're waiting? What would make them feel special? Flatter them? Increase their own self esteem?)

Exercise: "Tango"

Tango's packaging broke a taboo of color in soft drinks.

What are the apparent taboos of our category?

List them (they will be pretty close, at least as polar opposites, to the rules that were listed at the beginning of the day).

Why might breaking one of these taboos be beneficial to us?

Exercise: "Galliano"

John Galliano used unusually evocative invitations to heighten his audience's expectations of the show they were about to experience. This exercise looks at how we might precondition our consumers before they experience or come into contact with us.

First we need to identify the following:

- The expectations the consumer has of us.
- The "gateways" they pass through to interacting with us (for example, landing at an airport or checking into a hotel if I am a car rental company).

How could we use these gateways to raise the level of expectation and favorable predisposition toward our product? (And what would we have to be sure we could deliver to ensure those expectations were met?)

Creating Symbols of Reevaluation (Credo # 4)

Premise: You need to force rapid appraisal or reappraisal of your brand, generating salience and momentum.

Exercise: "Hayek"

Phase One

Agree on the key consumer complacencies that stand between the company or brand and rapid growth—or, indeed, success at all.

    Of all of these, which is the dominant consumer complacency?

Phase Two

What single piece of communication about our brand would change, puncture, or reverse this complacency? (You may want to make this three communication points, as Swatch did with "Swatch. Swiss. 60DM")

    In particular, suppose you could put some incarnation of your product on the tallest skyscraper in the city for two weeks:

- What product or idea would it be?
- In what form would it appear?
- What three things would you write on it?

The Second Day

Stage Three: Translating Strategy into Challenger Behavior

Preliminary to the Day: The dust of yesterday's discussion having cleared, reconsider the Big Fish. Does everyone agree that it is still the same as yesterday? Are there any refinements the group would make?

    If there is a change, write it up again as the central chart, dominating the room.

Sacrifice: What Are We Going to Sacrifice? (Credo # 5)

Premise: One or two marketing actions are going to make 80% of the difference in the fortunes of the brand next year. The rest must be sacrificed in order to make achieving these priorities possible.

The question of what those one or two things actually might be, when taken in isolation, is obviously much easier to answer in retrospect than in advance. There may, then, be value in beginning with the past: When reviewing all the marketing activities that took place last year, what were the one or two that made 80% of the difference? What real difference would it have made to the performance of the brand to have sacrificed *everything* else?

Then apply that learning to this year: Does this give us an indication of how we can decide what the critical points will be again this year?

It may be useful to distinguish between goals and activities:

1.   Write the year's goals for the brand up on the wall. If it helps, break these goals down into the marketing areas discussed in the the first stage of Day One (Audience, Distribution, Media, etc.).

Which is the least important?

Cut it.

The next least important?

Cut it.

Cut them down one by one, until we are down to two.

Stand back. Using last year as a guide, how much have we really lost?

2.   Write up all the marketing activities aimed at achieving these two goals.

Cut them down to two.

If you could only commit to these two activities, on these two goals— but could *over*commit on them—how successful would the brand be?

Overcommit (Credo # 6)

In principle, this is not a complicated task, having already identified the two tasks we absolutely have to achieve in the previous session.

First, we ask ourselves: What is the level of resistance and dilution we will have to overcome, and where does it chiefly lie?

Exercise: "Whitewater"

Ask yourself, for each core marketing task, the three irrefutable reasons it will fail (or be diluted into mediocrity). Then brainstorm the most effective way of neutralizing or reversing each of them.

What does two feet below the brick look like, then, in overcoming that resistance?

The second exercise we shall call "Jannard," after the founder of Oakley.

Exercise: "Jannard"

Jim Jannard started his new business with $300 and a wife who was eight months pregnant. This contributed to a formidable urge to succeed at every critical moment in Oakley's life.

This exercise is relatively simple; it consists of asking the same question three times, but raising the stakes of the outcome a level each time:

1. How should we ensure this activity succeeds?
2. How would we approach ensuring that success if our career depended on it?
3. And finally (and this is, if you like, why it is called Jannard), how would we approach it if it was our business, we were down to $300 in the bank, and our family's livelihood depended on it?

Using Advertising and Publicity as a High-Leverage Asset (Credo # 7)

We said in Chapter 10 that word of mouth usually arises because the consumer has found themselves in one of four situations:

1. **Bragging Rights.** They have discovered something valuable; they feel they are one of the first to unearth—a new brand, a new band.

2. **Product Enthusiasm.** They have come across an aspect of product performance about a brand that is startlingly impressive (or poor).

3. Aspirational Identification. They have found a brand with a strong identity and ethos (perhaps aligning itself to certain social issues, for instance), which they admire or would like to be identified with.

4. News Value. They have come across a piece of marketing activity that has surprised, strongly entertained, or shocked them, sufficient to prompt conversation with their peer group.

While it is clearly premature to discuss how our future advertising is going to help achieve our goals, we can at least assess how we are performing.

Exercise: "Water Cooler"

What could we do, as an extension of our identity, possibly as an extension of something we are doing already, to create water cooler conversation for *each* of the four reasons above?

Summary and Plan

The purpose of the final part of the second day is to pull out the key strands of thinking that everyone agreed on, without yet attempting to judge irrevocably the thoughts that were thrown up, or prematurely fixate on any new connecting tissue that emerged from one exercise to another.

Three questions, then, will serve as a summary at the end of the second day:

1. What is the Big Fish?
2. Who are we?
3. What are the three ideas in each section that have the most opportunity to transform our business?

(Note that there are no exercises over these two days for the implementation of the Eighth Credo. This process will be begun at a rather later stage of the overall journey.)

What Next?

Arrange a follow-up day for two weeks later. Give over a third of that day to pulling everything together: Which ideas and concepts continue to seem to be central to your future as a Challenger?

Spend a third examining how well equipped you are as a company to make the journey, in terms of the following:

Partners.
Passion.
Knowledge.
Ideas.
Titles and remits.
Culture.

Spend the last third of the day preparing an initial Plan for the next six months, to cover both external (consumer) marketing and the signals and briefs that will herald the beginning of adopting a Challenger mind-set internally.

Then Overcommit to it.

16

Apple, Risk, and the Circle of Rope

"Guts! Guts! Life! Life! That is my technique."
George Luks

When Channel 4 launched in the United Kingdom as the fourth network channel in 1982, it enjoyed some success in showing for the first time sports from other countries—American football, cycling from France, Australian Rules football, and so on. Shortly after launch, the channel tentatively added Sumo wrestling to this cosmopolitan lineup, and—as it had with each of the other minority sports new to the British armchair sportsman—prefaced the beginning of the Sumo season with an hour's introduction to the rules, history, and vocabulary of the spectacle in store. Reviewing the great Sumo champions of the last decade, the *yokozuna* (all of whom revelled in popular nicknames like "The Dumptruck" and "The Ox"), Channel 4 interviewed the aging trainer of the current title holder (called, I think, "The Tiger"), an occupation known in Sumo parlance as a stablemaster, and asked him the secret of his protégé's success.

The old man was very clear. There were, he said, three things that were important to be a great Sumo wrestler. The first was physical strength—and yet, he observed, while "The Tiger" was strong, there were other fighters that were stronger. And they cut to film of the champion, no bantam himself, being towered over by others twice his bulk.

261

The second important requirement, said the stablemaster, is excellent technique; but if The Tiger was strong on technique, he noted, there were other *yokozuna* as good or better. And there followed film of our champion gamely holding his own in a intricate barrage of handslaps with an opponent.

However, the third requirement, said the stablemaster, is *shin*—Japanese for "spirit." It is this that makes The Tiger the champion: He never gives up. He never loses the will to win. And they showed an extended clip of the champion, seemingly about to be propelled beyond the circle of rope that delineates the Sumo fighting area, yet always somehow recovering, fighting back, twisting his opponent's strength to his own advantage until he was the one left inside the ring while his adversary toppled gigantically out of frame.

Now there are actually a number of important dimensions to Challenger brands that we haven't touched on at all so far. Chance, for instance: Marketing is not a science, not a matter of plot and counterplot, like a game of chess. Being lucky, and how one exploits that luck when it falls one's way, can be a critical part of a Challenger's ascent. (Who would have thought, for instance, that Adidas's three stripes would suddenly become cool again on the streets of South Central Los Angeles, or Harlem, or Cleveland? And provide a springboard for the brand to bounce back from the brink to threaten Nike?)

But the more I interviewed the people behind Challenger brands, the more that particular image of the circle of Sumo rope came back to me— the sense of spirit being the true delineator. While I had embarked on a book to identify how Challengers use a more intelligent technique, if you like, to overcome an opponent's superior strength, I realised increasingly that what I failed to discuss was the real differentiator, which was something far harder to write about. *Shin*. Spirit. The emotions of those I talked to, the way they expressed themselves rather than what they actually said. The medium, not the apparent message.

It is hard, of course, to write about these sorts of emotions without opening oneself up to charges of penning the business equivalent of a Hallmark card. The reader may feel that we are veering horribly off course from the territory of case study and analysis into the world of self-improvement aids: They envisage any moment the onset of soft focus shots of eagles, or swans with broken wings, or Labrador puppies, and italicized quotes from famous Native Americans about the potential that lurks in every human heart.

Yet at the same time, how does one leave unmentioned the extraordinary moment when the founder of a company, retelling for the thousandth time the story of his own company's journey to a complete stranger, still finds himself so moved in the storytelling that he finds he literally has goosebumps on his arm? (He was as startled as I was. "Look," he kept repeating as he rose to his feet and shook one shaggy forearm repeatedly at the PR Director and myself, as if we doubted him, "*goosebumps*.")

How does one omit the propensity to embrace risk, the love of the unequal competition, the obsession with quality or innovation, the intense desire to win, the certainty of superiority, the sense of *fun*, that color so strongly the way these people talked about the business they are in. How, in fact, does one leave out talk of all these qualities without falling oneself (god forbid) into the fear of emotion, the "zero-defect" philosophy characteristic of the Establishment brand? It is not just that spirit is inspiring; at a more pragmatic level, it is that it seems to be the driver in the difference between Challenger intent and Challenger behavior. And we are not interested in intent; we desire a whole new way of thinking and behaving. So it might in principle be possible to summarize the book by listing the Eight Credos and the four stage challenger process they represent. And we might, for instance, essay a summarizing table of the differences between the brand leader and the Challenger brand that goes something like this:

Brand leader	Challenger
Reassurance	Identification/Enhanced self
The same	Different
Mass	Momentum
Innovation	Ideas
Recognition	Anticipation
Mainstream	Alternative
Stable	Unstable

We might talk of the future of Challengers as recognizing that the future lies in "the experience business." We might attempt, then, to redefine the old algebraic formula for value. Not $Q/P = V$, but $Q/P \times E$

The Challenger Program: A Four Stage Process

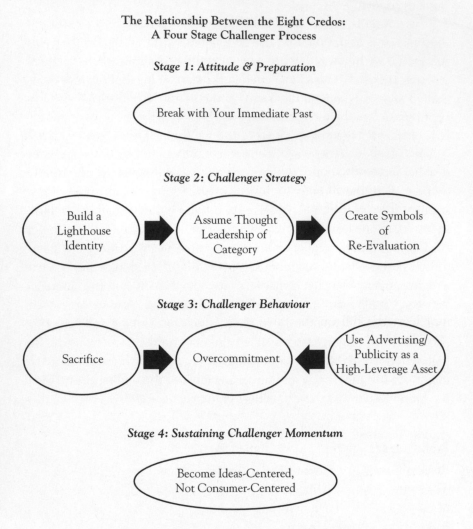

The Relationship Between the Eight Credos:
A Four Stage Challenger Process

Stage 1: Attitude & Preparation

Break with Your Immediate Past

Stage 2: Challenger Strategy

Build a Lighthouse Identity ➤ Assume Thought Leadership of Category ➤ Create Symbols of Re-Evaluation

Stage 3: Challenger Behaviour

Sacrifice ➤ Overcommitment ◄ Use Advertising/Publicity as a High-Leverage Asset

Stage 4: Sustaining Challenger Momentum

Become Ideas-Centered, Not Consumer-Centered

(experience) = V. This, we might predict, is the Challenger value equation and the battleground of the future.

But these kinds of conclusions, whether the reader finds them valuable or not, are missing something crucial. Herb Kelleher puts it well. When asked about the impending battle in California against Shuttle by United, he replied that, what would keep them on top was their "hearts and their guts." To take another example, when asked why he invested behind Howard Schultz, the chairman of Price Cost Co replied, "The look in his eye."[1]

Very little is written about the role of emotion in organizations and business. It is as if, now that IBM has defined itself as being about solutions, it is we humans that have become the International Business Machines. Yet emotion is a key variable. Whether it is a positive desire, like John Galliano's, or fear, like Grove's, doesn't seem to really matter, but you need a healthy dose of one or the other.

This goes beyond the old truth of people doing well what they love to do. It is about how one develops the personal impetus to fight through the moments when one feels one is about to be thrown out of the circle of rope. A story will serve to illustrate this.

It is Quebec, 1984. A winter's morning. Four people are sitting in a room with a phone bill they can't pay.

The four make up all but one of the executive group of Cirque du Soleil, a new circus made up predominantly of ex–stilt walkers, which has just finished the first year of its new life. The company is heavily in the red, and it is their money. They are discussing hard practicalities— not least the bill on the table from telephone company, which their overdraft will not cover. As they talk, the phone rings. Ironically, it is a collect call. From Italy.

They accept it. At the other end is Guy Laliberté, the fifth member and founding partner of the group, and he is in a state of some excitement. Great news, he tells them—he has just bought a new Big Top from a man he has struck up a friendship with in his travels in northern Italy. A huge tent, much bigger than the one they have now.

The room in Quebec is appalled: This is a disaster. The overdraft, they remind him. The bank, the debts. Even the wretched phone bill, for god's sake.

But the excitement from Italy is undiminished; they are looking at this the wrong way round, Laliberté tells them. This has been a year of just establishing themselves. Next year they will be better and better known: In order to recoup the money they owe, they will need a bigger seating capacity at each show. This Big Top is almost double the size: It will seat 1200 people. It is, in fact, the only sensible way forward.

Guy Laliberté is a very persuasive man and, at last, the four in the room in Quebec allow themselves to be persuaded. They agree to buy the Big Top in Italy with money that they do not have. Within a year they are back in the black.

This pattern repeats itself. Three years later the group argues again about expansion—should they move outside Canada, try the U.S. market? Many vote no: They have dabbled just across the border in Niagara Falls, and it was at best a mixed success. Laliberté pushes for yes—they should go to the United States. They have to keep moving.

There is considerable disagreement: After years of financial difficulty, many of them at last have families, mortgages, pension plans. The founding partners have their way, but at a cost—some of the company part ways.

They open the Los Angeles festival. By the time the opening night comes, they have exhausted all their available funds preparing for the show. If it goes badly, they do not even have enough money to get the trucks back to Canada.

It is a success.

And so it goes on.

What Cirque du Soleil illustrate is that being a successful Challenger is not simply question of taking one initial, enormous risk; a Challenger will only flourish if it has the courage to *continue* to take risks—even in the face of adversity. Indeed, it needs to foster within it a risk-taking culture that will continue to remain bold as it achieves higher levels of success, rather than falling back into conservative self-protection, forgetting the very reasons for its initial success. Fostering this culture is one of the primary responsibilities of a leader in a Challenger organization—for the culture as well as vision have to be exemplified at the top. Jonathan Warburton, owner-driver of Warburton's bakery, observes: "One of the great responsibilities of owner-drivers is to stick their necks out and be seen to take risks, because they're fireproof. What chance is there of the hired help taking risks if the guys at the top they are looking up to, who are fireproof, won't stick their necks out?"

And this preparedness to take risks—informed, educated risks—throughout the organization is important not simply because it is a vital part of an idea culture (where the courage to champion and pursue a new idea is as important to its success as the ability to have the idea in the first place), but because the old methods of reducing risk and putting copper bottoms on marketing decisions are looking ever more unsound. The Hollywood screenwriter William Goldman is given to remark that in show business, "Nobody knows anything," meaning that no one can predict what is and isn't going to work; one could be forgiven for thinking that, at the speed at which our markets are changing, the same could be true for Challenger brands.

Yet risk and reward are so hard to calculate. Ask yourself this: Which of the following three decisions would you have taken:

1.   You offer a mail-order service. There is a postal strike that lasts days, not months, crippling your business. What do you do?

2.   You are in the music business. You are given the opportunity to stake the fortune of your entire company on a new album that, instead of consisting of the regulation 10, three-minute songs, is made up instead of one piece of music per side, and no lyrics at all. What do you do?

3.   You are standing next to the Princess of Wales at a party to celebrate the launch of a new fleet of Airbus A340s joining your airline. She has agreed to take off her green jacket and put on the livery of a flight attendant of your own airline. You have in your hands a bottle of champagne; with anyone else you would shake it vigorously and spray them—but this is, after all, Princess Diana. What do you do?

Richard Branson was in each of these decisions. He took three decisions most of us wouldn't have taken, and that is one of the things that has made him the success that he is. Some of us might have made that move into music retail when the Postal Union went on strike, very few of us would have put our shirts on *Tubular Bells*, and none, I suspect, sprayed champagne at the Princess of Wales.

Now one of the purposes for creating a structure such as we have done is precisely that we are not Richard Branson, or Michael Dell, or Ian Schrager, or Herb Kelleher. As someone working on second-tier brands, who is not the founder of a company, we need entrepreneurialism, but structured entrepreneurialism. Entrepreneurialism on a set of guiding rails. And that all the individual examples we have discussed have been transposed into a system that is a postrationalization, rather than the path that anyone deliberately wrote for him- or herself from the beginning, is something that makes us *more confident*, because it spans the learning from a number of different categories, from launches to relaunches, from luxury to mass-market brands.

But it does not replace the need for some aspect of *shin*. Even if we may not possess the apparent fearlessness in the face of risk that one sees in the great entrepreneurs, at the very least there is the need for will. (I have been long fascinated by the power of will: the fact that among the Jewish community in New York, for instance, death rates decline before Passover and rise afterward—people have *kept themselves alive* through will alone to attend an important event). This at least we must have; behavior will be difficult to implement, and it will take time.

In fact, it is not a process that ever finishes. Once you have started being a Challenger, you cannot stop. Once you have started to create momentum within the eyes of your own company, let alone in the eyes of the consumer, to stop moving suggests death: better to have never started moving at all. Which is why, if we are looking to become genuinely ideas-centered and genuinely maintain momentum, we will need to practice *regularly* a kind of analysis entirely different from the kind we do now. At the moment, our tendency is to look regularly inward: We seek strategic direction every year from competitive analysis *within* our own category.

But what the examples contained in this book suggest, if nothing else, is that while such analysis of our own category is obviously an important prerequisite for thinking about how we defend our business, if we wish to gain a genuine competitive advantage we should be looking *outward*. What we should, in fact, be doing is the systematic and frequent analysis of:

- Number-Two Brands.
- Outside our category.
- Who are demonstrating rapid growth.

This analysis will look for three things. The first is, of course, individual ideas that we can simply appropriate and transpose into our own category (who says "Friends and Family" can't work for categories other than telecommunications: preferential rates on certain kinds of financial services, for instance, or even fast food?). The second thing such analysis will look for is insights into how they have achieved breakthroughs in an individual category, and then attempt to translate that into implications for our own category by turning them into the kinds of exercises we saw in Chapter 15. So, for instance, when we discover there is an outdoor clothing retailer called REI, which offers a shower room in which consumers are able to test rainproof clothing, two thoughts immediately begin to occur: How can *we* make the retail experience match the pleasure of the usage experience? And then how can we turn trial, and the experience it offers, at our point of purchase into a source of differentiation?

The value of the analysis is to refine the overall model, the Challenger Program. I said at the beginning that we should regard the Eight Credos as if a software program. What we are using here is, then, just the first incarnation—as new information comes in and new thinking is done, it will be refined, developed, made more user-friendly, enhanced. The core function and usage will remain the same, but the interaction will become easier on the one hand, and generate better output on the other (just as we update Office or Windows software even two or three years). As new examples come in that question or refine the model, we will develop and refine it, until, in eight years time, this initial version will seem amusingly prosaic and crude.

And in looking outward, we don't just mean outside our category. We mean outside our culture. It doesn't matter where these brands come from—Johannesburg, Tokyo, Los Angeles, Amsterdam—we should look all over the world. But particularly, I suggest, at the West Coast of the United States. Because context is crucial: The soil for even the most vigorous plant must be fertile for it to grow. Which is why the closing contention of the book is that the U.S. West Coast is the most fertile soil for Challenger brands in the world.

I recently asked an eminent anthropologist, Bob Deutsch, to define the essence of the United States in one sentence. His answer was this: "Everything is up for grabs all the time." Apparently simple, this reply seems to me remarkably profound, for the more one thinks about it, the more it illuminates culture and success in personal and corporate United States: the disposibility of language, for instance (compare the rate of introduction of new words in the United States to France or Britain), the fascination with sport (distilled in Phil Knight's observation that sport is U.S. culture), the continually renewed belief in the American Dream, the myth machine of Hollywood, the love of the open road, the Frontier mentality, and so on.

And at a business level, this is what makes the United States such fertile ground for Challenger brands. This very sense of flux and possibility is why so many of the iconic Challengers of the past 15 years begin in the United States: There are any number of individuals with a dream, a garage, and a belief that it can happen. And provided you can puncture the consumer autopilot with ideas on a big enough scale, it means there are also consumers who have shown themselves open to the most rapid adoption and championship of new ideas and ways of living, from Starbucks to the Internet.

And of all the United States, the West Coast is the capital of ideas. From the technology of the future in Silicon Valley, to the factory of popular culture that is Los Angeles, to the cradle of grunge and coffee that is Seattle, the West Coast believes in ideas in the way the East Coast believes in numbers. Suggesting, obviously, that if the United States is the most fertile soil for number-two brands, and the West Coast the most fertile soil for ideas, then every company in the world that regards itself as a Challenger rather than an Establishment brand should closely monitor the West Coast over the next 20 years. This is where the other great Challengers of the next 20 years will be born and grow, the new brand and business icons. And this in turn means that this is where we will find the stimulus to ideas and inspiration that can help us change gear within our own category. Eat the Big Fish. But only if we systematically find a way to let them have some influence on us.

Which leads us back to Apple again. The West Coast, a will that refuses to give up, the continual possibility of change—all these bring us, by one of Negroponte's curious "intersections," back to the brand that made the Number Two an icon again for today's generation of managers. Things famously went adrift at Apple for a while after 1984: Losing the hunger and single-mindedness that had made them the successful iconoclasts, they also lost sight of their core values and who they were. By 1997 analysts said they were way outside the circle of rope.

But Steve Jobs knew better: at the time of writing, his team had publicly "toasted" the Pentium II with the launch of the significantly faster G3, announced three quarters of profitability, and with the announcement of the iMac seemed to have Apple stepping firmly back into the ring. The iMac in particular marked a return to not just innovation, but the kind of leading edge conceptual thinking that had given Apple its initial following: at its launch both founder and inventor commented on it in vocabulary entirely new to the computer industry—because that vocabulary came from two entirely different categories altogether. Jonathan Ive, the senior director of Apple's Industrial Design group, noted in an interview that the language people were using to describe the translucent iMac was not the language of high-tech industry, but the language of food. And Steve Jobs himself unveiled the iMac in May 1998 with the words "Today we brought romance and innovation back into the industry." Romance? Food? In the computer industry? At last Apple was thinking and behaving like a Challenger again.

However, the first piece of mass communication that appeared from Apple under Jobs' return, a 60-second television commercial, was not an advertisement about product, or speed, or design at all. It was about something far more fundamental—a restatement to the world and to themselves of Apple's identity and purpose. This decision was a risk—with time to turn the company around slipping away, many commentators felt they should have been spending their limited advertising resources on more direct, pragmatic product communication—but the emotional declaration of who and why the brand was set the foundation among Apple users and staff alike for everything that was to follow. Over a black and white montage of people who famously broke the mould in their individual fields, from the arts (Martha Graham, John Lennon, Maria Callas) to business (Richard Branson and Ted Turner) to science and sport (Albert Einstein and Muhammed Ali), a voice celebrates their greatness in terms of their ability to see things differently, the scale of their ambition, and their absolute self-belief:

> Here's to the crazy ones. The misfits. The rebels. The trouble makers. The round pegs in the square holes.
>
> The ones who see things differently.
>
> They're not fond of rules. And they have no respect for status quo.
>
> You can quote them, disagree with them, glorify or vilify them. About the only thing you can't do is ignore them.
>
> Because they change things. They push the human race forward.
>
> And while some may see them as the crazy ones, we see genius. Because the people who are crazy enough to think they can change the world, are the ones who do.

It ends very simply, with the Apple logo above the two words "Think Different."

And although in this piece of communication Apple was speaking single-mindedly for and about itself, its spirit epitomised, just as in 1984, that of Challengers all around the world.

Postscript:
The Challenger Project

A number of people have offered opinions on the thinking and ideas in this book. Some were stimulated by it, others saw it as derivative, and one eminent advertising statesman memorably labeled it "half-cooked." Of all these opinions, I am most interested in the last.

Much of this thinking is indeed very raw. It needs development and argument, a broader database, and a more developed and cohesive set of ideas. For that reason this book, although finished, is not an end but a beginning, and hence the Challenger Project.

The Challenger Project is a continuous study of Challengers all over the world—mostly in the area of business, marketing, and brands, but also in related fields such as military strategy and sport. Its purpose is, through the continual enlargement and updating of its database, to:

a) Refine and develop the core hypothesis (the Eight Credos, and the Four Stage strategic process they represent), and

b) Develop further a range of strategic frameworks, tools, exercises and other catalysts which can allow that learning to be translated to any brand in the world.

The desire is to constantly evolve, so that, looking back from a more developed framework and set of ideas in five years time, the thinking and hypothesis in this book will seem crude and, well, "half-cooked." Like the first version of Windows might to a PC user today.

If you are interested in adding to the database of Challengers, offering evidence that refines or disputes the key hypotheses, or would like to offer feedback on your experience using the Offsite Program and the individual exercises it contains, please feel free to email the Challenger Project at eatbigfish@aol.com.

References and Sources

Chapter 1   More Blood from a Smaller Stone

1   Robert Miller, "OFT Investigates Dixons over Strong Arm tactics," *Times*, May 20, 1997.

2   This is one part of a greater body of unpublished work into this area by Udo van de Sandt, whose thinking this is.

3   I owe this observation—and graph—to Cindy Scott.

4   A.S.C. Ehrenberg and M.D. Uncles, "Dirichlet-type Markets: A Position Paper," (1998). I am grateful to Professor Ehrenberg for allowing me to reproduce this from the publications of the R&D Initiative.

5   Kurt Badenhausen, "Blind Faith," *Financial World*, July 8, 1996.

Chapter 2   The Consumer Isn't

1   I owe much of this line of thinking to original observations by Marty Cooke and Sally Reiman, and some of the substance to subsequent work by Anne Truscott and Fred Sattler.

2   Taken from a series of studies for the Newspaper Advertising Bureau. Approximately 1,000 viewers were queried in each study. Quoted in *TV Dimensions*, 1996.

3   Virginia Valentine and Malcolm Evans, "The Dark Side of the Onion: Rethinking the Meanings of Rational and Emotional Responses," *JMRS* 35.2, (1993).

Chapter 3   What Is a Challenger Brand?

1   *Ad Age*, June 30, 1997.

Chapter 4   The First Credo: Break with Your Immediate Post

1   *Fast Company*, October–November 1996.

2   William Taylor, "Message and Muscle: An Interview with Swatch Titan Nicolas Hayek," Harvard Business Review, March–April 1993.

3   *The Face*, April 1998.

4   This section owes much to a conversation with Gill Ereaut.

5   The company is Muse Cordero Chen.

Chapter 5   The Second Credo: Build a Lighthouse Identity

1   Tom Patty influenced many of my thoughts about identity. Kate Edwards helped develop the concept of Lighthouse Brands.

2   As quoted in "From Heroes to Losers" by Professor David Marc, speech to the Account Planning Group Conference 1996, Los Angeles.

3 Greg Braxton, "How Fox Outran the Hounds," *Los Angeles Times*, March 30, 1997.
4 Peter Doyle, "Building Successful Brands: The Strategic Options," *Journal of Consumer Marketing*, 7 (Spring 1990).
5 "Message and Muscle: An Interview with Swatch Titan Nicolas Hayek," *Harvard Business Review*, March–April 1993.
6 Jeanne Sather, "Starbucks Captain," *Business Journal*, Portland, March 3, 1995.
7 This observation is Leslie Butterfield's.
8 Much of this section came from an interview with Robin Wight, and his own thinking on Icon brands.

Chapter 6   The Third Credo: Assume Thought Leadership of the Category
1 The whole concept of Thought Leadership came from Matthew Shattock.

Chapter 7   The Fourth Credo: Create Symbols of Reevaluation
1 *Autoweek*, October 6, 1997.
2 "Message and Muscle: An Interview with Swatch Titan Nicolas Hayek," *Harvard Business Review*, March–April 1993.

Chapter 8   The Fifth Credo: Sacrifice
1 Brenda Paik Sunoo, "How Fun Flies at Southwest Airlines," *Personnel Journal*, June 1995.
2 Larry Light, "The Battle for Brand Dominance," Advertising Research Foundation 35th Annual Conference, April 10–12, 1989.
3 Andy Farr and Gordon Brown, "Persuasion or Enhancement: An Experiment," Millward Brown International, MRS Conference 1995.

Chapter 9   The Sixth Credo: Overcommit
1 Edward J Noha, CNA Insurance, address to Professional Insurance Agents of Connecticut, 1990. I am grateful to Bob Ceurworst for drawing my attention to this.

Chapter 10   The Seventh Credo: Use Advertising and Publicity as a High-Leverage Asset
1 Elizabeth Bumiller, "Counterculture Shock," *New York Times*, February 13, 1997.
2 My thinking in this area was greatly helped by discussion (and the development of a speech with) Mark Barden and Dan Baron.
3 This came from an interview with Nigel Jones of BMP DDB, London, whose research it was.
4 Conversations with John Stuart and Megan Kent were a considerable influence on this section.

Chapter 11   The Eighth Credo (Part 1): Become Idea-Centered, Not Consumer-Centered

1   William H Miller, "Gillette's Secret to Sharpness," *Industry Week*, January 3, 1994.
2   "Reading Matters," *Cover*, November 1997.

Chapter 12   The Eighth Credo (Part 2): Flying Unstable

1   Renzo Rosso, "Forty," *Diesel*, 1996.
2   Kenneth Labich, "Is Herb Kelleher America's best CEO?" *Fortune*, May 1994.
3   Renzo Rosso, "Forty," *Diesel*, 1996.
4   *The Independent*, November 18, 1997.
5   "Changes," *Chicago Tribune*, May 2, 1993.
6   This information stems from an interview with Barrie Berg, Booz, Allen & Hamilton.
7   "The Shoe Must Go On," *Frank*, October 1997.

Chapter 13   The Relationship between the Eight Credos

1   This is an observation of David Fong's.

Chapter 14   Challenger as a State of Mind:
Staying Number One Means Thinking Like a Number Two

1   Gina Imperato, "Harley Shifts Gears," *Fast Company*, June–July 1997.
2   This section is another that owes much to Robin Wight and his observations on the meaning of Brand Leadership.

Chapter 15   Writing the Challenger Program: The Two-Day Off-Site

1   See, for instance, Erik Calonius, "Garage," *Fortune*, March 4, 1996, Barbie Ludovise, "The Start of Something Big," *Los Angeles Times*, May 30, 1996.

Chapter 16   Apple, Risk, and the Circle of Rope

1   "Starbucks Captain," *Business Journal, Portland*, March 3, 1995.

Acknowledgments

When I told a colleague I had been commissioned to write a book called *Eating the Big Fish*, he asked me if there was going to be a recipe section. This is it.

Many people contributed to the content of the book, but there are four people without whom it would never have actually have seen light at all. Although the book as a whole is, almost by definition, a collection of other people's ideas, the first and most important idea of all I owe to Kate Marber; Kate came up with the initial concept of Challenger brands and was instrumental in developing the early research and thinking that gave the whole idea impetus and life. Ruth Mills, my editor, was generous enough to commission the book, and sympathetic enough to forgive my serial postponements of deadlines; it and I benefited enormously from her calm, advice, and love of a criminal pun. Georgia Garrett of TBWA Chiat/Day Los Angeles gave up evenings and weekends to help me research many of the themes and brands that appear in the book; I only wish I was ingenious enough to have found a place for all the rest of her serendipitous discoveries. And I owe a considerable debt to Alasdair Ritchie, twice over. His enthusiasm and championship of the idea at the outset was inspiring and infectious enough to make me think there might almost be a book in it, and his refusal to let it rest almost a year later allowed me to pick myself up after one particularly dark moment almost consigned the manuscript and myself forever to the bosom of the Thames. Thanks, Al.

After these, the most considerable debt of gratitude is owed, of course, to the people who agreed to be interviewed for the book. From them came all that is of interest and value within it. In particular, I learned a very great deal from the following: Jean David, Manuel J. Cortez, Jim Jannard, Mike Parsons, Tim O' Kennedy, David O'Hanlon, Barrie Berg, Gary Duckworth, Leslie Butterfield, Jack Supple, Ron Galati, Mike Parnell, Bob Thomas, Lynne Franks, Richard Lewis,

Jonathan Warburton, Steve Hayden, Rosi Ware, Janni Hofmeyr, Robin Wight, Bob Ceurworst, Andy Bird, Linda Firey-Oldroyd, Paul Southgate, Pam Keehn, Laurie Coots, Tim Delaney, Tod Rathbone, Megan Kent, and Mark Aink.

Where there has been a particularly influential piece of general thinking that these interviewees added over and above their insights on the brands they had worked with (as with Robin Wight's brilliant observations on Icon brands), I have tried to acknowledge this in the text or in the references indicated throughout. Six other people connected with, or working for, Challenger brands mentioned in the book were also generous enough to allow me to interview them but requested not to be named.

Once I had developed the idea for a book, it was the omniscient Bonnie Lunt who suggested I might want to put it in front of Andrew Jaffe and John Wiley's Adweek series, and Andrew who encouraged me to discuss it with Ruth Mills; without Andrew and Bonnie, it would still be a dusty proposal. Bob Kuperman was sympathetic enough to give me a sabbatical to begin writing it, without which I would still be somewhere around the bottom of the contents page.

Many of the colleagues at TBWA and TBWA Chiat/Day I have had the pleasure of working with over the past five years have profoundly shaped my views and the thoughts directly expressed in the book. David Wright in particular did a lot of the early background work with Kate and myself, after we had been further enthused by the ideas and enthusiasm for the subject contributed by the individual talents of a group of TBWA international planners over two days in New York (there are too many of the latter to name, but they know who they are). Velda Ruddock added her time and enthusiasm to Georgia's and taught me intelligent use of the Internet as a search tool—no mean feat. Conversations with Marty Cooke one winter led to much of the thinking in "The Consumer Isn't" section; I still miss those afternoons in Maiden Lane.

In preparing the manuscript, Monika Jain and Kirsten Miller of John Wiley were efficient and kindly guides, and Gabrielle Sheehan, Heather Carr, and Megan Sanders of TBWA were energetic and resourceful in their search for illustrative material and permission.

Of those who read the book while it was being written, Claude Bonnange and Uli Wiesendanger were generous enough to chew it over when it was barely digestible, and I am grateful to them for their advice and ideas, both of addition and subtraction. Rebecca Munds read the book twice at different stages and was invaluable in her inimitable combination of enthusiasm and honesty. And, most of all, I owe more than I can say to the support and ideas of Matthew Shattock and Sue Sheldon, who read it at several different stages, and whose enthusiasm from beginning to end fanned my own whenever it started to flag.

I said at the beginning of this section that above all the individual thoughts and ideas themselves, the book owed its life to just four people. I lied, of course; that list would be incomplete without three more. I have dedicated this book to my wife, Ruth, for only she and I know how much of a sacrifice it became for her to let me finish something I had always dreamed of doing. Until I am able to write poetry, the prosaic dedication to a book on business will have to act as a symbol of my gratitude and love. Lastly, I would like to acknowledge the more spiritual contribution of my four year-old sons, who every day find new ways to teach me that size and experience are no match for energy, enthusiasm, and a really strong point of view. Thanks, boys; the computer's finally free to play Pocohontas.

Photo Credits

Illustration	Page	Company	Credits
Jack as Icon	59	Jack in the Box	With permission of Jack in the Box.
Quidam North American Tour 1996–1999	64	Cirque du Soleil	Cirque du Soleil Photo: Al Seib
Hoops Cloud Swing	65	Cirque du Soleil	Cirque du Soleil Costumes: Dominique Lemieux.
Lobby of Royalton & Paramount Hotel	70	Dan Kloref Associates	© Todd Eberle.
Body Shop Bergamot Body Wash & Lavender Oil	91 92	The Body Shop	The Body Shop International PLC.
Jack in the Box: Boardroom	110	Jack in the Box	With permission of Jack in the Box.
Swatch on Commerzbank	118	Swatch	With permission of Swatch. Photo: Swatch.
Absolut Venice	128	The Absolut Company	Absolut Venice © 1995 V&S Vin & Sprit AB. Photographer: Vincent Dixon.
Absolut Aprils Fools'	131	The Absolut Company	Absolut April Fool's © 1997 V&S Vin & Sprit AB.
Sullen Fish	165	Tesco	With permission of Tesco.
Oakley Entrance & Oakley Atrium	200 201	Oakley	Eric Koyama

Index